Museum der Moderne
Salzburg

KUNST HALLE KREMS

Fiona Tan
With the other hand
Reader

Edited by Gilda Williams

snoeck

Preface

In Dialogue

Artist's Texts

Critical Overviews

Writings around Selected Works

Appendix

Thorsten Sadowsky
Florian Steininger
Foreword

This publication assembles for the first time the most important published essays by renowned authors, curators and art historians on the work of photography- and film-based artist Fiona Tan, thereby offering comprehensive insight into her complex artistic output. Her particular appreciation of language and literature is reflected in Tan's personal letters, essays and manuscripts, a selection of which enriches this volume.

Over the past decades Fiona Tan has produced an extensive oeuvre linking issues of postcolonial hybrid identities to in-depth archival research, art-historical reflection and a subtle poetics of memory. She has a fondness for archives, warehouses, collections and the encyclopaedic fantasies associated with them, and she uses her finds to conceive new narratives. Her filmic images focus on historically aware encounters with the Other and are often embedded in literary references. Accordingly, the oeuvre of the Indonesian-born, Australian-raised and Amsterdam-based artist is characterised by the thematic and aesthetic hybridity that might evolve between cultures and, in so doing, evokes the transcultural third space so poignantly described by critical theorist Homi Bhabha. This 'third space' means nothing less than a remapping of the world that transcends the polarities of West and East, North and South, globality and locality, tradition and modernity. This utopian restructuring of relations renders the world a larger and more complex place; precisely this experience is conveyed by the work of the far-travelled Fiona Tan, who brilliantly understands how to deconstruct and polyperspectively resolve stereotypes of perception and narrative.

We are very grateful to Gilda Williams who, as editor, has been responsible for selecting and editing the texts, while also contributing an insightful introduction. This reader is a pioneering feat and a major contribution to understanding one of the most prominent practitioners of contemporary art.

Thorsten Sadowsky
Director
Museum der Moderne Salzburg

Florian Steininger
Artistic Director
Kunsthalle Krems

Gilda Williams

Open Letters: Writings by and about Fiona Tan

Saskia Bos: *When [while making your films] do you write your texts?*
Fiona Tan: *Before, during and after.*

Rarely do we encounter a visual artist whose work is as rooted in language as Fiona Tan's. As this Reader celebrates, her nearly thirty-year span of art-making has attracted some of the finest art-writers of her generation, and is moreover regularly associated with eminent literature. In her art and writings Tan often takes inspiration from literary sources, from W. G. Sebald's *The Rings of Saturn* (1995) to Ariosto's epic poem *Orlando Furioso* (1516–32). David Campany associates the artist with T. S. Eliot, linking Tan's extraordinary fusion of antithetical media (moving and still image) with the poet's 'collisions of almost-opposites'. Jorge Luis Borges and Italo Calvino are repeatedly cited; Stéphane Carrayrou's essay notes how Borges' magical experiments in overlapping past, present and future – as Calvino discusses in his *Six Memos for the Next Millennium* (1988) – centre on 'a growing and bewildering network of diverging, converging and parallel times', comparable to Tan's multi-temporal artworks.[1] Often drawn from distant times and places, her art nonetheless belongs resolutely to the here-and-now, embedded by the artist's hand in present-day debates and technologies.

This Reader pays special attention to Fiona Tan's own texts, across the variety of formats she inhabits: research, scripts, diary entries, statements of intent, cultural theory. Just as Tan's camera imitates varied gazes – that of tourist, observer or researcher, as Sabine Maria Schmidt importantly notes – the artist's writing adopts multiple tones. What unites all her texts, however, is Tan's consistently uncluttered, honest and probing written voice. 'There are two works', the artist writes in 2005. 'The one in my head, or in my desires, and the one it will become.'[2] If the major retrospective that coincides with the publication of this Reader exhibits Tan's finished artworks 'as they became', this volume is the expression of that earlier artwork: the one composed of the artist's thoughts and desires.

In her writing Tan proves an indefatigable researcher, forever tracking down her subjects in the depths of dusty libraries, secretive museums, bottomless archives. Research-writing in her hands becomes a hybrid and highly pleasurable genre, a cross between fact-finding and personal discovery which (as Lynne Cooke describes) 'erodes the boundaries normally drawn between so-called amateur observation and "scientific" recording'. Her investigation into Théodore Géricault's *Portraits of the Insane* (c. 1819–24) in the essay '10 Madnesses' (2018), for example, combines 'straight' factual research with personal reflections on the French artist's painted-yet-living subjects; Tan sensitively notes how Géricault somehow 'caught their lostness ... which slips past and away from any easy grasp'. At times Tan's research is spoken by characters in the voice-over, such as Hiroshi's explanation in *Ascent* (2016) of how images of Mount Fuji were exploited during World War II by both Japan and the US to induce feelings of patriotism and longing among homesick soldiers. Voice-overs sometimes conceal a sly humour: at the close of the (male) Architect's self-aggrandising step-by-step account of his working process in 'Folly One' (2010), the Female Commentator describes the finale as the 'stage of shameless megalomania'.

At times the tone is work-a-day and diaristic, at others the words are filled with wonder. Sometimes her texts unwittingly reveal distant origins for later artworks; Tan's accidental discovery of Rembrandt's third, unsung daughter Cornelia van Rijn during her investigations for *Provenance* (2008) became the springboard for the subsequent work *Nellie* (2013). Tan moreover proves an insightful theorist; in 'Women in Storage' (2019) she brilliantly captures the paradox at the heart of Agfa's archive of 1950s commercial photography:

> *A woman in the '50s was said to have only two questions in life: What shall I wear? and What shall I cook? But the reality of daily life across much of Europe [...] was that there was nothing to wear and no food to cook.*

Tan plainly loves to tell a good story. In *Ascent* she shares the tale of the lovesick Japanese Emperor enamoured of a beautiful but fleeting moon goddess. With *Depot* (2015) she recalls Voltaire's *Micromégas* (1752), a myth centring on two colossal space-travellers who, having glimpsed only a portion of ocean on a visit to our planet, determine that Earth is inhabited solely by 'tiny' whales. Often Tan recounts the true stories of forgotten but inspiring historical figures whom she encounters in her investigations. In '10 Madnesses' the artist introduces readers at length to Jean-Baptiste Pussin (and his wife Marguerite), the warden and former inmate who unchained asylum inmates and initiated humane psychiatric care in the late eighteenth century. In 'Women in Storage' Tan tells of Shirley Polykoff, the talented but overlooked female advertising copyeditor and real-life inspiration for Peggy Olson's character in TV's *Mad Men* (2007–15). We sense the artist's desire to bring broader attention to their valuable yet neglected lives, generously loaning the space of her texts to pay them due homage.

Above all Fiona Tan's writings reveal an ongoing process of ethical self-scrutiny. She explores systematically her fascination with the young Balinese boys puffing on a cigarette in *Smoke Screen* (1997), meticulously putting into words their complicated – and potentially problematic – attraction for her. In examining her ambiguous curiosity with these images, Tan is recognising the delicate balance she must tread in order to avoid retracing the voyeuristic paths of the long-ago colonisers who originally took this footage. How can Tan revisit pictures without re-inhabiting an exploitative gaze? This crucial 'moral dilemma', as defined by Cooke, is broached by numerous critics (including Godfrey, Monk, Chan and Gioni): how to avoid trespassing on the photographic lives of distant strangers, the subjects of Tan's art? She responds with gratitude towards them, for example describing an image appearing in *Vox Populi Norway*'s family snapshots as 'a lovely gift'. 'I feel that I owe this much, at least, to these anonymous individuals and to my own artistic integrity', she writes, explaining her copious research into the lives of the unfortunates depicted in Géricault's *Portraits of the Insane*, in '10 Madnesses'. Surfacing again and again in her written words is Tan's abiding feelings of indebtedness towards all her subjects.

With the other hand gathers three kinds of art-writing clustering around Fiona Tan's art: firstly, the artist's own voice ('Artist's Texts') and secondly, commissioned essays ('Critical Overviews'). The final section ('Writings around Selected Works') draws together the artist's words alongside initial commentary and, on occasion, its critical reception in the form of exhibition reviews – the third art-writing type here. This work-by-work discussion of selected artworks from multiple perspectives reflects the project-based progression of Tan's artistic life. Critical essays can provide much-needed context, such as Joel Snyder on the American incarceration catastrophe behind *Correction* (2004); or Adelina Vlas' detailed account of Sir John Soane's life and collection at the heart of *Inventory* (2012). Others embed Tan within broad art-historical contexts, for example Mark Godfrey's discussion of portraiture's perpetual capacity to renew itself, as articulated by art historian Benjamin Buchloh, in analysing the 200 Berlin-based portraits that comprise *Countenance* (2002). Still others analyse Tan in relation to film theory; Thomas Elsaesser recalls Gilles Deleuze's discussion around the agency of the human face in relation to Tan's *Facing Forward* (1999). Okwui Enwezor contextualises Tan's work within Homi Bhabha's postcolonial framework which asks that we now favour the archive, over tradition, when addressing the cultural past. A commonly recurring – and, arguably, overused – soundbite is Fiona Tan's self-description as a 'professional foreigner': an evocative early interview comment that has perhaps adhered excessively to her. Better summaries of the artist have since been articulated, such as Massimiliano Gioni's encapsulation of Tan as an 'untiring cataloguer of gazes'.

While some writers pin Tan's work to notions of physical *space*, such as Doris von Drathen's discussion of 'exile' in the work *Island* (2008), it seems to me the richest and most frequent topic is *time*. Tan herself reflects continuously on time: the way it lasts forever in Chantal Akerman's films; the way a moving projection of still photography arrests time; the inherent short lifespan of digital data.[3] Many note how time seems to slow in her art, from 'the unhurried slowness with which [Tan] looks at people' (Frankel) to the lingering gaze Vlas describes in *Inventory*, whose images of the ageing Soane House Museum's peeling paint and cracked windows draw attention to time's relentless passing. For Adrian Searle, Tan's revisitations of old imagery suspend the viewer in an impossible and even supernatural time, staging a ghostly 'encounter with the dead'. Brian Dillon describes the multi-styled Brighton Pavilion in *A Lapse of Memory* as a 'time machine', while Christophe Gallois considers how *The Changeling*'s timeless young women exist 'beyond Barthes' "that-has-been" to assert that the image is never frozen in time'. Taken together these writers articulate the 'staggering network of diverging, converging and parallel times' (Borges, cited by Calvino) that consistently marks Tan's complex art-making, as Carrayrou wisely recalls.

Perhaps Tan has attracted such high-quality writing because of her own palpable appreciation for language. She seems actively to cultivate relationships with words: some she loves (the Dutch word *sinaasappel*); others she resists (the English term 'medium'); still others need defending ('For me there is nothing derogatory in the word "study"').[4] Critics have commented on Tan's careful attention to language; Midori Matsui notes the telling repetition of the pejorative 'savages' in *Disorient* (2009), taken from Marco Polo's 1298 travelogue. Tan is a skilful inventor of similes – 'The film screen is a like an empty bowl'; 'Memory is a fold in the fabric of time'[5] – and her commentators similarly display some exquisite word-smithing. Enwezor describes the character of Henry in *A Lapse of Memory* (2007), ceaselessly wandering the empty Brighton Pavilion, as occupying 'the iron cage of his failing memory', while Denis Gielen imagines a beached whale – mountainous in scale, stubbornly immovable – as 'a landscape'.

Writers often evoke senses other than the solely visual, from Hettie Judah's 'smell of tar [that] smacks of the harbourside' accompanying the marine ropes suspended in *Circular Ruins* (2019), to Juliana Engberg's description of maritime Venetian sounds 'that roll like a tide around the walls' and suitably accompany her canalside viewing of *Disorient*. Reviews can feature powerful visual descriptions – perhaps because aimed at readers who may not have seen the art – such as Laura Cumming's detailed roll call of *Depot*'s watery onscreen imagery:

> *Fish, eyeless and lacquered, vector forward like spiky bronze dragons; seahorses ride high in their glass vitrines; nameless serpentine forms turn gold in the museum light.*

I note two special formats that recur in this Reader: lists and letters. Tan has recognised in her attachment to list-making a desire for order – despite the corresponding recognition that even compulsive list-making will never counter the world's prevailing chaos. Many of Tan's most admired figures are consummate list-makers and cataloguers: Umberto Eco, Paul Otlet, August Sander, Aby Warburg. Lists join people and things together without judgement, allowing relationships to be forged unremarked. *Depot* lists all the marine species that begin with the word 'sea', producing a wave-like rhythm: *'sea star, sea lily, sea cucumber ...'*. The long list of supplies needed to climb Mount Fuji spoken in *Ascent*'s voice-over reflects the climber's respectful preparation when approaching that majestic mountain.

The other crucial format is epistolary writing. Opening this Reader is the exploratory letter she pens to writer and artist John Berger which set off an engaged, and eventually quite affectionate, conversation. The chapter comprising the artist's texts begins with her published 1986 letter to Chantal Akerman: a letter about letter-writing. Philip Monk takes advantage of the letter-writing format to ask open-ended questions, and consider varying types of 'correspondence' – from conversing on paper, to forming personal connections with images.

All Tan's writings are perhaps like open letters, addressed to her audience and laying bare her sources, methods, hopes, worries, heroes, perplexities and even doubts – 'put[ting] her own gaze on show', as Gioni writes. 'Framing is a choice, an act of selective reality' she 'confesses' to her readers,[6] and Tan repeats throughout the Reader that she wants viewers to become aware of art's artifice: the text-and-image's inherent manipulation. Fiona Tan's writings offer a site, parallel to her visual art, where this essential admission is candidly and emphatically made.

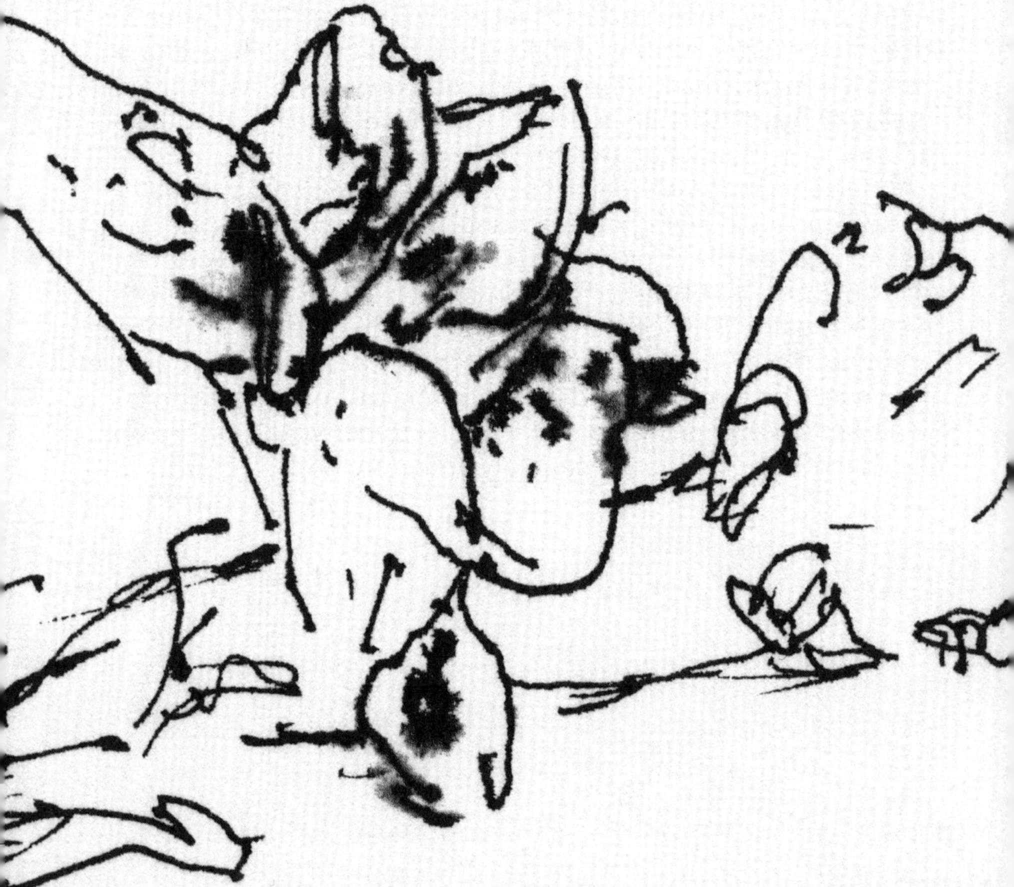

In Dialogue

John Berger, *Drawing for Fiona*, 1999

John Berger and Fiona Tan 'Exchange of Letters'

Fiona Tan: Scenario, Amsterdam: Vandenberg & Wallroth; Rotterdam: NAI Publishers, 2000, 51–83.

Amsterdam, 16 July 1999

Dear John Berger,

When I was an art student some ten years ago, a friend and fellow student recommended your books to me. *Ways of Seeing* (1972) was my first encounter, and I found it fascinating and stimulating reading. That paperback, now dog-eared and soiled, still has an important place on my bookcase, standing next to all the other novels, articles and essays from your hand which I have been able to find.

It is for me no easy task to explain the stimulating role of your writing for my artistic work. Together with the books of other writers and thinkers, it aids me in defining both my artistic practice and my artistic desires. Found footage is often a starting point for footage I subsequently shoot myself. And I try to find unexpected but meaningful montages through the juxtaposition of the old and the new material. The results are videos, films and audiovisual installations.

I look at the way we look, particularly at photographs and moving images. This undertaking can never be scientific but is a personal in-depth inquiry. Recently I have been thinking more and more about what history is made of, how it is constructed. I try to grasp how and why particular moving images fascinate me, effect my perception, my memory and my sight. And in the images and montages I make, I reflect on this.

Currently I am working towards a publication entitled *Scenario*. In this book – a scenario itself – my work is intended as merely a point of departure. The idea is that seeing my work can trigger, in an associative way, texts from a select number of authors. Beyond its singular approach, I wish the book to intertwine various ways of seeing and thinking. Embedded in this publication is the desire to stimulate a broader and yet more precise reflection and discussion about cinema, art and their role in social history. Hence the reason for this letter. Would you be interested in seeing my work and thinking about writing a text for *Scenario*? I would be truly delighted if you could.

I was particularly moved by the final passage of *To the Wedding* (1995) and was struck also by its very effective structure – a parallel montage. And indeed the blindman's cinematic storytelling I find very inspiring. By no means do I wish to dictate the structure or contents of your contribution, but at the same time I do hope that I can describe clearly enough the planned publication.

I hope to hear from you soon.

Sincerely Yours,

Fiona Tan

9 September 1999

Dear Fiona,

If I may be so familiar.

I watched your two videos last night. I shall watch them again tonight. And on other nights. They are of a tact, a precision, an unsaid, and therefore a beauty, that gives wings.

It occurs to me – off the top of my head – that these '49 Questions' might be a way of contributing? You could use them in any way you wished. Or we can think of something else.

In solidarity,

John

49 Questions

Where are you?
If you're beside me, why can't I see you?
What do you mean by nobody is nowhere?
Is there no nowhere?

Why did you let them?
You regret it now?
Why do you answer 'everything,' to every question?

And the agony?
Why did you let them?
Couldn't you lend a hand to shelter the flickering candle?
Do you think I could still make you laugh?
Maybe the secret is to remember you like your mother as a boy?

Shall I make you laugh again?
Do you remember what it is like seeing so little light?
Where are you?
In the night, tell me: what is small?
You say nothing, nothing?
Your silence is like a lance, you know that?
Tell me, in the dark, what is small?
In the dark how to learn to touch the difference between illusion and faith?
Where are you?
You want vinegar?
Is it your breath?
In the night we pray to begin again, no? With just one small thing?
Jesus! Why don't you answer?

Has it occurred to you that you, with your pain, ask too much?
Do you believe it will be easier one day?
It happens all the time, say what has to be done to make it different?
Do we have to begin again all the while?
Why can I never touch you?
Begin with what?
What would happen if we met?
Do you believe I can still make you laugh?
You say we have been saved?
Saved?

Why is there no reflection in the water?
What is missing?
How do stones undress?
Where to find what is missing?
You used voices to build a house, didn't you?

Around the undressed stones there is no end at all to the space?
And if now I open the door of the house?
You are asking me a question?
My answer is yes. Yes.

Why is every song about loss?
Can we keep nothing?
Only the melody?
Is the melody the one small thing in the dark for beginning again?
Only this?

You know I know that you are here now?
You don't have to answer.

Amsterdam, 14 September 1999

Dear John,

I was very pleased to find your letter yesterday, and opened it impatiently. Thank you for the swift reply. I am truly delighted that you would like to contribute to *Scenario*.

Thank you for the '49 Questions' which I shall reread again in the coming weeks. I find it intriguing how they read so differently with each reading.

I am enclosing a few simple questions – an echo. Maybe this is a way to move towards a text.

What do you remember most?
(Have you been here before?)
Seeing through a camera? Seeing before, after or without a camera?
What you do remember from thirty years ago?
What do a blind man's images look like?

Sincerely,
Fiona Tan

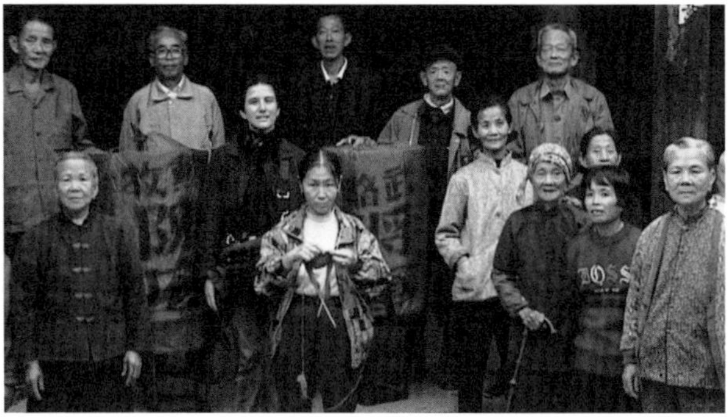

May You Live In Interesting Times (still), 1997

September 1999

Fiona,

What do you remember most? — Arriving in this world.

(Have you been here before?) — Yes.

Seeing through a camera? Seeing before, after or without a camera?
— Cameras were invented by the dead, so they can remember.

What you do remember from thirty years ago? — Imagining today.

What do a blind man's images look like? — Like tattoos.

For your video of the flower clock I send you a drawing. We can go on?

John

October 1999

Dear John,

Thank you for your drawn gift of flowers.

We can go on; I would like to go on. Moving, but not it seems in a forward direction; not as one perceives a linear progression. Is this how written scenarios for future films might look? Not a straightforward development, not one film but many. Hints and inklings and gaps to be filled in.

Who (what) makes the tattoos of the blind man?

Some people describe my work as 'poetic'. What can that mean?
What can be said about unsaid?
I was talking to a friend yesterday about the old Biblical concept of image worship.
Do I make images? (It doesn't feel that way)
Does a camera make images?
Can one really worship images as gods?
Do you have a favourite image, one you love above all others?
Sincerely,
Fiona

October 1999

Fiona,

Thank you for your letter. So fast. And it could be a question of speed. At a certain point speed cancels out linear progression, no? Anyway it's a way of describing something that is happening and you feel.

Who makes the tattoos of the blind man? His desire, don't you think?

When they say your work is poetic they mean that you're making very fast, unforeseen connections which are nonetheless not arbitrary (the way a cat jumps on to a table is 'poetic').

The prohibition of images. Biblical/Islamic and others.

I don't think you make images. With your video sequences and montage you surround something. You measure up to it and away from it (like the cat!) but you leave it, to be itself. You do not substitute an image for it. Or so it seems to me.

Do I have a favourite image? Perhaps something to do with blackness. Do you know Nick Cave's song *Black Hair* (1997)? Could it be that when the blackness is gone, one has to invent an image for consolation?

John

November 1999

Fiona,

Last night I watched your 'documentary', *May You Live In Interesting Times*

(1997), and I liked it very much. What is marvellous is that you talk in a direct way about yourself and, in doing so, talk about a whole world that is very seldom or never talked about. And it is this capacity (along with other things) which makes you a poet. The film has so much life in it. Like a fire in a snowstorm.

Now I ask you a question: I think you have three eyes. (Perhaps more.) Where is your third? What does it see?

John

December 1999

Dear John,

Thank you for your note.

To your question: my third eye. Several theoreticians have referred to the camera as a third eye. At once this seems to overrate a mechanical or electronic camera's ability and to underrate the human (or animal) eye. But it is true that the camera, photographs and films, show us things in a different way and things we sometimes could not otherwise see. I guess in some ways my third eye looks at this 'third eye' with both admiration and suspicion. It would be tempting to say my third eye is in my gut or my breast – somewhere more removed from the brain, but I flatter myself too much, I fear. Maybe my other eye is located in that odd but also utterly normal no man's land I sometimes occupy culturally. The slight shift – a gift given – which can result in a new camera position (an altered lens, a distorted depth of field). How has your move to France, to the Alps, to a village, affected you and your vision?

I am reminded of Roald Dahl's gruesome tale of a scientist who, upon his death, has his brain and eye removed and kept alive, only to be tormented by his vindictive, cigarette-smoking wife. (A just reward?)

Why this association here? The disconnection, the pain, the powerlessness of that eye? If I have another eye I would like to think that I cannot control it. It thrusts sights upon me that I can never describe and often not comprehend. And that is wonderful. A red spiritual spot right in the middle of and beyond stereoscopic vision? No, not that – a distanced eye (sight always requires distance). Does it reveal to me my blindnesses or does it help me create them?

Certain blindness, as we have already discussed, is very desirable, I think.

Fond regards,

Fiona

24 January 2000

Fiona,

Maybe we're getting somewhere with our 'third eyes'. Where? you ask after a pause. And then, after a longer pause, we both laugh, for we guess that the answer is a joke. *Elsewhere!*

Let me try to explain, but you know it as well as I do. To show something either in a story or in an image or on a reel, one has to observe intently. Most art that fails, does so through lack of observation. This has nothing to do of course with naturalism. I am not talking about copying details. I am talking about observing the essential in something, and this essential has its own energy which has little to do with the balancing act of art. It's an energy that lurches disconcertingly, and it's that lurch which has to be so intently observed with both eyes, repeatedly. Two eyes for that observation, two eyes for the forgetting of everything else. Two eyes for shutting, and still seeing what you have observed! You know all this ...

Then comes the question of accommodating what has been observed within the balancing act, the trapeze performance, which can never be approached straight on. Not something you can aim at. Rather something that happens. Sometimes, if you have enough trust.

Nevertheless it's here where 'the third eye' comes in. The third eye looks at what the other two eyes are intently observing, from elsewhere, from faraway, from another place, from another time. The third eye looks at *what is*, as if it were only *what might be*. It looks at *what is*, as if it were imaginary.

I am making it sound complicated and abstract. Whereas in practice it functions very simply. You are watching a flower opening, and your third eye watches this opening as if it had never before seen this flower! Yet its reaction has nothing to do with surprise or naivety. If the third eye belongs to another life, it's a life in which more is known than we know in ours. The third eye, which is somewhere else, records what it sees, and we perceive this recording rather as we hear an echo. It forces us to be in two places at once, or, perhaps, many places at once. And it is from this being-in-two-or-many-places-at-once that poetry begins.

You talk about the man you love and what has happened to you both. You are thinking intently about him and yourself, but you tell the story from far away. Otherwise there is no destiny. (Destiny is always a question of where something is placed.) And this faraway is the work, the production, of your third eye.

Or you go searching for your extended family in Indonesia and in China and you place your story with you at its centre – in a certain perspective. Yet the perspective is not an historical one, it is far more immediate. It is the perspective offered by the evocation of another, simultaneous world or life to which you do not and cannot belong, but to which, somehow, the story might. And in this simultaneous, alternative version of the world the story being enacted could have been otherwise! (There is a similar proposition in all the dramatic speeches of Greek and Shakespearean tragedy.) What happens has to be weighed against what is not happening, and vice versa. All this is the work of the third eye, no?

You ask me how the mountains have affected my vision? And I'm inclined to reply by quoting a sentence from the great Portuguese writer, Miguel Torga. The sentence, I must emphasise, doesn't in any way refer to what I have or have not achieved; it speaks simply of the way I have come to see things. 'The universal is the local without walls.'

Work well, being elsewhere, Fiona.

John

An instant that goes on and on – like what can happen in music. Charlie Parker playing Tiger Rag or Beethoven's one from last piano sonata ...

What is this world for you now? – Arriving in this world.

What do you remember most?

(Have you been here before?) Yes.

Seeing through a camera? Cameras were invented by the dead, so they can remember.

Seeing before, after or without a camera?

Perhaps So they can remember the living who came after them.

So they can remember ~~to~~ the living?

Photos are dead

What you do remember from 30 years ago? Imagining today.

And have things turned out very differently to the imagination/expectation?

Very differently, and in a way which puzzles me. So much has radically changed, and I expected things to change in one way or another. What I did not expect and what I now feel very strongly is that almost nothing has changed.

despite the changes, almost nothing? What does that almost nothing mean?

What do a blind man's images look like?

Like tattoos. Why? How?

Fiona,

For your video of the flower clock I send you a drawing.

We can go on? I think so

FIONA TAN

John.

His skin reads them. Perhaps he can make them move with his muscles or his breathing. Also because braille is like a script of needle-points to be read by touch.

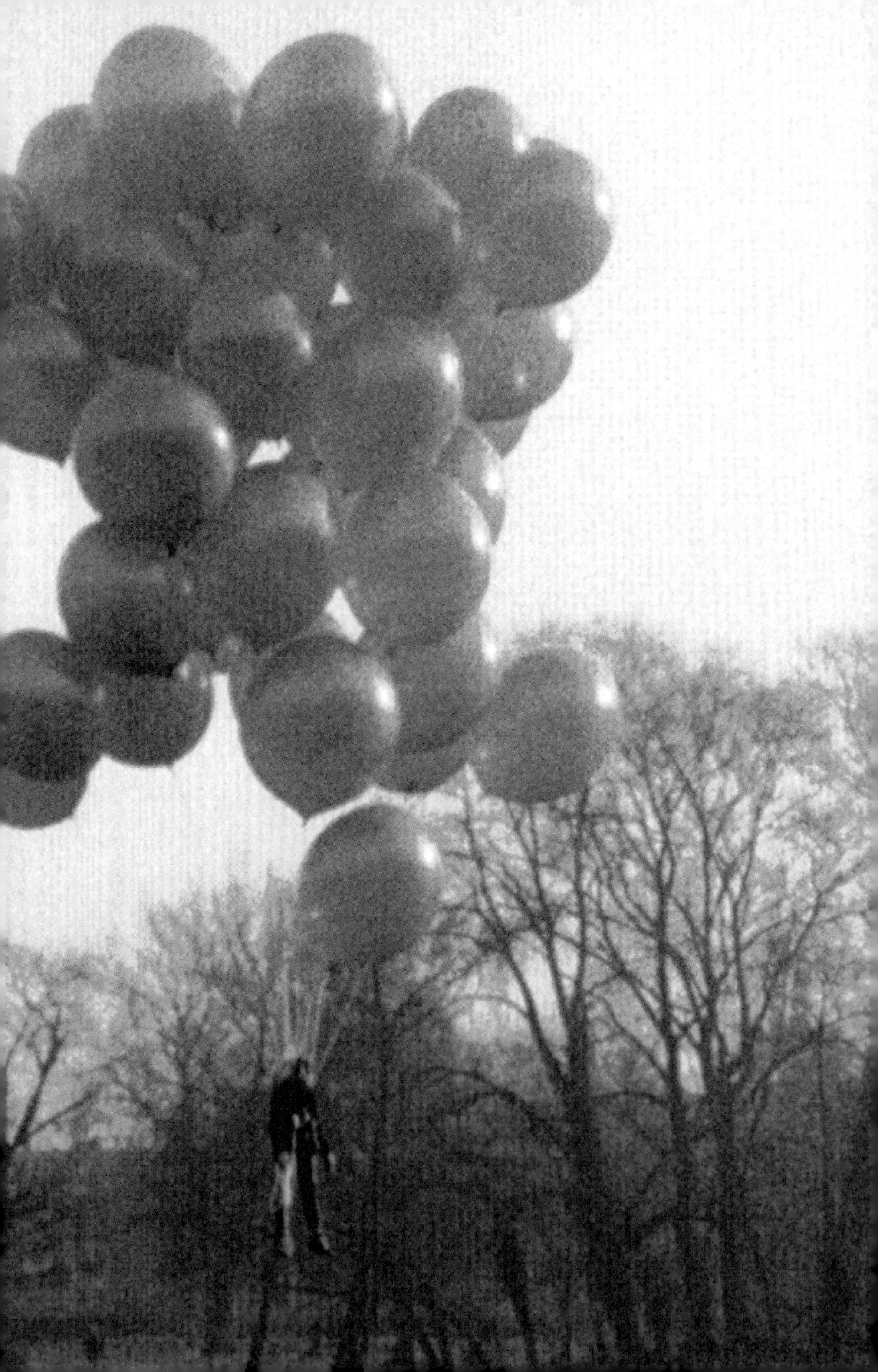

Artist's Texts

Lift (still), 2000

Fiona Tan
'Letter to Chantal Akerman'

'Brief aan Chantal Akerman', *Skrien* 228, November 1998, 56. Translated from Dutch by Frans van Woerden.

Dear Chantal Akerman,

I have been thinking recently about letter-writing and about films.

In your films people write and read letters and wait. Waiting is a virtue. As if life is an empty bowl waiting to be filled. Films can be 'visual letters', epistles posted in the void. The film screen is an empty bowl waiting to be filled; filled not so much with the intentions of the filmmaker, but with what the public thinks they see. A personal history 'full of holes' – that is how you describe your biography at the start of *Histoires d'Amérique* (1989). But in your films I think I can see a lot of you: missing scenes, lost images, intimate and personal and yet remarkably anonymous. The camera as an unmoving eye that records seemingly insignificant moments. Never before has the emptiness been so full.

Sicilian storytellers say: time takes no time in a story. In your films, time lasts forever. Your endless scenes confuse my sense of time; I have had to throw my view of 'real time' overboard. Sometimes I love it, sometimes I can't stand it, but never can I take it for granted. I think I've never seen a film as timeless as *Jeanne Dielman* (1975) before. And every time I see the endless line of people waiting at the bus stop in *D'Est* (*From the East*, 1993), I learn to love those images more.

My own history is also full of letters – electronic nowadays, but for years handwritten letters were my only communication with my parents. Writing letters has become increasingly important to me. Letters are written to distant loved ones but sometimes also to close beloved, to bridge distances and to fill holes. But in the end, letters are also addressed a bit to yourself as well. You just hope that the recipient understands enough to read between the lines.

If you were to make *Histoires d'Amérique* in thirty years' time, would it be any different? Or would you, as a lover, refuse to change a single frame? [...]

Sincerely,
Fiona Tan

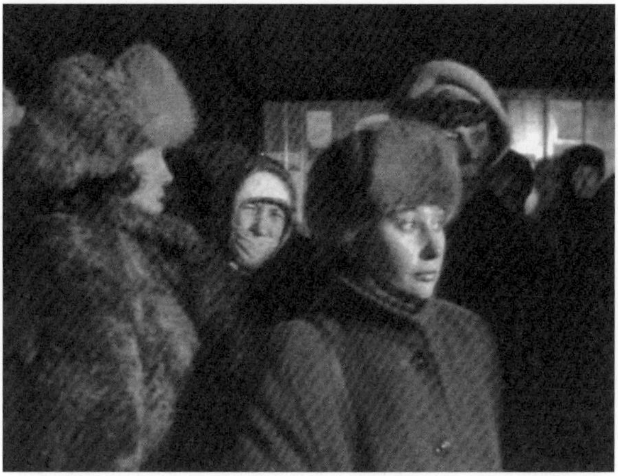

Chantal Akerman, *D'Est* (still), 1993

Fiona Tan
'Fragment II: Towards a Self-portrait of a City (Hong Kong)'

'Fragments towards a Self-portrait of a City I, II', in *Hong Kong*, Rijksakademie van Beeldende Kunsten, Amsterdam, 1998, n. p.

THE EAR

Every Sunday, under the impressive Norman Foster building of the Hong Kong and Shanghai Bank in the Central Business District, hundreds of young women gather together. They spend the whole day there, picnicking together in groups, singing songs, chatting. Reverberating through the building, the high-pitched loud chatter of all these women sounds like an incredible bird song. The women are all Filipina housemaids. Elsewhere in the city the other groups of housemaids – the Indonesians, the Malaysians – gather at their usual haunts.

If anything the incredible volume and noise of Hong Kong is something the Western ear finds difficult to withstand. Noise seems desirable to the Chinese. The Cantonese speak their speedy dialect with great volume and gusto. Hong Kong as a city is an incomprehensible conglomerate of sound. During my first stay the hotel windows could not be closed and I was sleepless in the initial nights. In my jet-lagged stupor there seemed no border between inside and out; the sirens raced across the room and the trams and buses screeched to a grinding halt at the foot of my bed. Firecrackers may be intended to frighten off evil spirits, but they must be accustomed to fewer decibels than the average Hongkongese.

My Chinese cousin, an acupuncturist, explained to me about the acupoints in the ear. The ear itself is a microcosm for the body. Acupoints in the ear can be very affective, but also very painful, if the doctor errs slightly. The trained eye can tell the personality from the shape and form of the ear. My ear can still hardly hear the inflections – the four tones of Mandarin – and I certainly cannot discern the six intonations of Cantonese, the official language of Hong Kong.

THE LIVER

In Kowloon, the oldest part of Hong Kong, wandering through the streets at sunset I had the feeling I was descending into the bowels of the city. It was humid and warm, the noise and lights of the shops enveloped me in a warm close heaviness. This was a city I could love. It definitely had a dark side, the clouded doors of the gambling parlours, the naked bulbs of the street vendors. Everything seemed like deep dark red velvet.

The thing I will remember most about Hong Kong are the smells, smells I know will still be there even after the British are long gone. Asian smells, smells of my childhood. The sweet tropical stench of rotting food and wastage, the intoxicating flavour of ripe mango, the steamy smells of rice, the fatty fragrance of pork wafting from so many makeshift street restaurants.

In Mandarin, the term 'food' is the same as 'medicine'. And the centre of feeling for the Chinese is not the heart but the liver. I have come to think that this is indeed a more apt place for feelings. Dark and silent but nonetheless large and swollen with blood, the liver is a very vital organ. But it is invisible; I could not point to its location in my body. This subversive position seems a very fitting home for feelings and emotions. Just like the back streets of Kowloon: this is where the city pulsates, absorbing the waste, purifying the body fluids.

In Chinese herbal medicine, with its unforgiving logic, the patient eats or drinks the infusions that he requires: tigers' bones for male potency; embryos for fertility; chilled foods and the medicines to cool the overheated; spices to heat the too cold. Health is a harmony and balance of warm and cool, yin and yang.

Western languages use other metaphors and analogies which reveal our image of the body: invasion, colonisation, resistance, foreign bodies, antibodies, germs, parasites, infections. A body at war from external influences: foreign diseases. A disease being by definition foreign, as Susan Sontag points out: syphilis – German measles, French fever, English ailment. Indeed Western medicine is based on interventions upon the body: pharma and surgery. The body as enemy. In the West we waste few thoughts on the less glamorous organs, those that perform functions we'd rather not think about. The Chinese in comparison are very grateful to their lower organs. An attitude I try to learn from.

THE HAIR

Hong Kong is a very vertical city. I am inclined to think of the city as a cross-section: underneath the pipes, the metro, then the waterways, the boats; the roads, pedestrians, the markets and shopping and eating areas; above that the living quarters crowded impossibly on top of each other. Then finally the dragon mountains above the city; the busy air space, the neon signs, the birds, the clouds, the aeroplanes. Its hair is blown by the occasional wind that comes down from the mountainous slopes flanking the island – the bones of nine dragons marking the hillsides. The high-rise buildings; the enormous and chaotic, knotted growth; the pencil buildings with their spectacular views combined with extreme lack of space and privacy. For a household of three to five people, the housing commission calculates a *maximum* requirement of 25 square metres.

Hair is the symbol for life. I get visions of Chinese water witches, their long hair flowing treacherously in the stream from which they have just emerged. To be trapped in hair as if constricted by tentacles. China is the number-one producer of human hair for wigs. I am lucky to say I have Chinese hair. My hair also knows a considerable growth rate.

Hong Kong was lost to the British as a result of the Opium Wars. The Emperor tried to stop them importing opium into China. My aunt explained to me that my great grandfather died young, weakened by the effects of opium addiction. This also is my inheritance of the colonial era. Later came the Boxer Revolution, when the activists cut off their long plaits in a sign of rebellion – a symbol of modernisation.

It was commonly thought that Europeans would get black hair if they stayed too long in China. I did it the easy way – I dyed mine temporarily black. The noisy and impolite Hongkongese did their best to rid me of the stereotypes and teach me that there are many varieties, shades and colours of Chinese thinking. Hong Kong remains a place for me to be trapped in my stereotypes and conventions; I cannot yet discard my clichés of East and West. Maybe I don't want to.

Fiona Tan
'Folly One' from *A Fool's Paradise*

Script-extract from four-part sound piece for headphones, *A Fool's Paradise*, 2010, a permanent public artwork commissioned by de Hoge Rielen, Kasterlee, Belgium. Each part corresponds to an imaginary architectural folly and a season; 'Folly One' is Winter.

Primary voices: ARCHITECT
FEMALE COMMENTATOR / ANALYST

ARCHITECT: Here we go. Deep breath now ...

Splash, the sound of someone diving into water. Gasps for breath upon surfacing:

Geez it's cold!

Gentle splashing sounds.

Japanese pearl divers hyperventilate before they dive. That way they can dive deeper and stay under for over a minute. Have you ever dived deep and looked up from under the water? The surface catches the sun and acts like a mirror.

The sound of frogs fades in.

Listen. It's getting dark now. That's when the male frogs start singing, competing to attract a female. Most amphibians are nocturnal. The singing usually stops about an hour before dawn. But during the day they wait.

A small boat rows past.

ARCHITECT: I'm waiting too. Waiting for inspiration. Waiting for the right moment in time. The right sort of waiting is very important for an architect. Something I only learned after architecture school. Building is a slow process requiring much patience. Stamina is indispensable.

The sound of flipping through radio channels, falling into a recorded conversation:

Folly comes from the French *folie*, meaning 'foolishness'. Generally a non-functional building erected to enhance a natural landscape.
Commonplace in gardens of the eighteenth and nineteenth centuries, but they have gone out of fashion nowadays.
Prime examples of an architecture about form without function! What is the point of a useless building?! *(Laughter)*

Water lapping.

ARCHITECT: I'm waiting for the winter to come, you see. I am waiting for the trees to lose their leaves. The frogs will then cease their song. Some of them will crawl into land and bury themselves in the mud. Others will sink to the bottom of the pool here and wait. Slowing their heart rate to four beats per minute, they will stop breathing through their lungs and breath instead through their skin. They must be sure to sink well below the ice or they will freeze to death.

Sound of heart beat slowing, changes into the sounds of sculpting and chipping at ice. An ice skater pulls in close.

I woke up early this morning. Early morning is the most beautiful time of day. Walk over to the wooden bench with me.

Sound of footsteps

If you wait with me and watch carefully we will be able to witness the first light when it touches the ice.

FEMALE COMMENTATOR: The question of where inspiration comes from, is a tricky one to answer. But it is feasible to presume that the situation and environment set off a chain of associations in the creator's mind.

ARCHITECT: As an architect I approach the creative process in four stages, and this here is the site of the first step. The primary idea stage is the most promising, the most exciting stage. Seen from here anything is possible. My imagination can conjure up the most amazing constructions in seconds.

FEMALE COMMENTATOR: This is a stage of shameless megalomania.

ARCHITECT'S VOICE, *heard from the middle of the water, panting because treading water*: When the time is right, you see, this will be the exact location for my most ambitious creation. You see the spot where the ripples are almost still? There! There I will build the most magnificent building to date.

FEMALE COMMENTATOR: Perhaps even a certain implausibility is necessary at this stage.

ARCHITECT'S VOICE: Originally I wanted to construct a glass cathedral. But glass is heavy and unforgiving. Suddenly it came to me: ice! Here I will build an ice palace that will rise up from the pool's surface, as high as the trees. The sunlight catching the ice buttresses will scatter tiny rainbows into the edge of your field of vision. The beams, blocks and strokes of ice will refract the view, breaking one view into a thousand. The ice will be bluish green in the shadows and orange and fluorescent yellow in the light! The building will be a weightless and graceful sculpture. Circumnavigate it and it will appear to shape-shift in front of your very eyes.

Sound of frogs calling fades outs slowly.

Fiona Tan
'Cloud Island'

Naoshima Note, no. 3, Benesse Art Site Naoshima, November 2011, 8–9.

My memories of Inujima, like a precious stone, shine and glisten quiet and proud.

Cloud Island (2010) depicts the small island of Inujima. This island is in many ways exemplary of Japan's last 400 years of industrialisation. Its surface bears marks and scars of history. Once an island of fishermen, Inujima then became a place of granite quarries and copper refineries. Now all the works stand empty; the quarries filled with water, factory chimneys crumbling. The island's aged population has dwindled to around fifty people who continue their day-to-day lives in this evocative and rather forgotten place where clipped trees and well-tended allotments stand next to abandoned homes. A story common to much of rural Japan.

I filmed on Inujima in May 2010 just as the first phase of Art House Project commissioned by the Naoshima Fukutake Art Museum Foundation was being completed. The architect Kazuyo Sejima has designed ten pavilions for the exhibition of artworks on the island. Four of which can now be visited. So this is a moment of transition for Inujima, and from time to time one glimpses the building works or one of the startling new structures whose shiny contemporaneity seems somehow at odds with its surroundings. This sense of change is felt almost more than it is seen. *Cloud Island* is a slow, quiet work: a film which is in many ways about waiting.

My memories of Inujima, like a precious stone, shine and glisten quiet and proud. Inujima is a place one can experience on a very human scale. It is as is if I can hold the island in the palm of my hand. The flowers, the sound of bees, ripples lapping at the wooden hulls of boats, wheelbarrows rolling down narrow streets, the islanders watering their gardens and chatting in Nakayama's tobacco shop, cumulus clouds blossoming in the late afternoon sky. Time has a different pace here.

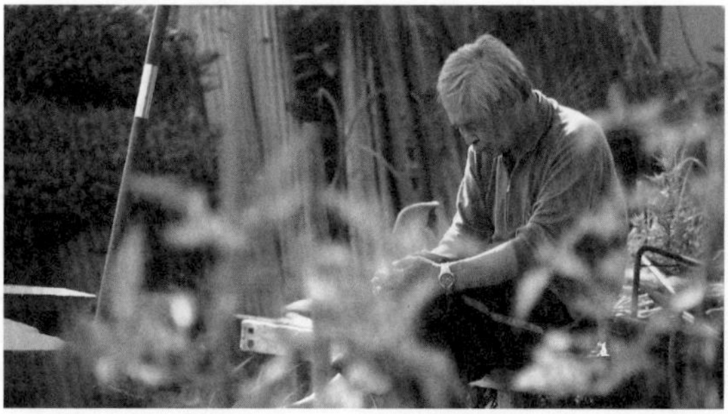

Cloud Island (still), 2010

Only memories remain locked, motionless as time passes. Life goes on. Pending change is unavoidable. With the local population on the smaller islands steadily depleting, this project comes at a crucial moment in time. People age, depart and die. Houses become abandoned and fall into disrepair and ruin. Nudging each other in surprising harmony, old traditional wooden houses nestle next to the exciting new pavilions of Kazuyo Sejima. A new chapter for this island is just beginning.

Fiona Tan
Excerpt from '10 Madnesses'

10 Madnesses, Amsterdam: Roma Publications, 2018, n. p.

PART ONE

On *Portraits of the Insane* by the nineteenth-century French artist Théodore Géricault. Five small oil paintings on canvas, c. 1819–24.

For years, I have been drawn to these portraits. I am fascinated and moved by them. To me they are haunting and strangely pertinent: unassuming, humane and somehow naked. They are portraits, but it is not clear of whom, or what their purpose was. They were painted shortly before the introduction of photography, and for me they are in a sense photographic: accurate and truthful observations, unmitigated registrations.

There is a text by John Berger, an essay he wrote after seeing an exhibition at the Grand Palais in Paris in 1991. On the streets of Paris, Berger notices that one of Géricault's insane, *Portrait of a Kleptomaniac*, (c. 1820) was chosen as 'mascot' for this exhibition's publicity. No written description I can attempt of these paintings can match Berger's masterful writing. Berger writes so well and so poignantly that I cut his essay out of the newspaper and fold it carefully away to keep in one of my drawers. This is the initial spark – Berger's essay 'A Man with Tousled Hair' (1991). The man in question is anonymous; we have never known his name – he is merely 'a' man and not 'the' man with tousled hair. I remember Berger writing about an image of humanity that was important and prescient, about humility and about compassion in a way that felt urgent and necessary. Perhaps now more than ever.

Some years ago I took the train to Ghent in Belgium to see *Portrait of a Kleptomaniac* for myself. It hangs in the Museum of Fine Arts Ghent together with some of Géricault's studies of amputated limbs. The *Kleptomaniac* is my favourite, but all five portraits have similar greenish hues and are approximately the same size. It is clear to me that Géricault painted them from life, without prior sketches and in a single sustained sitting. Furthermore, he painted them on-site, in the hospital. They are studies, but wonderful ones, unsigned and unpretentious. To me they are strikingly contemporary, as if the paint is still wet. And they are carefully observed. He paints what he sees and feels directly, swiftly but unhurried, and in the process, he paints without pretence. Compassionate and unadorned, Géricault lets no overt painter's virtuosity or ego get in the way. [...]

Géricault's five *Portraits of the Insane* – known in French as *Les Monomanes* – are said to be all that remain of the original ten commissioned portraits of insane patients from the Parisian hospitals of La Salpêtrière and Bicêtre. Each painting depicts a particular mental condition, a so-called 'monomania'. According to the attributed titles, these are portraits of a kleptomaniac, a woman addicted to gambling, a child kidnapper, a man with delusions of military grandeur, and a woman mad with envy.

Perhaps my most blatant consternation is the obvious discrepancy between the paintings' titles and what I actually see. To my contemporary eyes, the attributed obsessions and madnesses appear fanciful, even ridiculous. I am not looking at illustrations of illnesses nor am I looking at posed portraits of self-assured personalities. I see poorly dressed men and women who have clearly fallen upon hard times. Darkness surrounds them. Although their mood is hard to distill, it feels as though Géricault has managed to capture an accurate mix of several emotions, including dismay, distraction, and, in particular, absence. Each of those portrayed is looking 'off-screen', away and beyond. Each personality appears to have lost its centre.

The *Portrait of a Kleptomaniac* I have used before. This picture became the leitmotif and model for MP, the main character of my first feature film, *History's Future* (2015). MP (short for 'missing person') is a man who has lost his moorings, a person adrift, afflicted with retrograde amnesia; MP is a man for whom the world no longer makes any sense, and that is disconcerting and deeply unsettling. So I came to imagine a contemporary version of this man as a homeless nomad rebuilding his image of the world and searching for the right identity to steal in the hope that it might become his own.

Mental illness is surprisingly difficult to visualise. It reveals itself in abnormal behaviour usually only apparent over the course of time. It is not easily portrayed by still images. Madness or insanity is often very verbal; it manifests itself in how a patient speaks, acts and reacts. This is something I am increasingly coming to understand, and probably explains why there are so few depictions of insanity to be found throughout art history. But our definition of madness seems to say so much about what we consider normal and acceptable – about who we think we are and who we feel we should be. Then as now.

These paintings were perhaps trying to fulfil the role that photography would take in the medical and legal fields shortly thereafter: that of proof and possibly as a basis for diagnosis. Inadvertently, they seem to tell so much more. But if these paintings were intended for medical instruction, I can't help wondering whether their stark verisimilitude fails to fulfil the prescribed commission. They raise so many unanswered questions. [...]

To me, Géricault's working method is much like a journalist's – with a keen eye for drama, he responds to and analyses current affairs. He makes first-hand sketches of wounded soldiers returning defeated from battle, of executions in Rome. He interviews eyewitnesses and survivors of the shipwrecked *Medusa*. In his studio in Paris, he paints studies of amputated limbs that he has been able to borrow from hospital morgues. He prepares preliminary sketches depicting scenes of the slave trade. He makes drawings of condemned criminals, beggars and cripples in the streets of London.

It is generally agreed that Géricault painted *Les Monomanes* towards the end of his relatively short career, after spending over a year researching and painting his most famous work, the masterpiece *The Raft of the Medusa* (1818–9). Having first exhibited that monumental painting at the Paris Salon in 1819, Géricault undertakes several journeys to Great Britain, and over the next two years exhibits the painting in London, Dublin and elsewhere. He returns to Paris for the last time in December 1821. I consider it most likely that Géricault painted his *Monomanes* portraits in the initial months of 1822. Shortly thereafter, he incurs a serious spinal injury from the first of several equestrian accidents from which he never entirely recovers. He becomes increasingly ill, and is bedridden in the last months before his death in January 1824 at the age of thirty-two. [...]

There is so much we do not know. The works are unsigned. Géricault never mentions them, and during his lifetime they are never exhibited, nor are they listed among his possessions after his premature death. Even the most fundamental questions cannot be answered. We do not know when, where, why, what, how, of whom, or for whom. Nor do we know for certain how many there were or still are. So all we have are these five remaining portraits, if portrait is an ac-

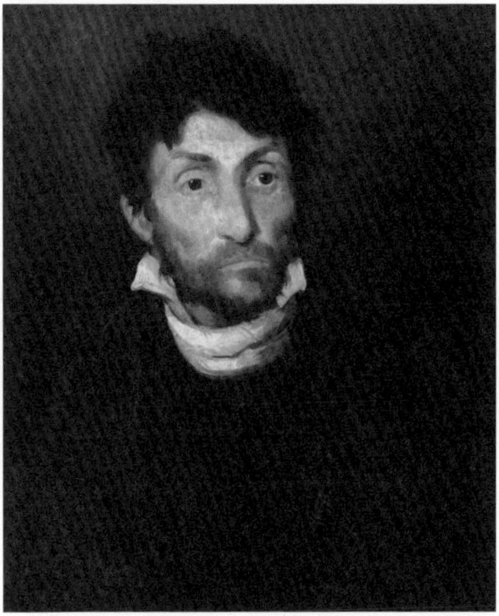

Théodore Géricault, *Portrait of a Kleptomaniac*, c. 1820

curate term for paintings such as these. No one doubts that they were painted by Géricault, and indeed neither do I. Despite the lack of information that surrounds them, these works – for all their silence – are wonderfully eloquent. [...]

I look again at the five *Portraits of the Insane*. Two years ago, I travelled to Frankfurt to see four of the five hanging together. They remain small and unassuming, particularly if compared to Géricault's famed *The Raft of the Medusa*. I look at pale skin and gaunt faces, at absent gazes. And I am struck once again by their immediacy. [...]

The old man with illusions of military grandeur is in his shirt sleeves; no man would appear like this in public, only at home. He is wearing a crushed and worn policeman's bonnet and the 'medal' around his neck is a simple metal disc strung on a leather thong bearing the number 121. I am inclined to think it is a label, as on a wine barrel. The child kidnapper is wearing a hat typical for the time and, although it is hard to see details, he appears relatively well-dressed. The kleptomaniac appears to be the best-dressed and youngest of them all, but his head is bare and his white, striped and possibly silken tie is wound loosely around his neck rather than neatly tied into a bow according to the fashion of the day. Having a beard is certainly unfashionable for that time, and his is a very scraggly, unkempt one.

In fact, now that I look closer at the male patients, I can see that they are all unshaven. They are all wearing quite heavy clothing, in layers as if for winter, but it is not possible to tell for certain what season it is. I am reminded of the many vagrants I see here on the streets and at traffic lights in Los Angeles who wear many layers of clothing regardless of the weather. [...]

I want to know, *really* know, more about the five people portrayed in these paintings. I want my knowledge to be as accurate as it can possibly be. I do not want to guess or approximate, nor do I want to gloss over and hastily fill in the gaps. Research and process might be fashionable terms in the current discourse on contemporary art, but surely that is precisely why there can be no excuse for half-hearted reconstruction or misinformed conjecture. I feel that I owe this much, at least, to these anonymous individuals and to my own artistic integrity. I am not sure what drives an art historian to undertake her research, but I know that, for myself, it can be a start of the creation of new works dealing with contemporary portraiture in lens-based, time-based, imagery. [...]

PART TWO

On 1 January 1822 the Parisian hospital of La Salpêtrière has a patient population of 4,856. Records of numbers of *aliénées* – the insane – have been lost, but in the previous year they had numbered 1,542. In comparison, the population of Paris was roughly half a million at the time. Over the course of 1822 there are 1,696 admissions, and 1,029 of these patients require care. There are 993 discharges and 726 deaths.

When I look at maps of both institutions, I see enclosed citadels providing all food, housing and necessary activities within their own walls. In a map from 1820, La Salpêtrière appears entirely self-contained. All functions and offices are neatly arranged in a neoclassical architectural structure. This enlightened layout would seem to contradict the dark reality of life for those incarcerated within these walls. The buildings for the prisoners are separate from the dormitories and workshops of the poor. Every ward has its own courtyard. There are many rows of small cells for the insane. There are fields for crops, vegetable gardens, forests for firewood, pigsties, workshops, courtyards, water cisterns, kitchens, a laundry, shower rooms, dormitories, cells. As would be expected, there is a church, an infirmary, a pharmacy, a mortuary, administration offices and housing for the employees. There is even a cemetery. A small city unto itself.

The organisation of life inside the hospital walls has been dutifully recorded. The populations of the elderly, the infirm and the poor are divided into five groups. There is a first division for the retired; a second for the blind, paralysed and infirm (staffed by a total of six employees); a third for the seventy-year-olds and the able-bodied elderly (with one employee per fifty patients); and a fourth group for those with dementia or cancer (one employee per twelve patients). The insane – *les aliénées* – make up the fifth division, comprising 670 beds in 1814, but by 1833 this number has grown to well over a thousand. All able-bodied residents and patients are obliged to work every day of the week without pay. Many work in the workshops, sewing and weaving or making ropes and string. Others work in the gardens and the kitchens. This arrangement is in line with the thinking of the time that charity should not be free.

Once every three years, the indigent are supplied with one winter coat and one white summer coat, as well as one petticoat and one linen corset. Each year they receive one pair of woollen stockings and one pair of cotton stockings. The laundries supply one shirt, one bonnet and one scarf every Saturday. Cotton and linen clothing that is more than three years old is handed down to the *aliénées*.

To my disappointment, most medical observation records have not withstood the ravages of time, and observations of only eleven patients still exist from the year 1822. It is clear that many patients are poor. Many arrived as children – perhaps orphaned or abandoned by their families. And they will stay in La Salpêtrière their whole lives. In the admissions register, I look through pages and pages of 'fools, idiots and cretins', epileptics, patients with dementia, patients undergoing treatment, patients receiving no treatment, the incurable. [...]

So allow me then to introduce to you here a few patients from this extremely random and small sampling. Meet Marie Louise Charlotte Grandidier – she is admitted to La Salpêtrière on 7 January 1795 (or *17 Nivose IV*, according to the French Republican Calendar) and dies there, aged seventy-one, on 8 February 1852. The doctor notes: 'Low intelligence, hereditary in nature. She cannot read, she cannot count, she does not know her age. Her perception of feelings has always been weak. A good person, she helps despite her age by washing the dishes.' The monthly reports duly note: 'Status unchanged.' From March 1852 on, they are empty. And meet Jeanne Antoine Crochet – admitted on 19 October 1796. Her notes report: 'Imbecile. Entered the institute at twelve years. She spent her whole life here. Incapable of any work other than combing wool or unpicking woven threads.' In November 1852, her monthly report notes a grave and chronic state of ill health. She dies on the 8 November 1852. And meet Victorie Augustine Bourgeois, who enters the asylum on 6 June 1815 and stays until 6 June 1852. Her notes report she is an imbecile, and that she was seduced with cake and subsequently gave birth to a daughter.

Venereal disease is rampant and incurable. Syphilis is a particularly nasty disease, which slowly but lethally affects the brain and nervous system. Late-stage patients are afflicted with severe delusions and eventually by complete paralysis. The French physician Antoine-Laurent Bayle first describes this general paralysis in 1822, but cannot yet link it to syphilis. Only a century later, after the development of penicillin in 1928, can the disease be cured. Many of the so-called insane have been mentally disabled either from birth or by misfortune – individuals with Down's syndrome or other genetic diseases, those with epilepsy, senile dementia and Parkinson's disease, and those who have suffered a stroke or other brain damage.

In the 1780s, before the French Revolution, La Salpêtrière was a huge place where as many as 10,000 women were housed. But even after the Revolution, both state-run institutions are many things at once: a hospital, asylum, prison and home for the elderly and the destitute. Just as before 1789, they still function as a place to confine and contain society's unwanted: the delinquent, the indigent, the ill and undesired.

Bicêtre (for men) and Salpêtrière (for women) are both associated with gloom and horror in the minds of the general population. Prostitutes who have been picked up off the streets are locked up in La Salpêtrière. These are places one goes, never to return alive. Female prisoners were moved to St. Lazare in 1794, but the former prison building at La Salpêtrière is still there in 1822. And in fact the Parisian police in Paris incarcerated 300 women in La Salpêtrière in the early 1800s. Arguably, the hospital is, in effect, still in use as a dumping ground, as one jail among others in the city. Mortality rates are high. Its population was struck by a typhus epidemic in 1814. Outbreaks of cholera and influenza will later follow.

In 1822, although Bicêtre's official title is 'Home for the Elderly', it is also still a prison. I find first a list of the names of all detainees in Bicêtre from 1831 through

1851. Is there any separation between patients and detainees, I wonder? Did doctors also treat inmates? Beautiful handwriting carefully notes each man's characteristics, and in the process details of tough lives are revealed. Scars, tattoos, pockmarks from small pox, missing fingers or limbs, branded like cattle with the letters 'TP' – forced labour (the sure sign of an escaped convict) – 'left hand missing', crippled knees, etc. In theory, both a kleptomaniac and a child kidnapper have committed a felony. I spend a long day sorting through the entries. Through a process of elimination, I end up with the names of two men, one of whom, for me, might possibly be Géricault's kleptomaniac. Enthusiastically, I attempt to give this portrait an identity – a name and a biography. But weeks later I am able to consult another archive, and I learn that all detainees wear the same striped uniform. Detainees are not asylum patients – there are other lists for those. [...]

The superintendent at Bicêtre is Jean-Baptiste Pussin, who works together with his wife Marguerite and was a former asylum patient himself. He is in charge of the day-to-day operations of the insanity wards. It is thanks to Pussin that chains were removed from the patients. The relatively humane and orderly conditions described in official reports of Bicêtre in the 1790s were the result of his supervision, care and management. Later, Pussin is transferred to La Salpêtrière at the request of the newly appointed chief physician, Philippe Pinel, considered the grandfather of French psychiatry. At La Salpêtrière, Pussin is able to reorganise and run the insane sections for the women in a similar fashion.

Eventually I obtain access to entry and observation records of patients at Bicêtre from this time. The number of entries is staggering, and many patients appear to stay for only a relatively short time. Numerous patients die within a few days or months. The doctors' observations are very brief and in marked contrast to those from its sister institution, La Salpêtrière. Perhaps this is due to that fact that Pinel was no longer head physician; Bicêtre certainly feels tougher and more anonymous. [...]

I go through the entry lists from La Salpêtrière once more. The duration of each patient's stay is dutifully calculated and recorded: 13,897 days, 16,348 days, etc. In the column listing the cause or diagnosis, I read: mania, profound melancholy, partial mania with fury, occasional religious mania, (incurable) imbecility, epilepsy. But nowhere do I see any form of monomania listed as a diagnosis. Is it perhaps too soon for this term to have entered these official documents?

So what is monomania? It is time to answer this question: the answer has been eluding me for months. [...]

PART THREE

Philippe Pinel was head physician first at Bicêtre, and then at La Salpêtrière from 1795 until his death in 1826. But in 1798 he also published a standard work of nosology: a systemic catalogue of medical diagnoses, which had gone through six editions by 1818. In the late eighteenth century, doctors believed there were four kinds of madness: mania (furious excitement), melancholy (depression), idiocy and cretinism. Pinel placed his insane patients in separate wards according to these categories. According to Pinel's student Jean-Étienne Esquirol, monomania was positioned between the extremes of mania and melancholy.

One should not forget that the very concept of madness as a mental condition was quite new at that time. In the age of reason, unreason and the irrational needed to be locked up and hidden away. Mind-body debates considered the rational to be human and the physical to be animal. For Descartes, mental illness was a contradiction in terms: illness could only be something physical and of the senses, and the mind was not something physical. '*Je pense, donc je suis.*' But if rational thought was disturbed, then 'I' no longer am, and a state of alienation becomes apparent. (Indeed, as already mentioned, psychiatrists in France were known as alienists.) To have lost one's mind was therefore to be only animal. It was merely a small step, then, to consider the insane to be impervious to extreme heat or cold and who could be exhibited like animals in a zoo, as they indeed were every Sunday at Bicêtre right up until 1789.

The new study of psychiatry and the manner in which the alienists grouped together illnesses and labelled them as mental illness nonetheless feels ad hoc and messy to me. It is also striking to notice how prevalent certain conditions are at certain times. Then it was religious mania, erotomania, homicidal monomania, and delusions of military grandeur (which we would now call megalomania). Now it is schizophrenia, depression, OCD (obsessive-compulsive disorder), autism, Asperger's syndrome, bipolar disorder and anorexia. Even today I can see that psychiatry is still struggling with the definition and the nosology of mental illness, and with the delineation of boundaries that separate psychiatry from psychology. There is an ongoing discussion as to whether schizophrenia is genetic or psychological, and as to whether it is a disease or not. [...]

I return once more to the hospital patient records, curious as to when and how monomania first appears in the lists as diagnosis. The La Salpêtrière admission records from 1822 never list monomania as a diagnosis. The earliest surviving comprehensive patient observation records I can find date from January 1827. These pages – written only five years later – are filled with it. Statistics show how swiftly the ideas of early psychiatrists Esquirol and Étienne-Jean Georget were being adopted. Considerable numbers of patients are diagnosed as afflicted with religious monomania or monomania of pride, with a *monomanie amoureuse* or with a *monomanie avec hallucination*. There are patients who believe themselves to be the daughter of the King of France. Other patients self-identify as empress and become furious if not obeyed. One woman 'refuses food, but has the power to make it rain or shine.'

How beautiful to believe you can control the sun, the wind, the rain! I cannot think of a more poetic or creative way of finding an escape for one's own powerlessness. In my notebook, I quickly make some sketches – this is an image I can use in my new piece. Sadly, I also read that in many cases the doctor recommends that these patients be transferred to the ward for the incurable, where they will receive only minimum care. The portrait of the elderly man with delusions of military command was initially the portrait which interested me the least, perhaps because, of all the paintings, his condition is the most obvious. But now I look at it with fascination and sympathy. […]

PART FOUR

Mental illnesses have much to do with absence. More provocative than presence, absence is also more unsettling. I have started working on filming five 'portraits' to take the place of the missing ones, but I am also developing plans for several other pieces.

10 Madnesses will be a project that will occupy my time for a while to come. I think about the young maid, Henriette Cornier, accused of murdering an eighteen-month-old infant in 1827. Her case was the first to be defended on the grounds that she was afflicted with a homicidal monomania. There will never be a satisfactory answer to the question as to why she committed this crime. I am still looking for the transcripts of her court case. Maybe I can find a way of scripting a monologue about monomania that deals with her story. The image of a sleepwalker traversing a dark and empty expanse – of someone who is both present and absent – is another night-time vision which will not let me go. I see a woman drifting across a landscape with that light sureness of foot that comes with the blindsight only a sleepwalker can possess.

Again I am struck by the theatricality of insanity. Madness is a mask; it can serve to hide oneself in an attempt to escape great pain. And there is intense loneliness. Over the last 250 years there has been less change in the way society deals with unwanted individuals than we would care to admit. From the confines of my car I look at the homeless people begging at busy intersections in Los Angeles as they struggle to survive at society's periphery. Their gaze is often off-centre. I was recently reminded that Ronald Reagan was sympathetic to the ideas of anti-psychiatry, and as governor of California closed down all state-run mental hospitals. Surely many homeless people also have mental health issues? I rather suspect that no government official would wish to know just how many.

I am unable to draw any definitive conclusions regarding these paintings. Any evidence I have been able to uncover is too circumstantial. To me, it makes perfect sense that the painter who painted studies of amputated body parts in all their ambiguity – as a *nature morte* or still life, simply and directly as they were before his eyes – would paint studies such as these. If Géricault had studied medicine he would not have painted these portraits in this way, and that is one of their great strengths among many others. They refuse interpretation.

It is time to take leave from my brief odyssey into the historical medical archives, for now at least. As far as I am concerned, these studies by Géricault are among the most evocative portrayals of madness ever painted. He painted these people and their conditions too well for any doctor to be able to use them merely as types or illustrations. He caught their lostness, the essence of their alienation, which slips past and away from any easy grasp. Insanity remains, in a way, an invisible condition. Words fail me when I try to get closer to any kind of *punctum* in these pictures, although a *punctum* – a piercing quality – is certainly there. The enigma which is their raison d'être I find fitting and appropriate. Sometimes it is good not to know for sure, and to be left hovering in uncertainty.

Let me end this essay where my search began, with 'A Man with Tousled Hair'. I would like to finish with a quotation from a writer who died earlier this year, in 2017, and whose memory I wish to honour here. John Berger, who writes of the *Portrait of a Kleptomaniac*:

> *So we face him today without an historical or a modern hope. Rather we see him as a consequence. And this, by the natural order of things, means we see him with indif-*

ference. We don't know him. He's mad. He's been dead for more than a hundred and fifty years. [...] The image pinched. In it there is a compassion that refutes indifference and is irreconcilable with any easy hope.
To what an extraordinary moment this painting belongs in the history of human representation and awareness! Before it, no stranger would have looked so hard and with such pity at a lunatic. A little later and no painter would have painted such a portrait without exhorting a glimmer of a modern or romantic hope.

And further on he writes:

There are historical periods when madness appears to be what it is: a rare and abnormal affliction. There are other periods – like the one we have just entered – when madness appears to be typical.

Fiona Tan

‘*Diagonal Composition*, Jeff Wall, 1993’

Affinities/Verwantschappen, catalogue of the Collection, De Pont Museum, Tilburg, 2019, 162–5.

This is a small work – a backlit slide. In the De Pont Museum it is tucked away underneath a metal staircase in an in-between room which provides passage between the front and main museum spaces. It appears quite at home in this narrow, purely utilitarian passage, a space which has retained much of the building’s original industrial character. Despite its modest dimensions, the lightbox frame protrudes quite a way from the wall. I am tempted even to describe it as clunky.

Without doubt, this work was made by one the most important photographers of his generation. It was purchased quite early in the history of the Museum, and as far as I can remember, it has always been hanging here in this out-of-the-way hidden corner. Jeff Wall made several of these compositions; all of them are still lifes portraying cleaning utensils positioned in forgotten and unnoticed corners. This piece is unassuming and unpretentious – qualities I admire in any artwork.

It took me a long time to feel that I had gained a good understanding of Jeff Wall’s work. But I have always felt a kind of unnameable fascination for his photographs. Even before I learnt about the classical references which Wall is inspired by and which he embodies in his photographs, I certainly felt them. This gives his photographs something paradoxical, both an appealing strangeness and an unexpected familiarity. A striking sense of timeliness and timelessness, which I could at once grasp and which at the same time still always escapes me.

Wall himself talks about this *Diagonal Composition* (1993) in his usual dry and cerebral manner: these pieces are like studies, but are not studies. He describes himself as a picture-maker and talks of how he resists the idea that small pictures are less important than big ones. Of how there is no narrative in his work, only suggestion. Like a painter considering the translation of the three-dimensional

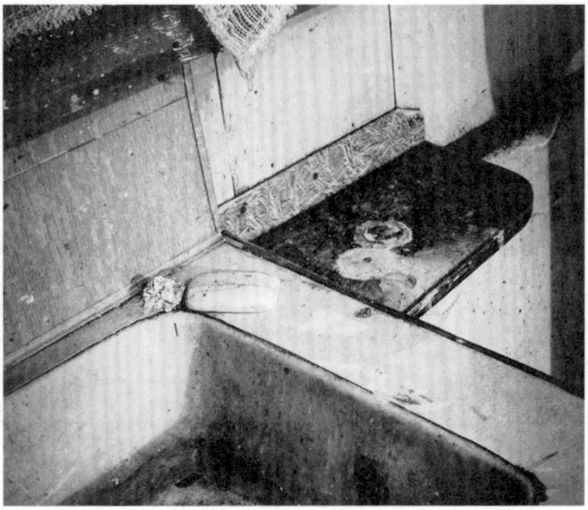

Jeff Wall, *Diagonal Composition*, 1993

onto the flat surface, he talks about the formal concerns of the rectangular composition and about his desire to 'make something happen within the rectangular'.

For me there is nothing derogatory in the word 'study'. I like to look at studies: I can feel closer to the maker, I can learn to better appreciate someone's motivation and method. Some speak of heightened reality when discussing Jeff Wall's carefully staged photographs, but this label feels less applicable when I look at this picture. It is a study of a corner of a workshop or studio. The image has a painterly quality – the conscious consideration of lines and composition, but also the pleasurable observation and registration of colour and of happenstance. I see a corner which one would normally pay no attention to: a place for washing hands, for cleaning up after the job is done. It is a grubby, perhaps honest depiction of something usually overlooked and considered unworthy, but the precise pictorial composition and lighting make me look again, and again.

Every time I come to the museum in Tilburg it hangs there quietly in its corner like a permanent fixture or a point of reference. Is it for me a kind of touchstone? I can look at it and recall all of Jeff Wall's impressive oeuvre. I find this reassuring and pleasing and indeed unusual in our fast-flowing, ever-changing contemporary art world. In fact I would very much like it if this work can stay hanging where it is, as it is. A still and unmoving work around which all the waves, ebbs and floods of contemporary art can come freely to rise up, shine or flicker, and eventually die down.

Fiona Tan

Excerpt from 'Women in Storage, or GAAF: Found Images from the Agfa Archive, 1952–68'

Fiona Tan: GAAF, Museum Ludwig, Cologne; Verlag der Buchhandlung Walther König Cologne, 2019, 52–75.

STORAGE ROOM

My first glimpse into the storage room is of a small windowless space. As the fluorescent tubes flicker on, I am confronted by several rows of rudimentary metal racks filled with folders and boxes and rows and rows of A5-format envelopes. Some of these are manila, but most of them are orange.

As the stock photo archive from the Agfa company's advertising department, these negatives would once have been neatly organised and catalogued, but the index has now been lost and I haven't been able to find it. Furthermore, a pipe burst several years back and damaged many of these photographs and negatives beyond repair. I'm told that although this forgotten archive has been stored here for over forty years, no one has ever really had a look at it.

I remove one of the orange A5 envelopes from a shelf at random. Attached to the front of the envelope is a small contact print of a colour photograph, and above that a handwritten letter and number. The 6 × 6 original negative is stored inside. The image I'm looking at is a medium shot of a woman wearing a green silk scarf and holding a brightly coloured umbrella. This is clearly a staged photograph taken by a professional photographer, and I strongly suspect that the woman is a model. Her clothing is immaculate, her make-up perfect, her shiny blonde hair clean and coiffed. Her smile and expression are bright and appealing but also disingenuous, managed. Although the resulting image is well-lit, colourful, and professional, it's also generic and impersonal. The image reminds me of the photos on my mother's knitting patterns when I was a girl. What comes to mind is the word *gaaf* – colloquial Dutch for 'neat' or 'perfect'. What am I looking at? And perhaps even more pertinently, what am I *not* seeing?

RETROGRADE AMNESIA

Since that first introduction to the storage room, I've been able to establish that the photographs from this archive were taken between 1952 and 1968. This was before my time, and its geographic location – West Germany – is not my country nor even my continent. I was born towards the end of this period, and into a different cultural mix; most of my childhood was spent in Australia. Nonetheless, these images feel familiar. I remember a colour studio portrait of my mother as a young university graduate, from 1960. She had just become engaged. Her portrait bears a striking resemblance to these images, and I see almost the same look, the same clothing, the same pose.

When I imagine life in the 1950s, I think of a uniform, conformist, homogeneous era. Social values were based entirely upon the family, and traditional stereotypical notions of male and female roles were reinforced. This was a period of rigid social cohesion and of official optimism, as Joan Didion so aptly described it in *The White Album* (1979). But what strikes me now is just how uniform and dominant this social conformity appears to have been across all Western countries. Whether in the United States, Germany, France, Britain or Australia scarcely seemed to matter: women dressed and behaved in the same way.

The historical narrative is common knowledge. Directly after World War II, just about every nation was affected by shortages and hardship. The European winter of 1945–6 was particularly harsh. National economies on both sides were battered or depleted. Even in Great Britain, rationing continued until 1954. However, within a few short years the global economy managed to recover and began to flourish. Economic growth in the 1950s and 60s was unbridled, and unemployment virtually non-existent. This was a period of ever-increasing prosperity. The baby boom led to the housing boom, and ushered in the consumption society. Above all, this was not a time to dwell on the past. The camera lens was most definitely pointed towards a brighter and better future. [...]

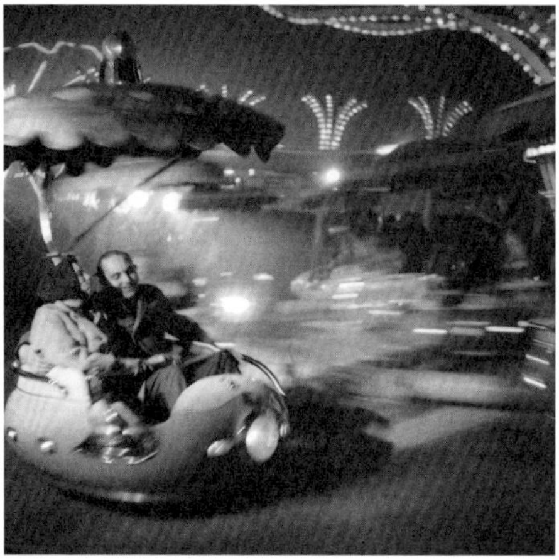

Agfa advertising photograph (CC 174), 1950s/60s

WOMAN – SUMMERTIME

I notice that the largest categories in the Agfa advertising archive are labelled AB and ABB. The subject of these categories is always a woman. Without exception, the woman in the photo is young, slim, pretty and impeccably dressed in colourful clothes. She is always happy and having fun. AB could perhaps best be described as 'Woman at leisure – Summertime'. The shooting locations are mainly outdoors, and the sun is shining. The model poses on the beach or in a field in the countryside, mostly in Germany, occasionally abroad. ABB portrays the 'Woman at leisure in the snow'. She poses with skis, or playfully holds up snowballs. [...]

It goes almost without saying that the images in this archive are exclusively white and Western. The photos before me show pretty young German women, sometimes in traditional Bavarian dress holding up a pretzel and a mug of beer, or perched on the hood of a shiny new Mercedes. Of the several thousand photos, only two show models with different racial backgrounds, and one of these, taken in Paris, shows a black man we see only from behind.

I will also zoom out for a moment and offset the life portrayed in these pictures with a few major events in the world at large during the same period: Mao Zedong declared the People's Republic of China in 1949, the same year the Netherlands finally recognised Indonesian independence after four bloody years of fighting.

A wave of decolonisation swept through Africa in the 50s and early 60s, and many African nations declared their independence. In 1955, West Germany welcomed an Italian labourer as the country's first 'guest worker', or *Gastarbeiter*. Nine years later, the millionth *Gastarbeiter* – Armando Rodrigues de Sá from Portugal – was welcomed into the German workforce and presented with the gift of a moped.

CELIBACY CLAUSE

Before pointing the lens more specifically towards Germany, I need to turn back the clock by a few years. At the end of World War II in 1945, an estimated eleven million people were left homeless and stateless across Europe. A year later, there were still over one million displaced persons in Germany alone. Major cities had been heavily bombed and lay in ruins. The coal and steel sector, military industries and factories were dismantled and divided amongst the occupying Allied forces.

The currency reform in 1948 marked the beginning of what came to be known of as the Miracle on the Rhine, or *Wirtschaftswunder*. In 1949, two German nations were established: the Federal Republic of Germany in the West and the German Democratic Republic in the East. The story for women was the same in West Germany as it was in Great Britain and the United States. During the war, women had taken on the duties and jobs traditionally done by men. The *Trümmerfrauen*, or 'rubble women', had helped clean up and rebuild the bombed city centres of Berlin and Cologne and Hamburg. But after World War II, men were returning home and to the workforce, and women were actively encouraged to give up paid employment and return exclusively to unpaid domestic chores at home. The cover of an issue of the German women's magazine *Für Sie* from 1960 displays a picture of an elegant young woman holding a feather duster. The headline reads, *Hausfrau – schönster Beruf* ('Housewife – the finest profession').

Laws were introduced or revised to the disadvantage of women. As a result of the *Zölibatsklausel* ('celibacy clause'), female civil servants lost their jobs as soon as they married. The *Doppelverdienergesetz* ('Double Income Act') meant that married couples who both worked paid higher taxes, a disincentive designed to ensure there would be just one breadwinner per household. Only in East Germany were women entitled by law to earn the same as men for the same work. West German marriage laws were revised only in 1977 when they were changed to state that 'both husband and wife are entitled to work'. All the way up to 1977, a husband was allowed to prevent his wife from working outside the home.

While all countries on both sides lost many young men during World War II, German losses were very high. In 1950, females in West Germany outnumbered males by four million. [...] Although women were clearly in the majority, this didn't seem to help them gain equal rights any sooner.

A woman in the 50s was said to have only two questions in life: What shall I wear? and What shall I cook? But the reality of daily life across much of Europe – and certainly in Germany directly following World War II – was that there was nothing to wear and no food to cook. [...]

THE HAPPY HOUSEWIFE

The women portrayed in these Agfa advertising photos never seem to work, never get their hands dirty, and never seem discontented in any way. Their life is one of leisure, of pleasure. The couples increasingly portrayed in the later photos from the 1960s appear to be romantically fulfilled. What of family life, the subject central to almost every photo album created since the introduction of consumer cameras?

As a writer for women's magazines in the 1950s and 60s, Betty Friedan interviewed many American women, and described and analysed what she called the 'problem that has no name': a pervasive crisis surrounding the role of women and the image of womanhood. Together with the English translation of Simone de Beauvoir's *The Second Sex* in 1953, Friedan's publication of *The Feminine Mystique* in 1963 is widely recognised as signalling the start of the second wave of feminism. Men, women and children were all required to adhere to rigid expectations and social norms. But a woman's identity was dictated entirely by her duties towards others: her role was, first and foremost, to be a housewife and mother. Even though a woman might have had a college education, she was required to stop working once she married, and her life was completely subservient to the needs of her husband and children. In the United States, the average age of marriage for women dropped considerably: by the end of the 1950s, this was 20, and fourteen million girls were engaged by the age of 17. Whereas in 1920, 47% of the college population was female, by 1958 this figure had dropped to only 35%.

'All I wanted', one woman told Betty Friedan, 'was what every other American girl wanted – to get married, have four children, and live in a nice house in a nice suburb.' Fighting for emancipation or chasing a career were not on these women's horizons. But housewives were increasingly coming to realise that despite how rosy and cheerful they appeared from the outside, their lives were not fulfilled. The happy housewife was a myth, a twisted fantasy. 'I feel empty somehow … incomplete.' And: 'I feel as if I don't exist.' One woman, who left college at 19 in order to get married, explained to Friedan:

> *I love the kids and Bob and my home. There's no problem you can even put a name to. But I'm desperate. I begin to feel I have no personality. I'm a server of food and a putter-on of pants and a bedmaker, somebody who can be called on when you want something. But who am I?*

DOES SHE … OR DOESN'T SHE?

The successful television series *Mad Men* (2007–15) is centred around the world of Madison Avenue advertising agencies in the 1960s. Peggy Olson is hired as a secretary; she is inexperienced, earnest and diligent. She soon learns that the role of secretary is one of mother, waitress and sometimes whore, and that discretion is the highest virtue. But Peggy is young and ambitious, and aspires to become a copywriter. However, Peggy can't have both a career and a marriage, and she has to work harder than her male colleagues to gain respect and achieve success. As a successful copywriter, she is doomed to remain a single, unmarried mother.

Only recently did I learn that the character of Peggy Olson was based on a real person, a successful copywriter from the 1950s and 60s named Shirley Polykoff. When Clairol launched its new campaign for hair colour in 1956, it was Polykoff who came up with the slogan 'Does she or doesn't she?'. Previously, dyeing one's hair had been frowned upon, but advertising like this changed all of that. Furthermore, the new hair dye products enabled women to do this in private at home. With mixed feelings, I note that some of the most well-known advertising slogans – in particular, those for beauty products for women – were in fact written by women. The Clairol campaign was hugely successful: sales figures rocketed, and letters of gratitude poured in. One of them read, 'Thank you for changing my life.' This was liberation through shopping, and women were deliberately targeted by many American advertising campaigns.

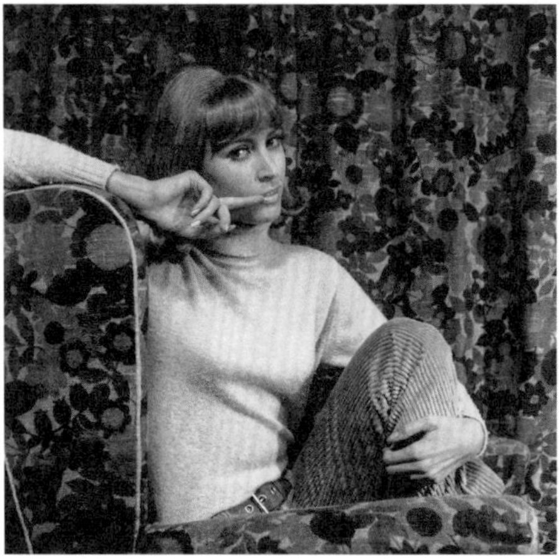

Agfa advertising photograph (AB 2445), 1950s/60s

Although Polykoff was creating new, confident self-images for women, they were still about how men looked at you. In 1973, another female copywriter, Ilon Specht, wrote one of the most successful slogans ever. It was for Préférence hair colour by L'Oréal, and it was to become the motto for an entire generation: 'Because I'm worth it.' If we're to believe Peggy Olson's boss, Don Draper, the art of advertising is quite simple. He says,

> *Advertising is based on one thing. Happiness. What is happiness? Happiness is the smell of a new car. It's freedom from fear. It's a billboard on the side of a road that screams with reassurance that whatever you're doing is okay. You are okay.*

So what of these photographs produced at the request of Agfa's advertising department? Advertisements for photography were aimed mostly at men, and indeed, perhaps still are. So it is only logical, then, that the photographs used in these ads would depict the subject that appealed most to this target group. In reality, men were using their cameras to take photographs of their young families, their children's First Communion and perhaps Carnival festivities, the new car, maybe a picnic by the side of the road. But despite this fact, without exception, the stock photos stored in the archive depict slender young women who are free and unmarried. These young girls are definitely in the marriage market, but they aren't yet hooked. Sometimes they even appear to show a certain independence and spirit. These women aren't bound by domestic chores or housekeeping. I see no mothers looking after the children, washing the clothes, cooking the evening meal. The photos from this archive that portray a mother and child can be counted on one hand. This is perhaps the strangest and most interesting paradox of all: Agfa cameras, film and photographic paper were being advertised with pictures that were, in fact, not being taken. But the image of a carefree young woman was undoubtedly an attractive and compelling one for both men and women, married or single.

These images exude only good vibes. The sun is always shining. Things are perfect. They contain the promise of the good life: this is what happiness, success, prosperity and well-being looks and feels like. A beautiful young girl – your beautiful young girl – scantily clad in a bikini, waiting for you in the wicker beach chair. The Instagram pictures young women and men currently post aren't all that different. They're equally fake, with one important difference: these individuals take the pictures themselves. The women portrayed in these Agfa photographs were never real to start with, but perhaps – even today – we somehow, very occasionally, still want them to be.

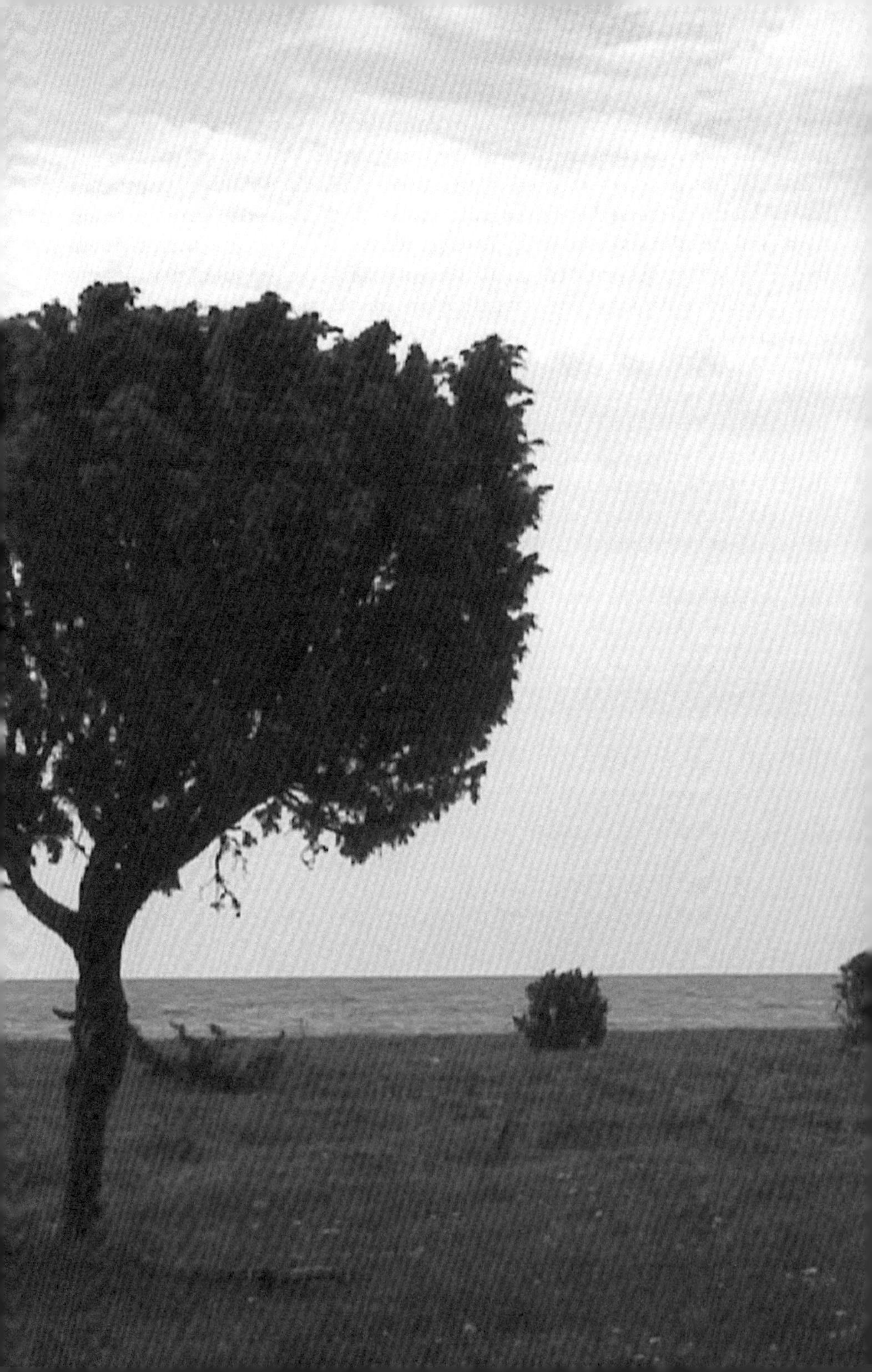

Critical Overviews

Island (still), 2008

Doris von Drathen
Excerpt from 'Aerial Roots'

Fiona Tan: Disorient, catalogue for the Dutch Pavilion, 53rd Venice Biennale, Heidelberg: Kehrer Verlag, 2009, 2.03–2.11. Translated from German by Matthew Partridge. Revised 2020.

Memory is vision tied to place. This paradox harbours its freedom. Even if memory is attached as though umbilically to the place of its origin, it nonetheless has no need of the site's objective presence to bring it to mind and to keep the ties alive. The fibres of recollection that issue from language, images, emotions and sense impressions are aerial roots[1] – they can abide in a context which dissolves the boundaries of time and space, which flows back and forth between past, present and future and joins them together. To be rooted in earth is not the norm: human existence is grounded in memory as its vital source of nourishment. From the earliest days of life onwards, while the remembering eye proceeds by creating an ever-expanding space of subjectivity based on its own proportions, designations, evaluations and criteria for selection, it is weaving an indispensable filter of orientation for the founding of the subject's consciousness and identity capable of accommodating all later experiences, assessments and reflections. This fabric of perception acts as the tiller and the depth sounder for navigating the unknown seas of life. A repressed, curtailed or damaged framework of remembrance is more than an unfortunate loss, it is a vital threat to an individual's development.

The space of memory – and hence the space of identity – that Fiona Tan explores harbours precisely this drama. Indeed, not only is her space of memory severed from the place of its origin but it has also lost its most important root: the language of this place. Her artistic work has enabled her to grow a vein of life that, for herself and for anyone viewing her work, opens up a new space, an actual space of exile beyond all affiliations. The Latin verb *exsilire* means to 'jump out' or 'jump off'. People in exile are by definition exceptions to the norm – a fact that is changed neither by the increasing preponderance of this way of life in the course of history nor by someone's voluntary choice of exile. It is not only the different nature of an expatriate's inner world, but also the experience of pain unleashed by separation, departure and a new beginning which the exiled individual embodies, and that fills the others – those who are 'rooted' – with existential insecurity and fears.

The reason why the following three works have been chosen to follow the journey undertaken by Fiona Tan is because, on the one hand, in an altogether exemplary manner they offer the possibility of sharing in various stages of the experience of exile,[2] and on the other because, beyond this, they also show the universally existential dimension of this experience and reveal its ethical and philosophical impact.

1. IN SEARCH OF THE ORIGINS

The interpreter says: 'They say you also belong to the family.' The artist and her film crew were coming to the end of a journey around the world tracing the history of the Tan family, and thereby completing the film *May You Live In Interesting Times* (1997). One of the final scenes shows Fiona Tan in China surrounded by residents in the middle of their village Shan Ho, in front of the Ancestor Hall. It is the village she thought she would never find, the place where her forebears were born and everyone has the same name. 'One big family', as they say in the film. Hearing this invitation to 'belong to us' that she yearned for so long, Fiona Tan smiles amiably, like someone who, on seeing the doors open, wonders why it had previously seemed imperative to enter inside. All at once the motor that had driven her on her year-long search simply evaporated, and with it, her inner haven of security. She had arrived – but where?

Fiona Tan was not born in her 'fatherland' but in her first place of exile, Indonesia, where the Chinese were called 'yellow Jews', as one of her uncles still living there recounts in the film. She speaks neither Chinese nor Indonesian, but English like her mother, who came from Australia, the family's second stage of exile. Today she lives in Amsterdam, her third place of exile. Anyone who knows the artist also knows her story. The film which documents Fiona Tan's odyssey following the trail of this story has itself travelled around the world.

So when her quest for her provenience – her *Heimat* – came to an end in the village of her father's birth she was confronted with her 'alienating' – *un-heimlich* – mistake: this was not her place of origin after all. This desire to probe the beginnings of her history, however, is something the artist shares with a lot of people. It is a fundamental moment of human experience that the awareness of being uprooted not only kindles a wish to return to the place where separation first occurred, but also stirs a desire to go even further back and uncover the very origins of these roots. It seems almost that exile brings alive an inner calling to retrace the thousands of footsteps which one senses might be resonating to the rhythm of our own steps, which we intuit as living in our cells, as dancing through our memory in unfathomably shifting, deceptive images. Sociologists consider this attempt to secure evidence of family origins to be typical of the first stage on an exile's path towards a new, reconstituted consciousness.[3] But the key difference between Fiona Tan and this general phenomenon is that she forms it into an artistic process. Transformed into film, her own path exerts an impulse on the viewer's path; her images built of language and film create sufficient space to stimulate other people's quest for identity and emerge as images of meaning and reflection.

Her fruitless search for her origins manifests an experience recognisable to the viewer, since it belongs to our collective reservoir of existential knowledge: the idea of arriving somewhere we might forevermore call our home is an illusion. Whoever nonetheless falls into the trap of imagining a possible return and endeavours to fulfil this by peeling back the strata of our veiled and multilayered everyday world, will strike into the midst of nothingness, similar to the experience evoked by Hermann Broch: 'The empty space between the epochs, the empty nothingness that yawns wide, the nothingness for which everything comes too late and too early, the empty abyss of nothingness beneath time and the aeons, which time tries to bridge over cautiously and on a hairline by stringing moment to moment in order to conceal the stony petrified crevice, oh, the abyss of unformed time must not become visible, must not be allowed to gape open; no interruption must occur, time must flow on incessantly, each moment simultaneously enclosing the end and the beginning, the moulded time ...'[4]

Consequently, what Fiona Tan exposes in her film is far more than a journey through the history of her family. The moment she realises that she could never live at the site of her family's origins, in her 'fatherland', and that she is excluded from the language in which she is offered this long yearned-for invitation to belong, she consciously or unconsciously touches on an elemental human experience: the encounter with rootlessness opens up a crevice in the immensely precarious edifice of what we commonly call everyday life. Anxiety-driven bustle betrays our dark premonition that only a single plank need become dislodged from this construction for the reality we inhabit to become precariously unstable. Meticulously engineered time and solidly built spaces cannot delude us into believing that this is where our existence is housed. Rather, our existence consists of a sequence of cyclical exile experiences which begin with the departure from the mother's womb and continue through the different phases of advancing age, each with its own face, as a succession of shed skins and freshly shaped identities, leading to the abandonment of our form of being, at least – if not of life itself. It is here, in the heart of this existence, that this search for loss and pain resides, without which we would not be who we are, even while it is gnawing at our consciousness. Exile is merely the overt proof of this dark foreboding that is inherent to our life.[5] This is why the issue of exile is such a powerful catalyst of self-reflection for everyone, even for those who are 'rooted'.

It is in awareness of this condition that Fiona Tan focuses her work on this theme, even if she articulates this insight with biographical images and diary-like poetry. Hence, in the aforementioned Chinese village, the artist grasps that her essential search should not be directed at finding the unattainable family source but at fathoming her own identity. On the odyssey through the changing terrains of her family history she discovered how chameleon-like this 'I' can be, from how many faces it is assembled, and how profound the desire in her is to shape this diversity into a coherent whole. Because people in East and West alike seem unable to place her physiognomy, she has been asked since childhood 'Where are you from?', and has let this question carry her from one end of the world to the other. As if within this question another were inscribed, asking 'Who are you?', her real journey began on her arrival in the place that was truly to cast her into the chasm of nothingness, not towards her source but to the mirror world of her identity, which had long since been searching for its roots in the aerial space of memory and in its lack of affiliations.

2. A FOREIGNER WITHIN ONE'S OWN SELF

The face of the Other becomes the mirror that the artist consults. In 2002, during a scholarship residency in Berlin, Fiona Tan tested the youngest of her many skins of identity, that of 'being a foreigner'.[6] When she set out to photograph the faces of people around her she asked herself, 'Do I look better at someone's face in a foreign city?' Thus she distinguished between her third place of exile, Amsterdam, where she had settled down, and some new foreign place.

So her life started all over again in a city where she knew no one and no one knew her. For her, alien places and people are the most familiar. In *Countenance* (2002), with her camera she began exploring the city – not in its architecture but in its faces. In an endless field study she sought contact with people from all walks of professional and daily life, filming each person individually and for the duration of about one minute: a metalworker, a social worker, a greengrocer, an architect, children in the street, a receptionist, a street sweeper and a magistrate, a farmer, a taxi driver, a barkeeper, prostitute, doctor, filmmaker and a beggar ... Her only stipulation was that each person stand motionless in front of the camera for an entire minute.

The people stare at her. One minute is a long time. As each second passes, the mask of their everyday activities slowly begins to slip and fall away, as if an eggshell were gradually metamorphosing back into a soft membrane. In turn, the faces interrogate the one scrutinising them: Why are you asking me that? – What do you want from me? – Who are you to ask me who I am? Some of her candidates, particularly the strongest, are beset by a kind of helplessness, a vulnerability that at times borders on tears. Accosted by this small exception to their daily practice, the people are unsettled and undergo an unanticipated sense of defenceless, prising open their 'hiding machines'.[7] Consciously or not, with the human images that Fiona Tan peels away from the people's active sense of everyday identity, she creates something like an exile. As the artist here skilfully demonstrates, the gaze into the countenance of these people translates into the dispossession of their belonging. But these faces' vulnerability now reveals the true significance of belonging, which is to provide shelter. In these portraits the 'I' is laid bare; an 'I' is rendered visible that lies beyond identity.

Resuming her almost obsessive search for the true countenance of the Other in her film *Correction* (2004), it seems that Fiona Tan discovered the presence of something in her own self that she had long suspected, a kind of mirror. Together, the face of the 'I' from her period before going into exile, from her remembered inner world, and the face of the 'I' from her real exterior world had long since formed a hiatus in her consciousness; these two faces gaze at one another incessantly, their mirrored dialogue rhythmically measuring her presence. But who exactly – a question that gives her no peace – speaks as 'I' between these mirror faces?

It is as if she had admitted a stranger into herself[8] and given this alter ego an abode. Instead of looking for where this alien 'I' comes from, in her subsequent films she went increasingly in search of her own self-portrait in people from foreign parts. In *The Changeling* (2006), for instance, Japanese schoolgirls are made to become her mirror; or in *A Lapse of Memory* (2007), an old man attempts to recall his memories but finds himself losing them more and more to a realm of dreams. The man's name is Henry, although in fact – as we learn from a gentle voice off-screen – he is called Eng Lie. He has a crumpled face and white hair. His skin is pale, his eyes are green, he has big feet and a pronounced nose – a description Chinese would commonly give to Europeans. The off-screen commentary introduces a second film; Henry's story could perhaps begin *there instead.* [...] His *principal* story is not the home he has been looking for. The departure into exile can now properly begin: 'His forgetfulness is perhaps his greatest virtue. His journey is one yet to be taken.' On this *new* journey, could perhaps his 'I' transform into the 'I' of a woman? Fiona Tan knows that the next stage of her quest must be to build an enduring place in foreign parts, but one she can take with her.

3. EXILE AS A CREATIVE ACT

Only when the uprooted individual bails out of the logic of the deracinated condition, only when the wish to reclaim the abandoned home is relinquished, when the insistence on the integrity of the subjective world is eschewed and the diversity of the 'I' is accepted, only then is it possible to create something new. To dwell or inhabit means to be a stranger. In Hebrew the word *ger* = stranger, derived from verb *gar* = to dwell.[9]

However, the plurality of the 'I', the complexity of being assembled from many different people and faces, is a phenomenon inherent to the human condition: 'The belief that a person only has one mind and one memory is an illusion. We are a coalition. The unity of the "I" is an illusion. We are not consistent. We don't decide things rationally. We have no idea how we decide nor "who" in us is making the decision.'[10] Exile simply lends greater emphasis to the plurality of the 'I'. But at the same time, this also raises the crucial question concerning exile and the multiple 'I', the question already outlined in Fiona Tan's films *Countenance* and *Correction*. Between the faces of the individual 'I's, which split the self through their mirror, who is the 'I' speaking there? And to which place does this 'I' from the hiatus, from the intervening space, sally forth?

Two ocean currents converge, and along the boundary of their meeting create a gently elevated crest whose ceaselessly spluttering foam and spray glints in the first morning light. Starting at an island, this demarcation line runs across the entire image and acts as a connecting line to the camera's eye, which thereby appears to be drawing itself in towards the island, while also pulling back a curtain to reveal the breaking day – thus the opening sequence of the film *Island* (2008). The island is almost entirely uninhabited: just two houses, a lighthouse and a round horizon. Fiona Tan came here alone. The island is duration in material form. Repeated time, repeated space: blasting wind, clouds in shapes resembling the craggy pines, the unvarying screeches of seabirds, hardy dune grass, a shoreline without beginning or end, the relentless breathing, in and out, of crashing waves as they roll up, then down the sand. 'This island is like a boat – noiselessly she can sail through an ocean of hours, days, weeks. Gaining distance is sometimes the only way to get close to what matters.'[11] The off-screen voice glides through her consciousness, which appears to lie bare and defenceless, bereft of protective skin. 'Slowly memories surface from time spent on another island ... She remembers the scenes only vaguely. It had a lost, timeless feeling ... too heavy and slipping away, something her memory could not hold onto.' The voice sounds like distant *recitativo* similar to the chorus in a Greek play. Like an interminable melody, it resumes the story of the gardener who keeps reiterating the refrain of that old question, simply because he has just started learning English: 'Where are you from? Is it cold there or hot?'

Once again, similar to someone imprisoned in silence and tormented by a fitful welter of thoughts, the voice laments: 'This place cannot contain her. This place cannot contain her unease.' The wind sweeps across the dune grass with unchanging vigour. Her inner self only gradually finds calm. 'This island is like a magnifying glass. No matter how far she retreats the world at large feels tangibly close. She did not come here to get away.' Her actual 'I' appears to be making itself increasingly at home in the place where it actually belongs, the place of its innermost being, beyond all familiar, cultural or national ties. 'Now the air feels cooler and she thinks: Perhaps this place is becoming my home. When she leaves she will fold up this place and put it in her pocket for safekeeping.'

The insular quiet of repetition is inhabited by a homogeneity of space and time; this homogeneity has the capacity to suspend the sensation of time which divides life's experiences into separate, equivalent sites. Henri Bergson, maybe more palpably than anyone else, elucidates the significance held by memory in our conscious processes within the present.[12] Namely, it operates as the selective, accentuating voice within a fabric of musical complexity, which would cease to resonate in fullness were this voice to be removed. Only when seen in these terms does it becomes clear what far-reaching insights Fiona Tan's film *Island* has drawn from her experience in exile, since her images built of language and film correspond perfectly with Bergson's philosophical notions.

From the perspective of this work, Fiona Tan's journey in search of her own place and, ultimately, of her 'I', resembles the age-old transcultural metaphor of the treasure hunt, which describes how restlessness can only find peace and security within the space of one's innermost, inalienable self, that most deeply concealed home which is most difficult to find and prompts some people to travel to all ends of the earth. With her films Fiona Tan has progressively constructed precisely such a place, steering towards this goal with almost blindly visionary precision. But furthermore, on her travels she has also constantly enquired into the value of memory and formulated her answer in *Island*. It is in this film that she opens up a space where the faces of the various 'I's resonate together to form a single time- and space-less 'I', an 'I' in which all questions about place or identity meld, a space where an 'I' can smoothly spread out between memory, the present and the future. She thereby creates a universal space for reflection for a manifold existential condition, whose aerial roots are transformed into strings that bring to life a single, vast chamber of resonance.

Thomas Elsaesser
Excerpt from 'Fiona Tan: Place after Place'

Fiona Tan: Disorient, catalogue for the Dutch Pavilion, 53rd Venice Biennale, Heidelberg: Kehrer Verlag, 2009, 2.20–2.33.

FACE TO FACE

Every thirty seconds or so another person looks at us, framed from the knees up. In the background metal railings, stretches of corridor, overhead strip lighting, glimpses of stairways, walls with a clock or a bulletin board. An institutional space, with a look and a feel distinctly American: a 'correction facility'. Warders and inmates, men and women, young and not so young, black and white, looking serious or expressionless, concentrated or casual, trying to keep their posture in place while they are being filmed. The rhythm of the successive video portraits imposes itself, modulates expectations, and one begins to notice detail: badges, tattoos, a baton, a white overall apparently buttoned at the back, a security wristband, a walkie-talkie; distributed across these often broad expanses of body, the items both link the persons with each other and distinguish them, not always along the lines of keeper and kept. After a while, nothing seems to divide them, except their individuality – and the screen. They look at us, held and locked as our gaze is by the eye of the camera, itself fixed and mounted on a tripod. What is not seen is the surveillance apparatus, human and technological, that keeps an eye on both the camera and the subjects. It is reproduced in the set-up of the installation, faintly alluding to Bentham's Panopticon.[1] The non-visible and its partitions and divisions haunt *Correction* (2004) while 'releasing' all kinds of associations in the viewer. Surrounding several of the subjects, for instance, is a kind of halo, backlit as the figures are, either by the film crew's halogen lights or by the institutional neon. It gives them an uncanny presence, compressing time to the moment of shared duration, while raising no more than a cursory flicker of interest in their backstory or personal narrative. Instead, attention is directed to the implicit and complicit knowledge that our camera-conscious society now has about the performance of self-image and self-presentation, even in the most unlikely locations. Whether in neatly pressed uniform, shirt-cuffs and belt, or a T-shirt and open jeans, there is the sense of intense concentration on appearance, reflecting perhaps the care of the self in prison, battling the boredom of life inside with body-building and self-maintenance, with status and self-discipline.

Correction, it will be evident, with its head-on style, undertakes several kinds of perspective corrections, in so far as the lines between inside and out, inclusion and exclusion are being redrawn and renegotiated. The observer, rather than shifting more or less safely between witness and voyeur, finds herself enfolded, repositioned, at once drawn in and kept at a distance. The circular arrangement of the six double-sided screens not only make the subjects look at us, even from where we are not looking; they make up a formidable collective, holding their own, back to back, against anyone gathered in the gallery. These individuals neither seek our empathy and understanding, nor does the camera solicit any on their behalf; we are 'free' to reflect more generally, and also to decide more personally, on what it means to have a face-to-face encounter with a cinematic image.

The face, the face-to-face and the close-up in cinema were among the first ways of defining the new medium of mechanical reproduction as an art form in its own right: 'In a truly artistic film the dramatic climax between two people will always be shown as a dialogue of facial expressions in close-up.' The phrase is from *Der sichtbare Mensch* (1924), by the German-Hungarian screenwriter and theorist Béla Balázs.[2] Balázs was convinced that the cinema would bring a momentous turn in human evolution, delivering us from a mixed blessing – books. These had made people so focused on depth and interiority that they became deaf and blind to the surface language of bodies and faces:

> *The discovery of printing has gradually rendered the human face illegible. People have been able to glean so much from reading that they could afford to neglect other forms of communication. [...] [But] our culture is being given a radically new direction – this time by film. [...] The whole of mankind is now busy relearning the long-forgotten language of gestures and facial expressions. This language is not the substitute for words [...], but the visual corollary of human souls immediately made flesh.*[3]

Similarly, in France, Jean Epstein tried to designate what was unique to the cinema with the term *photogenie*, defining it as the 'moral character of every personal and mobile aspects of the world, beings or souls that are enhanced by filmic reproduction' and specifying the close-up of the face as its privileged instance.[4] Balázs and Epstein's ideas became hugely popular – a kind of *doxa* – with Carl Theodor Dreyer's *The Passion of Joan of Arc* (1928). There, the story's drama seemed to rest entirely on the close-ups of the protagonists, and all the moral weight of the suffering world came together on the face of Maria Falconetti, who could still bring tears to the eyes of Anna Karina more than a generation later in Jean-Luc Godard's *Vivre sa vie* (1962). Some years earlier, Roland Barthes had eulogised 'The Face of Garbo' in terms that echoed those of Balázs and Epstein:

> *Garbo belongs to that moment in cinema when capturing the human face still plunged audiences into the deepest ecstasy, when one literally lost oneself in a human image [...], when the face represented a kind of absolute state of the flesh, which could be neither reached nor renounced.*[5]

Later, in the early 1970s, the face as mirror and the mirror as face saw another conceptual turn: no longer the mirror to another being's soul, in which I try to lose myself, the face onscreen now directed attention to the mirror-function of the cinema as such, inviting the viewer to regress and catch his/her own idealised self-image, and project it on to the other, in the form of 'identification'. Taken from the writings of Jacques Lacan, and especially his 'mirror-stage as formative in the function of the ego', this notion of the screen itself as both mirror and face has in turn become a sort of *doxa* within cinema studies.[6] It complemented and reinforced Michel Foucault's critique of classical representation, who in a sustained, subtle and much discussed study of Diego Velásquez' *Las Meninas* (1656) tried to demonstrate how this famous painting, commissioned by King Philip IV of Spain, used the idea of window and mirror (on which much of our post-Renaissance idea of the image as a framed view is based), to show how the gazes of painter, subjects, spectators and king sustain and balance each other only at the price of cancelling the very space that any of them thought they occupied.[7]

More recently, and in apparent contrast or even deliberate opposition to the almost mystical transubstantiation that the cinematic image of the face once received, as well as to the psychoanalytic and pictorial deconstruction of its mirror function, an entire ethical philosophy of 'otherness' and asymmetric power-relations became founded on the face-to-face. For Emmanuel Levinas, encountering a face is to be called upon to acknowledge the radical otherness of the other, to the point of resistance, and at the same time, to recognise my obligation to this other, to the point of giving up myself for the other's care and protection. As Levinas specialist Bettina Bergo writes:

> *The defenceless nudity [of the other's face] is therefore a passive resistance to the desire that is my freedom. Any exemplification of the face's expression, moreover, carries with it this combination of resistance and defencelessness.*[8]

It is into this confusingly contradictory, philosophically charged, partly dystopic, partly utopian history that Fiona Tan's preoccupation with faces has found itself enmeshed, and to which it answers, sometimes obliquely, sometimes implicitly, and from which it also – this would be my tentative thesis – begins to extend itself. But first one needs to remind oneself just how much and for how long the face has been the strongest unit of organisation in Fiona Tan's work, the bedrock of her art, her ethics and aesthetics. Not only that: the face is also her 'minimal unit', in the sense that it allows Tan the richest combinatory on which to play very different variations, from close-up to frontal staging, from a circling camera to slow tracking shots, from *plan américain* to the medium shot that embeds a person in their surroundings. The face has also given a common denominator to the diverse historical and pictorial sources from which she has taken either her materials or her inspiration: Japanese school pictures (*The Changeling*, 2006), family snapshots (*Vox Populi*, 2004–), ethnographic film of tribal physiognomies (*Facing Forward*, 1999), 'found footage' in *News from the Near Future* (2003) or August Sander's famous photographic taxonomies of Germany from the 1920s and 1930s (*Countenance*, 2002). Faces and people, mostly looking at the viewer, seem to occasion the deepest and most sustained meditation on her own engagement with the world: the look into the camera initiating an open, dynamic, sometimes disturbing and discomfiting relay of points of address between maker, subject and viewer, each aware of the other's burden in the exchange yet neither able nor required to share this burden in equal measure:

> *I am more aware of […] the artificiality of the encounter and simultaneously (in) voluntary resistance against it. It is as though as a viewer, I cannot own and cannot pocket the image in the same way I imagine I could if it were only a still photograph*

hanging on the wall. When looking at a video portrait, I am looking at something, which is constantly escaping me.[9]

Thus, time and again in Tan's work, something not unlike Levinas' paradoxical asymmetry of otherness and selfhood is being enacted. Yet the viewer is also aware of how rich and important an instrument or probe these encounters with faces are for Tan herself, in the ongoing self-interrogation of her craft as film-maker and video artist, working with, and therefore necessarily in the interstices of, the photographic image, cinematic projection and the gallery installation. Her special *forte*, the form she has made her own, is the video portrait or filmed photograph, which some might consider a hybrid or even a concession to the digital technologies of the day. However, it possesses its own aesthetic challenges, opens up a different dimension of spectator engagement, something Tan is well aware of:

> *A filmed photograph stretches time, and in those often uncomfortable moments a lot happens. The viewer can see the embarrassment, bewilderment and anger, or the curiosity and shyness due to the confrontation with the camera.*[10]

But it also ensures that her work is at the cusp of one of the most important transitions in the visual arts: today, as in the days of chrono-photography, we are able to recognise that a photograph has always been as much a 'stilled' image as a 'still' image, setting free the possibilities of an entirely different way of thinking not only about images in the present, or images of the past in the present, but of past images in the past. [...]

Gilles Deleuze [is among those who] provided both the urgency and the concepts for rethinking the relation of stillness and motion, the instant and duration in the image, contrasting (in his two *Cinema* books) the movement-image and the time-image, and cutting both loose from the problems of representation, the mirror-effects and the geometry of the subject, briefly discussed above.[11] Not since Roland Barthes' reflections on photography in *Camera Lucida* (1980) (developed by design only with the still image in mind) has there been such fertile thinking as Deleuze's on the nature of the image as agent, *movens* and agency in its own right.[12] Deleuze's conjunction of moving image and the body, his implication of the motor-sensory apparatus in any act of viewing not only makes (conceptual) room for how we experience moving images in the museum, once the old

Marlene Dumas, *Chlorosis (Love Sick)*, 1994

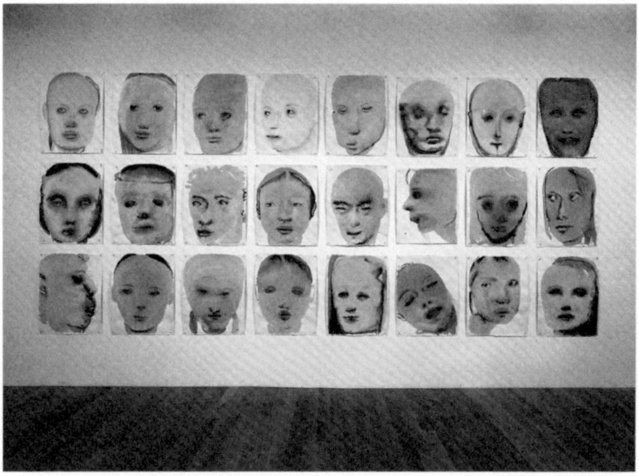

divisions between cinema (moving image / immobile viewer) and museum (still image / mobile viewer) no longer apply, but he redistributes and recombines the linear sequential order of perception, affect, sensation and action, and allows for a different 'organisation' of time, affect and perception. It is not surprising then, that Deleuze would turn to the face and the close-up for proof of such a different interplay of perceptual energies and intensities. For Deleuze the face is not just an enigma, a surface to be 'read' either as the expression of some yet-to-be-revealed interiority, or for a language prior to and inaccessible to verbal language that needs to be deciphered like hieroglyphs, as it was for Balázs. The face can also be a pure phenomenal presence, an 'entity' in and of itself, presenting 'a surface that is sensible and legible at the same time'. And, one might add, it animates the filmic image, lending it the power to communicate into the future, across past temporalities and those yet to become actual, in the act of being remembered, replayed or repurposed, while still retaining its moment of eternal present.

A good example of a Deleuzian flow of energies stored in time itself, that can be made to pass back and forth between viewer and face in archival footage, is Tan's *Facing Forward* (1999). Culled from the Amsterdam Filmmuseum's collection of Dutch East Indies moving-image material, it features a series of very different faces, bodies and postures displayed before the camera: a line-up of white hunters seen with their indigenous servants, in a kind of trophy parade; a group of tribal men and women, posed before the camera, their faces in medium close-up, inaudibly answering to the person behind or next to the camera; three unclothed figures in medium long shot, being ordered to turn around and present themselves from all sides. There are also shots of a cameraman turning the handle and smiling, as if to assure the viewer of his innocuous intent and to protest his innocence. Whether capturing moments of the colonists' pride or documenting ethnographic 'specimen', the camera's look now strikes us as obscene to the degree that it makes visible too many of the hidden motives that frame the colonial gaze. But the temporal gap between this look and us, looking through this look, also effects a reversal: those who were once looked at in such an objectifying way, now look back at us, inducing discomfort, shame. It is as if these faces take their revenge, precisely by looking at us the same way they did then, seemingly untouched by the knowledge we now have, and thus unable to either absolve us or to forgive. The faces that here look at us have a gaze so naked, almost as if such a face is more naked than a naked body. And faced by such unprotected looking and being looked at, it makes *us* more naked than these naked bodies ever were.

Concentrating so insistently on the face also gives Tan another pedigree and a lineage, this time putting her in the company of painters, photographers and filmmakers from her adopted country, the Netherlands. I would call it 'the Dutch way of seeing the face', and while it has many different facets, one very strong tradition is, famously, that of portraiture, from Hals, Vermeer and Rembrandt in the seventeenth century to van Gogh and Charley Toorop in the nineteenth century and twentieth century. Tan has inserted herself with seeming ease into this ancestry, with a series of filmed portraits of family members and friends, commissioned by the Amsterdam Rijksmuseum, entitled *Provenance* (2008). There is arguably an equally salient link to contemporary photographers and painters who have rediscovered the full-frontal, head-on body, among whom, for instance, Marlene Dumas and Rineke Dijkstra would be two prominent Amsterdam residents, whose figures have similarly direct, often shockingly open, naked and unguarded faces. Yet the closest affinity that Tan's work has in this respect is with a filmmaker, the late Johan van der Keuken. Van der Keuken, who started out as a portrait photographer before becoming an internationally renowned documentary filmmaker between the 1970s and 1990s, is one of the most prominent if perhaps less remembered exponent of this 'Dutch way of seeing the face'. Capturing unsuspected moments of the unveiled gaze and the frank stare on his many journeys, and catching them or being caught by them in places like Amsterdam

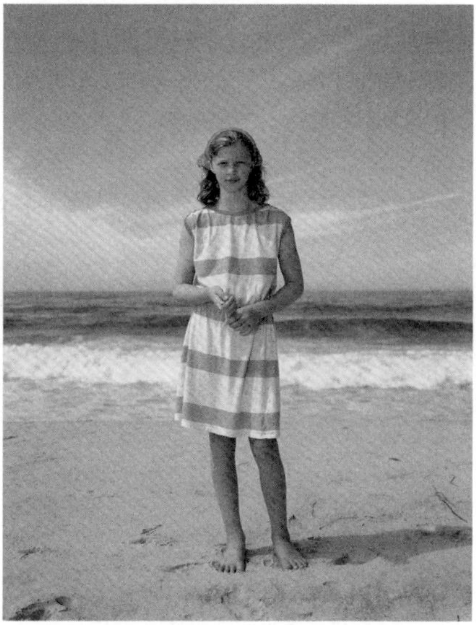

Rineke Dijkstra, *Maddy, Martha's Vineyard, MA, USA, August 5, 2015*, 2015

and Lima, Hong Kong and Lhasa, puts van der Keuken in the tradition of Dutch portraiture. Films like *Face Value* (1991) make this evident in the title, but *Lucebert* (1994) or his photo-series *Women and Children in Madras* (1988) show much the same 'tender and cruel' observational-confrontational realism with which Tan, with a combination of ethnographic dedication and aesthetic detachment, faces her subjects. *Provenance*'s subtitle might be *Amsterdam Generational Faces*, Tan's answer to van der Keuken's most famous film: *Amsterdam Global Village* (1996). For all their differences, then, van der Keuken, Dumas, Dijkstra and Tan are loosely but importantly connected: ever so often in their work, we encounter that steady, and in its forthright candour disturbing gaze, with which the sitters of classical Dutch painting return our look. The Calvinist self-confidence of having nothing to hide (an often noted feature of the Dutch burghers of the Golden Age) translates and mutates in their work into a provocation that is little short of physical: haptic, tactile and erotic. [...]

Brian Dillon

'Different Voices: Memory, Exile and Cultural Heritage in the Films of Fiona Tan'

Frieze, June 2010.

In his *Confessions of an English Opium-Eater* (1821), the Romantic autobiographer Thomas De Quincey – the first writer in English to posit that the mind has 'unconscious' provinces – recounts a series of intoxicated dreams in which time and space seem to shrink and swell with awful realism. De Quincey is lost in visions of a boundless architecture drawn from his study of Giovanni Battista Piranesi's series of sixteen copperplate etchings, dating from the 1760s, 'Carceri d'Invenzione' (Imaginary prisons), and thrust back ('like a person drowning', he writes) into regions of his own past which he had quite forgotten. But his most tormenting dreams concern an enigmatic Orient of fathomless age and sublime expanse. Haunted by images of a China he has never actually seen, De Quincey finds himself menaced by imaginary birds, snakes and crocodiles – not to speak of the very decor in this monstrous country of his own invention:

> *I escaped sometimes, and found myself in a Chinese house, with cane tables &c. All the feet of the tables, sofas, &c. soon became instinct with life: the abominable head of the crocodile, and his leering eyes, looked out at me, multiplied into a thousand repetitions: and I stood loathing and fascinated.*[1]

De Quincey's nightmare is of course just one instance of the weirdly aestheticised racism that would dominate Western representations of Asia during his century – he writes elsewhere, almost with admiration, of the fabled 'cruelty' of the Chinese. But the appearance of this Orientalist grotesque in the midst of his opiate musings on geography and memory is complicated, if not mitigated, by the fact that it is wholly fantastic: most likely based on his reading of the travels of Marco Polo and the dream Orient in Samuel Taylor Coleridge's 1798 poem 'Kubla Khan'. More to the point, the passage is clearly inspired in terms of imagery by the contemporary English taste for chinoiserie: the kind of lurid fakery that was even then being installed at ruinous expense by the former Prince Regent (newly crowned George IV) in his holiday home by the sea. The Royal Pavilion in Brighton – the setting for Fiona Tan's film *A Lapse of Memory* (2007) – is an absurd confection of disparate styles: mock-Indian outside, with cod-Chinese interiors and a very English oppressiveness. The building seems to ravel up several threads of imperial ambition and envy, while its decorative fabric has been stripped and restored so many times that the Pavilion is a time machine of sorts, compacting historical periods and whole continents into one lavish but somewhat shabby edifice.

In Tan's film, the Pavilion appears at a further mythological remove. Its hoard of authentic and invented artefacts, its painted serpents and carved dragons that soar like superheroes, its delicate depictions of an imagined daily life in China: all of this becomes a solid projection of the mind of Tan's protagonist, an old man who haunts the Pavilion's elaborate showpiece rooms and enigmatic side-chambers. *A Lapse of Memory* is notable for combining two innovations that have marked Tan's recent films: her use of off-screen actors as narrators and the appearance of fictional 'characters' on screen. Here, the voice-over tells two competing tales about the old man: he is named both Henry and Eng Lie; he has travelled from Europe to China or perhaps in the other direction; he enacts, in the tea ceremony that we see him perform in the apparently abandoned Pavilion, either a custom from his lost home or a learned habit that denotes a different life of adventure and discovery. 'Restlessly, he moves between his various selves' – at times, he seems to have been dreamt up by the building itself.

When *A Lapse of Memory* was shown in the Dutch Pavilion at the Venice Biennale in 2009, Tan described it as an unexpected return to the topics of cultural hybridity and postcolonial identity that she thought she had left behind: 'But here, all of a sudden, was this building, which refused to go away. It felt like full circle, like a way of completing a sentence.'[2] But given the weight of geopolitical history and cultural fantasy that informs its setting and stories, the film is surprisingly elusive, less a 'hybrid space' (as the voice-over puts it) as a set of nested narrative spaces whose order or hierarchy is unclear. The narrating voice coils about itself like one of the Pavilion's serpents, telling us: 'Henry's background is unclear. In the voice-over this also remains ambiguous.' The old man, bedding down in a fragile pool of light amid the building's looming decor, is both Marco Polo and Robinson Crusoe, with echoes of Shakespeare's exiled magus Prospero. But he also recalls the sole character of Samuel Beckett's one-act play *Krapp's Last Tape* (1958), who drifts disconsolately from one version of his past to another as if they were adjacent rooms in which he can find no solace. In a way that seems newly irreducible to the historical specifics of exile in Tan's earlier work, there's a sense here, as in Beckett's play, that outside the Pavilion 'the earth might be uninhabited'.[3] [...]

A certain drift has been evident in recent years, away from geo-cultural complexities and from documentary modes, towards fictions that seem at first glance more straightforwardly universal or existential. A case in point is *Island* (2008), a fifteen-minute black-and-white video that again deploys the motif of solitary exile, this time on the (actual) island of Gotland off the east coast of Sweden. It was the location for Andrei Tarkovsky's last film, *The Sacrifice* (1986), but it is neither named nor its history exploited in a voice-over that tells us of a woman who has gone there for obscure reasons and whose angst is unexplained.

> *She did not come here all that long ago, but already she's lost track of time ... Slowly memories surface from time spent on another island ... Today she can find no peace of mind. Despair puckers at the smooth surface of her days. Feeling very small, feeling very useless, she paces in circles.*

The island itself remains mysterious too: seen mostly in static long shot so that black trees compose a wind-slanted calligraphy against grey skies, a few houses and a lighthouse are distant and unexplored; only the sounds of wind and water and seabirds suggest that there is movement or life here at all. The island, we're told, has become a prison; in one of the few mobile images in the film, Tan's camera hares through colourless undergrowth: flying, so the voice-over implies, from the memories that assail the exiled mind.

It's in the artist's two-screen video installation *Rise and Fall* (2009), however, that Tan's turn towards a more implicit (and ultimately temporal rather than geographical) sort of exile becomes clear – or rather ravishingly unclear. The two upright ('portrait' orientation) screens appear to show doubled lives that are actually one: two women whose bodies, actions and pensive moments brush up

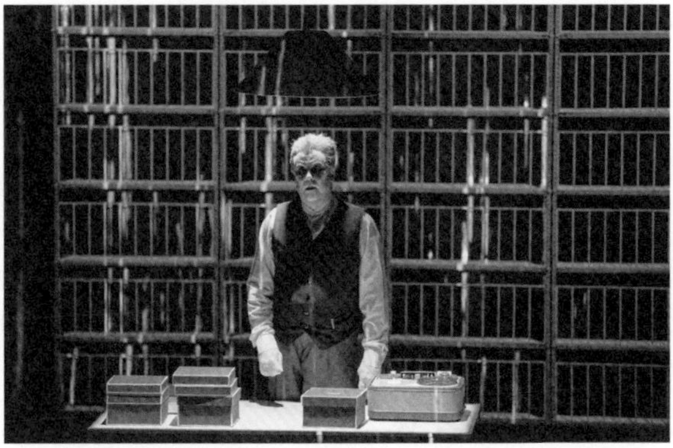

Robert Wilson performing Samuel Beckett's *Krapp's Last Tape* (1958), 2012

against one another in ways that suggest a biographical unity, and yet depart sufficiently from one another to introduce some doubt. The older woman, who may be remembering her younger self, wakes slowly in bed, bathes, stares from a window, sits by a table in a lush, half-wild garden. The younger woman, who may be imagining her future self, and whose face remains obscured much of the time as though in a frustrating dream that will not give up its secrets, does not quite rhyme with her older double: when she stares out of a window, the camera pulls back to reveal her lover, and a startling vista on the Niagara Falls.

The parallels between the two screens in *Rise and Fall* are managed with some delicacy, even if there are occasional hints – such as twinned images of the women walking in woods, the older in spring, the younger in autumn – at a more explicit or literal-minded structure that, at some point, Tan abandoned, or let subside deeper into the visual fabric of the work. She had originally written a script, to be read as a voice-over, which suggests that the mnemonic, affective traffic between the two women, no matter how complex, all moves in one direction:

> *She would like to repeat in her head her favourite scenes. Re-member, re-collect, re-trieve, revive. After careful consideration it is becoming clear that to remember something is not to repeat. For her, a memory is a fold in the fabric of time. Forgetfulness leaves gaps, picks holes in the picture. Holes, nonetheless, that she can look through.*[4]

Instead of a work manifestly 'about' memory and its slippages, *Rise and Fall* is itself patterned with odd eddies and currents that will betray the viewer. One such, which is also an emblem of the process of mis-recognition at the level of character or narrative, is the recurring image of roiling water which is suddenly revealed – a steaming void descends from its top left corner – to be speeding towards the edge of the Niagara Falls. (There is a reminder here of Tan's 2001 video piece *Saint Sebastian*, with its phalanx of female archers approaching the moment of release and flight.) A surface that had seemed exercised in situ by localised depths turns out to be irretrievably part of some vaster process of becoming and vanishing. It would be easy, and too hasty, to call that process 'life' and conclude that Tan turns here, and more generally in her recent work, towards a merely humanist reflection on Time, Memory, Age and Death. In truth, what *Rise and Fall* leaves one with is the question of what constitutes a 'life' in the first place: where exactly among the half-remembered instants of action or lassitude, the stalled desires and fearless projections of self into the future, the texture of habit and accident, we can discover ourselves.

Midori Matsui
'Terminology: Themes in the Art of Fiona Tan'

Fiona Tan: Terminology, Tokyo Metropolitan Museum of Photography; The National Museum of Art, Osaka; Bijutsu Shuppan-sha, Co., Ltd, Tokyo, 2014, n. p. Revised 2020.

ATTRIBUTES

Depicting her subjects in relationship with their possessions and as reflections of their personal qualities, Fiona Tan demonstrates how people attain their singularity, not in isolation but through their relationships with others and with objects. In this respect, the stationary camera effectively directs the viewer's attention towards certain objects, and manipulates the distance between the person holding the camera and those captured by it. In *Provenance* (2008) and *Levensloop* (2011) filmed portraits of men and women of different ages are juxtaposed as individual tableaux. The frontal views of their faces and bodies are augmented by the focus, one by one, on the objects they surround themselves with, and on the activities undertaken in the environments which contain those objects. This shifts our perception from an initial encounter with classic portrait 'types' to individuals – people who change in space and over time. In *May You Live In Interesting Times* (1997), a documentary of Tan's visits with her relatives of Chinese descent scattered all over Asia, the subjects' invisible ties are suggested through the distance between their frontally captured figures and the camera, and through the accrued fragments of their unseen activities.

CLOCK

Memory in Fiona Tan's works is portrayed as an inner reality that transcends the changes and losses that occur with the passage of time. With the two women in *Rise and Fall* (2009), for example, the young woman seems to be the elderly woman's younger self of memory, yet we sense that the older person's 'now' is not empty. Conversely, in *A Lapse of Memory* (2007), an elderly man suffering memory loss grows disconnected from the objects around him that suggest a rich and colourful past, leaving him to repeat empty ritualistic actions. In *Linnaeus' Flower Clock* (1998) a woman fearing that the intensity of her present happiness will fade over time repeatedly evokes images that embody physical and emotional fulfilment in order to extend 'now' and etch it in her memory. In doing so she attempts to construct a personal clock showing her own inner time, rather than the mechanical passage of time. Her failure to halt time is shown in the temporal continuity of the video, and the sight of the flowers opening and closing over time. Accepting that life goes on and that all things must pass impels us to concentrate on the present while providing life with its memories.

COUNTERPOINT

Filmed image and narration in Fiona Tan's works do not necessarily overlap, but can develop independently in different directions while commenting indirectly on each other through metonymies. Through the confrontations, partial correspondences and displacements between image and spoken text, new meaning is created. The discrepancy between narration and images in *Island* (2008), for example, suggests overriding one's sensual consciousness (as will be discussed in the following section). In *Disorient* (2009), the juxtaposition between passages read from Marco Polo's *The Travels* (1298) and images of exotic Oriental curiosities are projected side-by-side with signs of contemporary Asian poverty, itself the result of uneven modernisation and the gradual breakdown of an exotic fantasy in light of harsh realities. At the same time, the repeated use of the pejorative 'savages' in Marco Polo's account and almost obsessive attention to spices and other 'characteristic' products allude to prejudices against foreign cultures and the introduction of an alienating materialism that distances Asian life from its cultural origins. This counterpoint between narration and images releases the viewer from preconceptions, helping to dispel the fantasy of 'the Orient'.

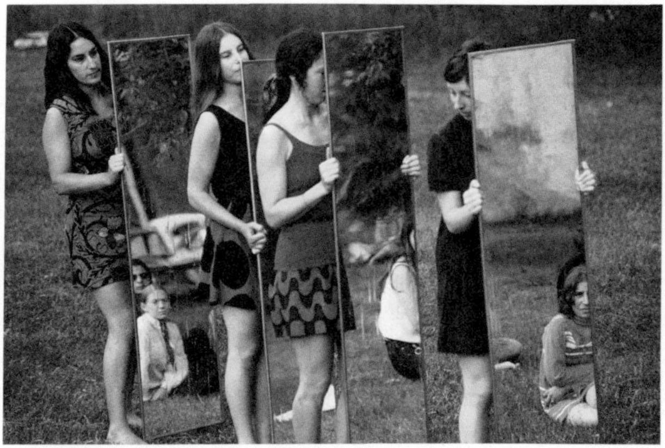

Joan Jonas, *Mirror performance III*, 1969

DISTANCE

The distance between Fiona Tan's cinematic images, filmed with a stationary camera, and the position of the photographer gives rise to multiple meanings. In *Island* that dynamic also forms the structural principle of the film. This effect is perceived in the varying degrees of distance between the subject and objects presented respectively in the film's narration and imagery, and perhaps even in the gap between the messages they convey. The image of an island captured frontally and of the wide stretch of sea that divides the island from the viewer suggest that we are approaching the island from a distance. The narration tells us that 'she', the film's invisible protagonist, came to this island to distance herself from her everyday life and meditate quietly, and that the internal concentration 'her' mind requires finds even the island's natural surroundings to be an obstacle. The camera, on the other hand, by taking varying degrees of distance from the frontally captured images of various objects, alludes to a process by which 'her' senses make contact with the objects on the island and gradually open up to them. Through this gap between word and image, consciousness and senses, one can sense the ambiguity of the line in the narration: 'gaining distance is sometimes the best way to get close to what matters'.

GRAVITY

In *Roll I & II* (1997) and *Lift* (2000), Tan demonstrates an extraordinarily direct and skilful handling of the body. *Roll* shows footage of Tan rolling down a slope, and *Lift* sees her body being raised up first by the hands of others, and then by a bunch of balloons. Though they depict two totally opposing phenomena – falling to the ground and floating upward from it – both videos are visualisations of gravity. Here the human body becomes subjected solely to gravity, liberated from socially limiting criteria such as age, sex and occupation, and acquires a presence as a solid form. Such performances (and their documentary footage) present the body as a singularity determined by actions, movements and contact with objects and natural phenomena, and connect Tan's early works to the minimalist experimental performances and postmodern choreography of artists like Joan Jonas and Tricia Brown in the 1960s and early 70s. At the same time Tan's early works prepare the way for the physicality of later videos from 2008 onward which fused social symbolism with actual spaces.

MORTALITY

Fiona Tan casts doubts on the idea that cultural artefacts and memorial-type structures transcend human mortality. By showing items in fragmented fashion, like a catalogue, from the collection of nineteenth-century architect Sir John Soane held in his private London museum, *Inventory* (2012) views precious ancient artefacts as mere goods, hinting at the rigidity of meaning visited upon things cut off from any organic relationship with human endeavour. *A Lapse of Memory*, set in Brighton's eclectically Asian-style Royal Pavilion, follows the eccentric personal rituals of an elderly man living a hermit-like existence. Because he suffers loss of memory, the fragments of cultural customs – such as the tea ceremony he performs – now hold only the bare bones of meaning. This corresponds to the way in which the style and decoration of the pavilion, built by a king and an architect who had never visited Asia, captures not the essence of a culture but its builders' fantasies. What is shown to transcend the death of the individual body is the relationship between the activities of the living spirit with people and objects.

MUJOKAN

The Japanese word *mujō* refers to the mutability by which all things change and nothing stays the same, and the transience of human endeavour: that is, the fact that even the most spectacular, rock-solid of civilisations will eventually crumble. These two states – permanence and transience – form the underlying tension across Fiona Tan's oeuvre. *Inventory*, which shows across multiple screens the collection of classical sculptures amassed by the nineteenth-century architect, demonstrates through the cold, fragmented display of objects isolated from living culture, the ambiguity of the museum's role in preserving humanity's heritage while amplifying our sense of loss. *Rise and Fall*, in which the everyday lives of two people, an elderly and a young woman, are shown alternately on two screens through acts common to both – waking up, putting on make-up, writing – contrasts the maturity that time endows with the youthful suppleness it steals away. Just as the flow of water around the pair hints at years that will never return and new life (see 'Water', below) the truth of *mujō*, that life can only continue amid the flow of time, is accepted.

PHYSICALITY

The reality of the body in Fiona Tan's videos is invariably viewed through the body's relationship to something. Through particular acts, or the effects or vestiges of contact with other people or objects, the body is experienced as a thing of definite substance. In *Roll I & II* the unique quality of the performer's body, rolling down a bank, is asserted by the speed at which it rolls and is subjected to gravity. The sand stuck to the palms of her hands as she lies face up at the bottom shows her bodily connection with the Earth.

In *Levensloop*, in the process of moving from a painting-like approach of filming face-on, to continuous filming of a person's actions, possessions and movements, portraits of seven men and women of various ages emerge as organic wholes linked to a specific history in time and space. In *Linnaeus' Flower Clock* (1998), as symbols of the certain existence of the 'self' – the suddenness of jumping into the water; the impact of falling in the male body diving into a pool; the weight of a woman floating face up into water – are conveyed with graphic immediacy, suggesting the sufficiency of sexual love that fuels their current happiness.

SENESCENCE

As indicated by the turtle laying eggs in *Linnaeus' Flower Clock* (1998), longevity signifies for Tan a necessary condition for achieving what should be achieved in life; advanced age attains dignity as a result of the accumulation of such acts. In *Levensloop* and *Provenance* (2008), in which images of men and women in infancy, adolescence, maturity and senescence are presented as unique portraits set in individual frames, elderly men and women are shown as autonomous presences engaged in sport or work, or in their unique aesthetic or intellectual pursuits. Such portrayals indicate different aspects of fulfilment relevant at each stage of life, from infancy to old age. In *Rise and Fall*, the juxtaposition between the figures of a young woman and an older woman, both engaged in the same everyday activities, highlights – beyond the body's ageing with the passage of time – the intellectual agility and sensual flexibility maintained through the continuity of actions and revived by the evocation of memories. An elderly woman's girlish gestures and both women's powers of concentration, each involved in the act of writing, reveal the existence of youth in the elderly, and the budding maturity among youth.

SUSPENSION

Provenance and *Levensloop* share the same structure. In the former six, and in the latter seven, men and women of different ages are positioned as independent and opposing tableaux. After filming them initially from front and back as portraits – close to stills – using a fixed or slow-moving camera, Tan films the objects around them (furnishings in the room; things they have collected; store-bought goods, and more) thus capturing their behaviour in this environment. By doing so, the subjects' lives are understood as multi-faceted wholes, each with a unique history. In contrast to painting, which views the subject from one direction and percolates it down to a single image, the operation of manipulating the audience's attention via the limited images produced by a fixed camera, and provoking the viewer with the slow filming speed, incorporates the viewing experience itself in order to emphasise the temporal continuity peculiar to film or video. Time does not come to standstill but stops as it progresses, capturing people as they exist in time.

Water for Fiona Tan is a medium for a woman's body and emotions. In *Rise and Fall* everyday acts performed by two women, one old and the other, alternate on-screen, thus contrasting the fresh dewiness of the young physique with qualities like maturity and refinement, and showing the passage of time which gives a woman a fulfilling life yet robs her of her youth. The flow of time is manifested in the ceaseless motion and transformation of water, surging and cascading, flowing then surging again, in footage of a waterfall surrounding the vignettes of the two women. At the same time, the overwhelming sense of volume and smooth flow of water – the sound of water roaring violently or burbling peacefully – aligns with the women's pulses and emotional currents, gently embracing them and causing the viewer to see their individual lives as part of a much greater flow. In *Levensloop*, as the elderly woman swims the water acts as an intermediary, transforming the heaviness of her body into buoyancy and allowing her to move freely; while in *Linnaeus' Flower Clock*, water takes the weight of the falling woman, conveying the intensity of her love as she casts herself outside personal autonomy.

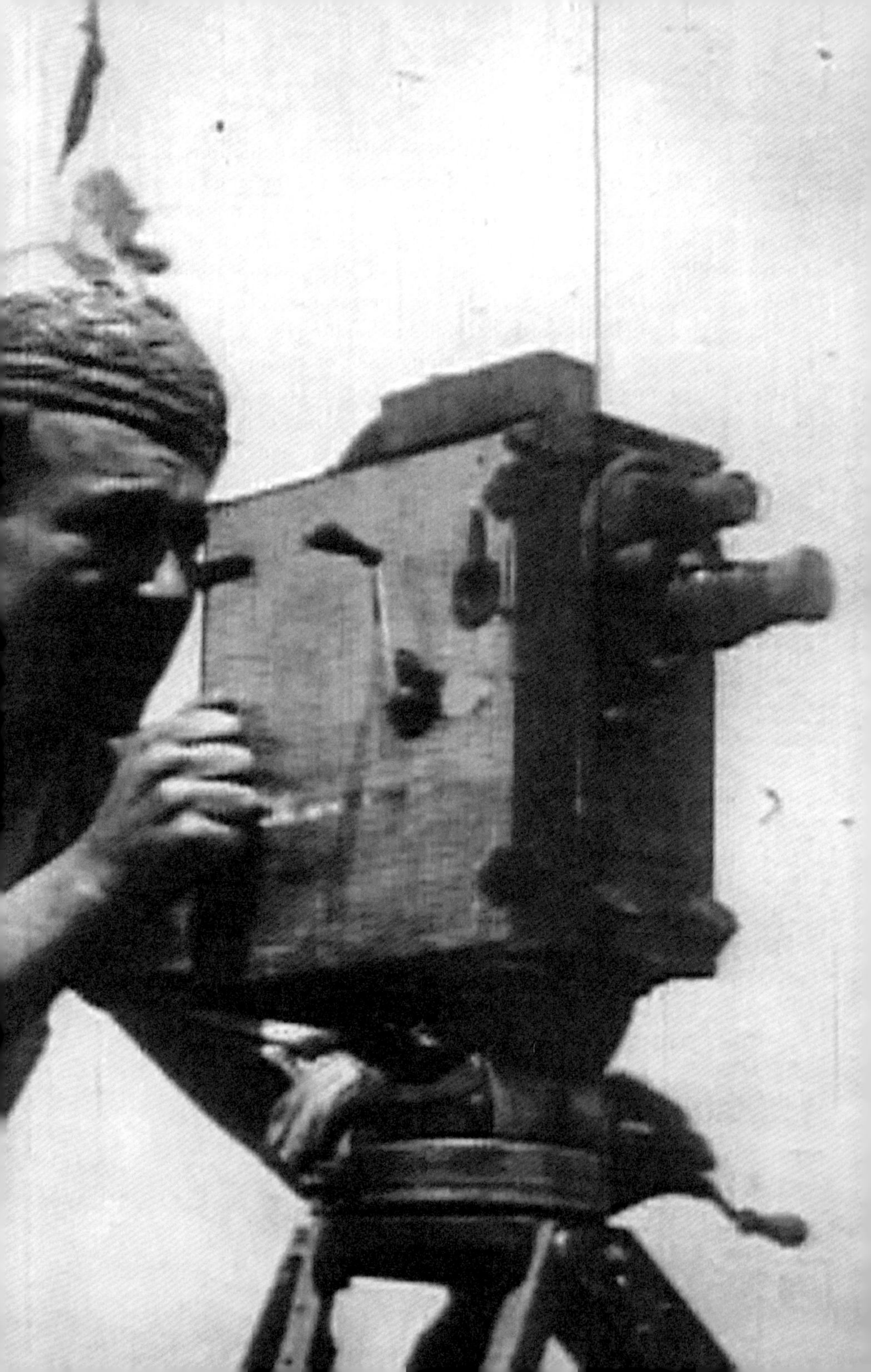

Writings around Selected Works

Facing Forward (still), 1999

Fiona Tan
'Smoke Screen'

Written 1997–8. Published in Dutch as 'Rookgordijnen', in *Lover* (Dutch feminist magazine), 1999.

ABOUT THIS IMAGE

Three children, scarcely dressed, are sitting outside. The sun is shining and casting strong shadows. The footage, in black-and-white, was probably shot at 18 frames per second and has a high contrast. It is also somewhat scratched. The old-archive quality of this film is probably the first thing one notices. I think it was probably copied already several times; there are now sections missing, causing the brief scene – which lasts altogether no longer than ten seconds – to 'jump'. The eldest child, possibly five or six years old, is seated in the middle and holds a young baby, maybe a year old. To the left sits a younger child, presumably brother or sister; he is maybe four. The children are dark-skinned, dark-eyed, dark-haired, clearly a scene from a tropical, Asian country. The two older children are smoking.

For me this image is powerful, polemic and problematic. Sixty years after it was made it is now a difficult image. And with this writing I am trying to understand better why I want to use this image within the art context and exhibit a film installation incorporating this image in the most public and arbitrary of art spaces: on the street at night.

To my mind this image is the intersection of several important but difficult issues.

1. It is about childhood. About how we see children.
2. It displays smoking in such an unabashed way, it is instantly about the taboo that smoking has become.
3. It is about how we look at other cultures and deal with colonialism now.
4. Connected with all the above-mentioned issues, it is about how our reading of this image has changed over time.

Finally, through presenting this footage on the façade of an ordinary building where one would otherwise imagine seeing a billboard or advertisement, this work addresses the issue of censorship and the limitations of the socially acceptable.

I can see now that this complexity of interpretation explains my fascination for this image. This extraordinary richness of issues which present themselves through viewing this image, transforms it into an image which leaves no one cold. So the point of my interest is not so much the image itself but the way you and I perceive it – what we think about it, how we react to it, how we feel about it. What does this image stand for, what do we do with it, what does it do with us?

THE CHILDREN

Whilst I dare make guesses regarding the intention of the director and cameraman with whom I as a filmmaker must identify, I grope in the dark when I try to place myself in the position of the children. I can only observe the few body movements and gestures I see during the ten-second-long fragment. The two older children can smoke without coughing; hence I can conclude that they are not doing it for the first time. I notice they do not inhale deeply and they seem to smoke hastily, although this may only appear so due to the slightly speeded up film motion (18 frames/sec projected at 24 frames/sec). The eldest one holds the cigarette with a certain ease; both seem to copy adult gestures – something we find touching and comical. He hands the cigarette to his younger companion. This one fumbles with the cigarette before he can hold it properly between his fingers. We notice how large the cigarette is in his hands, adding to the comical effect. This seems to be the major impact of the image: the children puffing out smoke quite 'professionally'.

What I see after repeatedly watching the film fragment is the frown of the child on the left, who repeatedly looks at someone offscreen to the left of the camera. Once or twice both children glance in this direction and then at the camera. It is the tropics, it is obviously hot, and the eldest child in the middle shades briefly the eyes of the baby in his (or her) arms. This small and tender gesture leads me to think that the children are in the sun at the request of the cameraman. Normally the children would sit in the shade, as would anyone else.

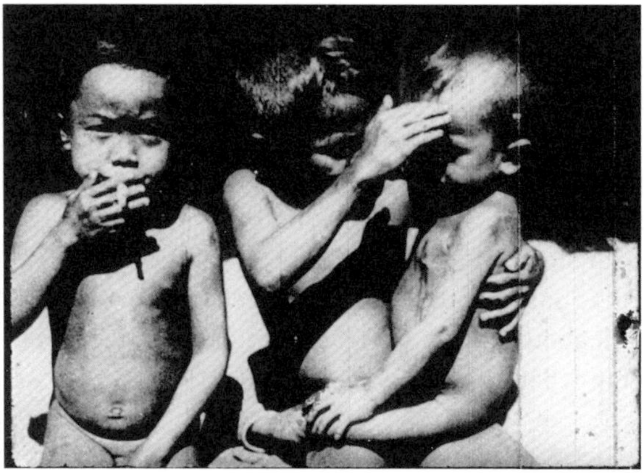

Smoke Screen (still), 1997

At the end of the fragment the child on the left has covered his face with his hands and then blows out the smoke out of the frame – in the direction of the unseen, anonymous director. There is something frustrated about this gesture; I begin to doubt even more that the child is smoking entirely out of his own free will. I am tempted to read the raising hands to his head as dizziness caused by too much smoking, possibly the child is headachy from the smoke. The manner in which he blows the smoke towards the offscreen director and his permanent frown look like anger or irritation. Also this leads me to think that this scene was set up, done for the camera. I can see that the children can smoke, I doubt that the film crew invented this, but the scene was staged for the sake of the camera.

CHOCOLATE CIGARETTES

I do not smoke, I never have. Nor do I have any children. It is difficult to know if I would see this material differently if I did, however I doubt it. When I was still a child every self-respecting housewife had a selection of cigarettes lying on the coffee table for guests, something which seems impossible now. At the local sweet shop I can still buy chocolate cigarettes, like the ones I remember from my childhood. Their brand names: 'Mild Heaven', 'Gorbachov Internationals', 'Fortune', 'Future', 'Sombrero' and 'London Mall'. I am surprised that these are not banned.

Cigarette commercials are forbidden from most media. As we now all know, smoking is bad for your health and it has become taboo. I am reminded of a book I once read where the writer in the book, who attempts in vain to stop smoking, used to write on his packets in large black letters: 'Cancer is painful.' To allow children to smoke is not done. To film them whilst doing it is not done. To incite them to do it in front of the camera is definitely not done. What excuses this film is its age. Then, people didn't know better, which immediately raises the assumption that we now do.

When writing about taboo and media I immediately feel myself on slippery ice. The whole mechanism of censorship rests on the idea: out of sight, out of mind. And the very tricky issue which lies at the very roots of this, is the power of the image. Can a visual image incite, influence, change people, cause them to misbehave? Personally I wonder whether that is such a good thing – out of sight, out of mind. We need visualisations in order to remember. I believe in the adage of attempting to learn from history. It is not a good thing when censorship works hand in hand with denial. Know thy enemy would be more my motto – not to copy his ways, but to learn how to recognise and avoid them. Paradoxically I taboo censorship; this does not mean however I stand behind the idea that anything goes.

SOURCE MATERIAL

The film fragment dates presumably from the 1930s, a time when a considerable amount of film was shot in Indonesia, at that time still a Dutch colony. This fragment I found in a film called: 'The Tropical Netherlands – A Journey with the Film Camera through the East Indian Archipelago.' In this two-hour cinema travelogue, published by Polygoon and accompanied by a jolly Dutch commentary, we are taken by boat on an extensive journey starting in Europe and docking at foreign ports such as Egypt, India, Singapore. Finally we arrive in 'the other Holland', in Batavia, and begin the journey overland by car through Java. After ten minutes in the rice paddies of Java, sighting the Borobudur and similar sights, we arrive in Bali. The smoking children are part of a run-down of typical Balinese, from old to young. The original commentary translates as: 'An old Balinese with striking features. A young court lady. These sucklings take advantage of the opportunity that mother has gone shopping. Women! At home, we children in a sling actually do much better. As soon as we wake up, we are turned around and then we are sweet for another hour.'[1] Notice that, when describing the smoking children, the commentary uses the term 'sucklings' instead of the more usual 'children': a 'witty' play on words.

The scene is interrupted twice; there are two clappers in this brief fragment. Why? How much longer was the scene originally? Did the children not cooperate? Did they not act as the filmmaker/editor desired and did the editor censor that 'misbehaviour'? Obviously when 'Tropisch Nederland' was made there was not enough material which could be used integrally without these cuts. Any shorter and the viewer has not enough time to see what the children are doing.

POSTCOLONIAL ACCOMPLICES

Did these children often smoke? Who taught them to smoke? Is this due to colonial influence, or did this sort of thing take place before the arrival of the Dutch, the German, the Portuguese? Tobacco plantations and export brought the VOC (*Vereenigde Oostindische Compagnie*, or Dutch East India Company) and Holland considerable wealth. Did people in Indonesia smoke a lot before the Dutch came? Because this footage was shot in Indonesia and not for example in Gouda, these questions concerning colonial powers arise. The children, so I am tempted to read the material now, seem not only to be copying adults but colonial gentlemen.

Did they smoke the way that street children in various parts of the world are now addicted to sniffing glue, in order to still their hunger? This is the association which our conditioning immediately brings to mind – the overkill of known images and charitarian clichés: of starving Ethiopian children, skinny Bangladeshi infants with ballooned bellies, bewildered Rwandan orphans. These children have become our responsibility.

People's reactions I have observed are either of reserved shock and concern, or laughter. The nature of this image makes it contentious, possibly offensive. The strange thing is that when this film was first made and shown to the general public, the reactions were very different. No one would have raised an eyebrow or batted an eyelid. It was shot for its exotic worth – *aapjes kijken*, or 'watching the monkeys', as the Dutch expression goes. And this was the way in which the audience saw it. The comic side of this material has survived, but ironically that humorous side seems for some viewers to have gone sour and contributes to making this image particularly wry to the taste.

Power immediately becomes an issue here: the power of adults over children, the power of the colonial ruler over its subjects. This seems to make the image doubly difficult. In the time when this footage was taken, would a camera crew have filmed the same in Holland? And would that footage have been received in the same way as this material? Ironically this fragment was lifted out of a film presented as a portrait of a part of the Netherlands. The general line of the commentary text is, 'These children too are Dutch subjects' – one of us, but filmed and compiled in an exotic travelogue most definitely as 'the Other': the unknown, the unusual, the exotic. The incomprehensible if charming; delightful if alien; the comical and curious. The comparison to the zoo and the Victorian rarity chamber is unavoidable. In the zoo in Hamburg I have seen photos of African tribal people in tribal dress displayed in an enclosure next to the zebras and elephants. I have seen advertisements dating from the beginning of this century advertising the sale of Javanese labourers together with oxen and other cattle.

This is the unusual postcolonial situation we are now in. We have become accomplices after the fact. Few of us were even born at the time this footage was taken and yet something akin to guilt is what we feel. And these complex feelings of shame, these uncomprehending but sympathetic attitudes, are present when we talk about multiculturalism, immigrants and social integration. Racism is definitely taboo.

I was born in Indonesia and am half-Asian – Chinese, not Balinese like these children. I think this leaves me with more kinship to these children than, for example African orphans, whose images I may equally have found in some other archive, had I looked for them. Being partially Indonesian does give me some more identification with these children. I have been to their island, I can imagine some things or their lives and times. I feel more connection to them and their image than for African and South American children. Whether my cultural background gives me more 'permission' to use these images I am not sure – that would seem equally a racist implication. Incidentally, I stumbled across these smoking children whilst researching a documentary film about my family and my cultural identity. In theory at least I straddle this juxtaposition of East and West. And I am doing my best to see things from both sides, with – I must admit – increasing doubts as to whether that is actually possible.

My mother has in her wardrobe an old fur coat of my grandmother's. Sometimes she wears it out. Is this a good or a bad thing?, I ask myself. The coat was already there, my mother didn't buy it. The minks had been killed and their fur made into this coat long before fur coats became an issue. It's a pity – a waste – not to use something you've got, my mother rightly argues. Recycling. But, I wonder, does the fact that she still wears it instil in other people's heads the idea that it is OK to wear it? After all they don't know it was originally my grandmother's. Only, I ask myself (possibly muddying this discourse by broadening the field too much), why do people make a fuss over fur and not over pigs, or chickens for that matter? Does a mink or a fox have more rights than a domesticated pig?

In a sense I ask myself the same ethical questions in this work. The question of moral responsibility – as image-maker and as spectator – are maybe too large to answer in the space of this work and this brief epistle. My responsibility as artist in this case entails the decision to show this material. The documentary-maker is always manipulating; framing is a choice, an act of selective reality. I want the viewer to be aware of this. And I chose the openness and the generality of the street as my forum – out of the protected haven of my studio or a gallery. Originally this material was intended for the general public.

I do not condone smoking – I do not want to advertise for smoking or for children smoking, but neither do I want to preach or tell the viewer what to think. I am trying to activate individual judgement and sensitivity towards difficulties in interpreting the visual. To make aware of the relativity and the manipulative power of film and of the limitations of the moving image.

Lynne Cooke
'Fiona Tan: Re-take', on works 1997–9

Fiona Tan: Scenario, Amsterdam: Vandenberg & Wallroth; Rotterdam: NAI Publishers, 2000, 20–34. Revised 2020.

Facing Forward (1999) opens with a slow, horizontal pan across serried rows of men, civil and military officials, and their subordinates, posed as if for a group photograph. The leaders are Europeans, the lower ranks 'natives', the moment sometime in the past when the still camera was the more familiar tool for recording. Most stare fixedly towards the lens, holding a pose, deferential to the strictures of documentary witness. Their conventional arrangement, with the senior uniformed figures comfortably seated in the foreground and the subalterns more tightly packed behind, conforms to norms long established for the recording of a commemorative portrait of society's authorities. A brief insertion of black leader separates this footage from a second fragment, structurally similar but thematically and typologically quite other. In this archival extract, a single line of naked male tribesmen posing in front of natural vegetation is again revealed by the slow pan of a camera. They, too, stand to attention, as if similarly habituated to the demands of documentary reportage. However, this time the framing conventions resemble those of early ethnographic representations, specifically those of 'first contact' photography.[1]

The paralleling of these two elaborately staged fragments – the historicised social record contrasted with the 'timeless' anthropological data – conjures two separate traditions rooted in documentary as a genre, and through that two distinct discourses. The accompanying soundtracks reinforce this methodology of contrastive mirroring, as the former fragment is overlaid with a composition that in its solemn regular tonal beat signals the unfolding of real time, and by implication, historical time, as well as the portentousness of the occasion; conversely, the 'primitive' warriors are immersed in a naturalistic ambient sound that is nonetheless also a later appendage. While the former asserts itself as a fabricated intervention devised in order to mark duration, the latter through its very unobtrusiveness instantiates an ahistorical realm.

Only now does the title appear. If '*Facing Forward*' would seem to reference the positions taken by these subjects of the camera's scrutiny, it quickly becomes evident that something more complex and problematic is implied by this phrase. For the third segment, the longest to that point, introduces an urban scene shot from a moving camera; unidentified, the place seems to be a city somewhere in Southeast Asia, sometime early in the twentieth century. As the hand-held camera glides along the streets, it follows various inhabitants in their daily activities, some of whom turn to acknowledge its presence. Leisurely wandering from one site to another, it mirrors the gait and pace of a visitor, the proverbial traveller curious and yet respectfully attentive to the passing parade. Roving casually as if in response to the kaleidoscopic character of the scene, the tracking shot is the antipode to the centrally positioned fixed lens, which was prioritised in pioneering sociological and anthropological documentaries on account of its purported neutrality and objectivity. A voice-over narrates a hypothetical exchange between Marco Polo and Kublai Khan in which the emperor quizzes his venturesome guest as to whether his understanding of the world – of his self and his place within it – is inevitably predicated on history: 'You advance always with your head turned back? ... Is what you see always behind you? ... Does your journey take place only in the past?' 'Possibly, ...', the first word uttered in this evocative text, establishes the provisional and speculative – the fictive – foundations on which the whole rests, at the same time as it gives credence to Italo Calvino's provocative contention that 'It is not the voice that commands the story: it is the ear'.[2]

The Khan's questions concerning the relation of the past to the present offer an entry to Fiona Tan's primary preoccupation here, as in many of her previous works. For they introduce the structure, the mechanisms and the discourses through which she probes her theme, the means by which self-awareness and, perforce, self-understanding may be construed. In *Facing Forward* the principal vehicles used in this enquiry are those proverbial adversaries, the traveller and the anthropologist. The figure of the anonymous white male camera operator may serve as a paradigm for each. Silhouetted against an empty expanse of sky, abstracted from place and time into an archetype, such a filmmaker appears twice in Tan's eleven-minute film installation. On each occasion he turns his camera, to point directly to the screen and to the viewer, as if indicating that the spectator is equally the subject of this work.

Short segments of 'representative' ethnographic footage follow: brief black-and-white shots of tribal peoples are intermixed with colour footage of village women and girls.[3] However, in certain other segments, for example that depicting three Chinese men, one in Western and two in traditional dress exiting the courtyard of a residence, the exchange between the camera(man) and his subjects betrays an air of informality and intimacy that belongs more to the vocabulary of the traveller who hunts the incidental, anecdotal and idiosyncratic than it does to the style of transparent scientistic reportage sought by the anthropological field worker. Such contrasting types of shots, including the pan and an iris fade, instil a reflexive awareness of the cameras' operations and aesthetics. Likewise, the juxtaposition of diverse extracts emphasises the heterogeneity of this material which, given its wide-ranging geographical origins, becomes a microcosm of the world at large.

The film ends where it begins, with an iteration of the footage of the group photograph, as if the pan had come full circle. This serves to raise the question whether retrospectively – that is, with hindsight – Tan's eclectic mixing of ethnicities and cultures might be read differently, whether the historical record might be examined from other perspectives. Appended to this collective portrait, as a kind of coda, is a brief close-up of two girls veiled with a blue filter and seen through an iris lens. This haunting filmic snapshot has an arresting, unique role. Unidentified and unidentifiable, placeless and yet rooted in the specifics of a recorded moment, these young women reconfirm the inherent ambiguity, the unknowability, of the Other and, at the same time, given their irreducibly affecting presence, affirm their singularity and individuality as subjects. That these contrasting scopic drives – the drive to survey, document and classify and the drive to look closely at and engage empathetically with, a human subject – may be incommensurable is intimated in the accompanying narrative, in which the two protagonists strive to communicate from opposing and often antithetical positions. [...]

A site of multiple displacements and rearticulations of what is allegedly either documentary record or subjective witness, *Facing Forward* deftly and incisively highlights a fundamental question which James Clifford, the noted scholar who combines anthropology, history and literature in his work, has also probed in relation to an ethnographic habitus: 'Is it possible that historical reality is not something independent of these differently centred perspectives, not their sum total, and not the result of critical sifting of different perspectives by independent experts "at the end of the day"?' he asks. 'Can we conceive of historical reality as an overlay of contextual stories whose ultimate meanings are open-ended because the contact relations that produced them are discrepant, unfinished?'[4]

Clifford's thesis, that 'in the wake of growing arguments over the cultural and political location of historical narratives, it becomes harder and harder to sustain a unified, inclusive historical consciousness capable of sorting and reconciling divergent experiences', is key to Tan's practice.[5] Amongst Tan's earliest mature works is a sixty-minute video commissioned for public television in the Netherlands in 1997, entitled *May You Live In Interesting Times*. Explicitly autobiographical in focus, this work pivots on a dialectic between roots and routes. At once the central protagonist and the author, Tan pursues a mode of self-imagining and self-definition that entails interviewing her immediate family, plus close and more distant relatives, in addition to travelling to the remote rural village in China from which her ancestors once migrated. Public affirmations of kinship alternate with more privately expressed anxieties about difference in the soundtrack which interleaves extracts from interviews with voice-over asides, soliloquies in which personal doubts are admitted. Via the tales of various members of Tan's extended but dispersed family larger issues deriving from irresolvable conundrums – between exile and migration, and between assimilation and diasporic existence – are limned. By contrasting personal perspectives, a matrix of experiences emerges that is as much marked by place (by the different countries and cities in which her relatives reside) as by time (the different generations to which they belong). Contemporary invocations of diaspora are made concrete and real, historical and particular.[6] From this richly woven tapestry of anecdotes, confidences and confessions, a portrait of Tan herself also begins to emerge, albeit obliquely and indirectly, for it depends as much on negative principles as did Marco Polo in his negotiations with the world through which he journeyed. And, like the Venetian before her, Tan, too, discovers that her point of origin cannot be the place she occupies, that she, too, is destined to remain a traveller, a nomad, a 'professional foreigner'.

Acknowledging that the information she gathers is plotted rather than collected, Tan highlights the ways that such data is prefigured and rhetorically communicated. Drawing on the dual modes of travel writing and anthropology, she engages a wide range of rhetorics and narratives, personal and impersonal, objective and subjective, embodied and disembodied. That there is an element of the undecidable at the core of any identity rooted in a hybrid ethnos is hinted at in various ways, not least by the title of this work, which in Chinese is akin to a curse but in English takes on a resonance that is disarmingly benign in tenor, and by the litany of Chinese names, that sound impossibly quaint in translation, which fill the opening moments of this intricately constructed search for identity. Frequent recourse to representations in other media, including still photography, a video monitor replaying footage just shot, together with extracts read from a diary, manifest Tan's wry acknowledgement of the circularity and reflexiveness of such an undertaking. Her admission, articulated near the beginning of the work, 'It started off as a search, now it feels as if I'm constantly in search of my search', reinforces the viewer's awareness that this is as much an act of generation as one of archaeological uncovering, and that the camera is neither an unobtrusive nor a neutral recording devise, but a catalyst or provocateur which intrudes on the pro-filmic event, its very presence stimulating and hence partially responsible for the reactions of those being filmed.

The consciousness of her dual roles – as subject and as filmmaker; as family member and as author – points to divided loyalties and potential moral dilemmas. This question of responsibility towards one's source material has continued to preoccupy Tan, most evidently in *Smoke Screen* (1997), which incorporates archival footage of an ethnographic character. Prompted by the subtle insertion of multiple voices in the inter-titles, doubts are raised as to both the authenticity of this brief episode, in which young Asian children are shown smoking, as objective documentary witness, and to the ethics of the original filmmakers and subsequent appropriators. Not only the shift in tone and idiom in this laconic commentary – 'With my own eyes'; 'Boys will be boys'; 'These sucklings [infants] take advantage of the opportunity that mother has gone shopping'; 'Indonesia, maybe 1930' – but also the uncertainty and mutability of the subject positions undermines belief in a single source of authority. Intercutting an image of a contemporary filmmaker (herself) into the original footage, editing paratactically so that nothing is fixed and all relationships remain contingent, Tan posits without actually instantiating a subjective ethnography. Two additional postulates emerge. The truth of a statement proves to be a function of the particular discourse in which it is embedded as opposed to something that can be unproblematically divulged. And fiction occupies a central place within the genre of documentary.

Based, as was *Facing Forward*, in material drawn from the holdings of the Amsterdam Filmmuseum Archives, *Tuareg* (1999) probes the basics of historical documentation by establishing a dialectic between imagery made by the still and the motion camera. With its focus on the 'photographic moment', defined by means of a juxtaposition of the prior, and hence incidental, with the chosen, and therefore significant, instant, itself shorn of ensuing consequence, it dramatises the complex relations between photography and film and their changing status as documentary media.

The installation itself reinforces these contrasting modalities. A transparent screen onto which is projected archival stock (that has been transferred to video) bisects a darkened room. While the visual imagery may be read from either side (one version mirroring the other), the soundtracks are quite distinct: one half of the space is permeated by 'real-life' ambient noise, the other by a desert wind. The filmed extract shows a group of children of various ages, from what the title indicates is a Northern African locale, who were invited to line up to be recorded by the camera. Barely five seconds in duration the footage concentrates primarily on the prequel, those scant moments before the children resolve themselves into the formal fixed positions dictated by convention and mechanical necessity. After this extended prelude a freeze frame mimics the iconic representation, the unique frozen moment of the desired shot. Ignorant of the expected codes of behaviour one very young child wanders casually away from her place in the front row, across the line of sight of the lens. By contrast, two adolescents, though far from unaware of what is required, still cannot resist squabbling and scuffling before being called to order – by whom it is not clear, for there is an adult partially concealed in the tent behind in addition to the cameraman who may also have intervened.

The climax of the piece is a wipe that follows the brief freeze frame, in which all are suitably posed as if for a still photograph. No traces of the aftermath are disclosed. The effect of this sly edit is to transform what was originally happenstance reportage into a structured fiction. *Tuareg* thereby not only emphasises the split between reality and the reproductive process but, more tellingly, it confirms the constructed character of all representation. At the same time, by preserving what might be described as the 'outtakes' alongside the 'official' record, and oscillating between them, it re-enacts the classic distinction between the aesthetic of the traveller who seeks the exceptional, the unexpected, the idiosyncratic by way of an informal, improvised and subjective approach, and that of the scientific reporter, whether anthropologist or historian or archivist, for whom visual data, inscribing a certain set of supposedly objective conventions and values, performs the role of extended illustrative notes that complement the field worker's written evidence. In short, here, as elsewhere in Tan's oeuvre, poetics overrides politics; film/video is celebrated for its expressive as much as its analytic potential, and truth is a product of fiction melded with fact. In *Tuareg*, as in *Smoke Screen*, and *Facing Forward*, the faith of a former era in the evidentiary value of the cinema as a document is rewritten in order to explore the ways in which information and knowledge of a different order may be conveyed, ways in which neither the medium nor the genre is regarded as transparent and direct in its relation to the ostensible subject.

In recent years the prototypical documentary has increasingly been called into question by recourse to fictional modes. Tan's creation of a dialectic between the traditional ethnographic film and its antithesis, the personal travelogue, erodes the boundaries normally drawn between so-called amateur observation and 'scientific' recording. Engagement and interchange between subject and object, between the filmmaker and the individual being recorded, call the received status of the photographic and filmic image into question, revealing it to be the product of a synthetic and hybridised encounter infused with mis-readings and counter-assumptions as much as with shared beliefs, contractual agreements and mutual convenience. A different, perhaps deeper kind of truth emerges in that trio of succinct and modest installations, imbued with a disarming potency, a terse yet haunting charge. Although governed by a rigorous economy and distillation appropriate to the work of visual art made for the gallery or museum as opposed to the cinema, they nonetheless recall the aesthetic of the celebrated French filmmaker Jean Rouch.

Repositioning the subject and object, the author and spectator, in his groundbreaking films of the 1950s, Rouch radically redefined the terms in which ethnographic and many other kinds of documentary film would thereafter be made. At the same time as he confirmed its participatory character and its fantastical aspect: 'Fiction is the only way to penetrate reality – the means of sociology remain exterior ones', he asserted in a much-quoted statement, arguing that 'the whole problem is to maintain a certain sincerity towards the spectator, never to mask the fact that this is a film', he contended. 'Once this sincerity is achieved, when nobody is deceiving anybody, what interests me is the introduction of an imaginary, of the unreal. I can then use the film to tell what cannot be told otherwise.'[7] The child of a hybrid ethnos and of a later generation, Tan is necessarily differently positioned from Rouch in relation to much of her source material. Capitalising on the complexities those differences introduce into her relationships with her subjects, she appears nonetheless to be refining a similar strategy. For her, as for her renowned predecessor, rather than a research tool whose methodology approximates to 'notes of enquiry', ethnographic film may be an eloquent vehicle for the subjective study of identity.

Cradle (1998), a work closely related to *Facing Forward* and *Tuareg*, attests that Tan's engagement with the specific properties of her chosen medium is not only an abiding preoccupation but one which, now, comes centre stage. Although it, too, draws on pre-existing film of similar origin, it is ultimately more engaged with the nature of the medium per se than with critiquing the underlying ideology and function of documentary material, regardless of whether it be geared to entertainment or pedagogy. It comprises a brief segment of several seconds' duration seamlessly looped so that it appears to be an unending action devoid of beginning, middle and end, that depicts a swaddled infant swinging from a tree by a rope. A 16 mm projector casts this sepia-toned imagery onto a white cloth that hangs freely in a darkened room. Uncannily, the shaft of light from the projector appears both to reveal and animate the still image. Propelled by air currents generated by the apparatus the cloth literally moves: fluttering gently, it sets the cradle in motion. An inert material form – a cloth – is miraculously transformed into a vera icon. Imprinting itself onto the textile, the *sui generis* image has mysteriously come to life through the transfiguring action of light: the baby rocks rhythmically, apparently of its own volition.

Tan's lyrical motif melds certain ancient beliefs and allusions into an extraordinarily resonant emblematic image. Vera icons, most notably the Veronica vernicle and the Shroud of Turin, were long considered 'true' not only in resemblance but in substance. 'The impression was "true" as Christ's shadow and blood. The cloth was as "true" as his body and skin', writes Ewa Kuryluk in *Veronica and Her Cloth* (1991), a fascinating study of the mythology and history of this subject. These true images were intimately related to Christ's death and resurrection: the portraits attained immediately prior to his crucifixion were considered analogous to his burial clothes, resurrected along with his body: 'What seemed dead became animated, what appears material became spiritualised', Kuryluk asserts. 'Turning into an *acheiropoieta*, the cloth metamorphosed into a double of Jesus: the image of his soul.'[8] Such body-shroud-anima metaphors inspired the development of iconic textiles, interest in which was also stimulated by cloth traditions concurrent elsewhere, in particular in Egypt where even in early Christian times the deceased continued to be interred in painted shrouds and masks, second skins and dresses for their afterlife.

Cradle weaves allusions from both Christian and Egyptian sources with more recent responses to the camera from tribal peoples and others, who regarded it as a stealer of souls and photographers as shadow-catchers and face-takers. While accounts of such reactions may be primarily hearsay, admits cultural historian Marina Warner in her vivid account of this recurrent notion, she nonetheless contends that 'it matches an uneasiness, it reflects a doubt, shared by both the subject of the image and its maker, that the photographic image may be more than dead matter'.[9] Given that, as she demonstrates, 'the photograph can act as a magical summons, aiming to enshrine identity, to create a memorial which pleads for deathlessness and issues a challenge to time', its iconic potential is undeniable. The photograph exists at the frontier of materiality and immateriality, a frontier which, Warner speculates, may 'correspond to the mysterious ungraspable frontier between body and spirit, between individual forms and the animating character of persons.' Rather than simply dissolving this boundary, the embodied cinematic image in *Cradle*, like the vera icon, literally incorporates these dualities into itself. With its ceaseless rocking, *Cradle* conveys the illusion of life endlessly prolonged in a perpetual 'now', of death forever forestalled. Overlaying deeply seated responses to photographic and filmic reproduction with far older beliefs rooted in traditions pertaining to death and the afterlife, it memorably instantiates that ever-present urge to create mimetic representations in order to compensate for what is bound to be lost. In its privileging of film's expressive powers over the analytical and evidentiary, *Cradle* stands apart in Tan's early work: primordial beliefs, fears and desires are here less represented than actively conjured.

Fiona Tan
'*Saint Sebastian*, Work in Progress'

First published in *Gagarin*, no. 2, 4–18, 2001. Reprinted in *Fiona Tan: Saint Sebastian*, Musée d'Art Contemporain, Montréal, 2005, 6–8, 20–2.

In August last year I travelled to Japan in order to install one of my works in a group exhibition in the Museum of Modern Art, Kyoto. It was my first visit to Japan. Although I am somewhat familiar with Southeast Asia and China, Japan struck me as being completely different from other Asian countries I know. Like any tourist I spent some time visiting a few of the many temples that Kyoto, formerly the historic capital, has to offer. It was at a visit to the Sanjûsangen-dô temple, famous for its thousand sculptures of the thousand armed goddess of mercy, that I chanced upon a postcard which triggered this project. The postcard showed a row of young women with stockinged feet and in kimono, each standing poised with tall bows and arrow drawn in their hands. The image struck me as unusual; in my daily walks around the city I had seen only women in high heels, jeans and Calvin Klein T-shirts, or in Chanel suits.

The postcard – it turned out – had been taken at the annual *Tôshiya*, a traditional ceremony which has taken place each New Year at the Sanjûsangen-dô temple for over 400 years. *Tôshiya* is a coming-of-age ritual. It is an traditional archery competition practised by women at age twenty, the age when adulthood is reached in Japan. Fascinated, intrigued and inspired I began scheming to find out more about this event.

COMING OF AGE

On 11 January this year, I boarded a flight from Amsterdam to Osaka Kansai airport with a modest film crew: my camerawoman, Claire Pijman, and soundman,

Hugo Dijkstal. Our goal: to film the *Tôshiya* at the Sanjûsangen-dô temple, which was taking place that coming Sunday. Prior to this I had been frequently emailing and faxing with Shinji Kohmoto, senior curator at the Museum of Modern Art, Kyoto, and curator of the Yokohama Triennial, in frantic attempts to gain permission to film an event I had never seen, knew little about, and was only scarcely documented. Thanks to the efforts of Shinji and the Triennial staff, permission had been granted a week before. *Tôshiya* is a religious ceremony in a sacred temple; permission to film the entire event had never been given before.

The more information I found concerning this event, the more fascinated and determined I became. To my mind this event embodied a surprising intersection of several themes: traditional ritual and modern-day young Japanese women; religious practice and military inheritance; youth and cultural history. Although I have always been drawn to archery, I hardly knew the first thing about it. Somewhere in the back of my mind lay half-forgotten passages of Eugen Herrigel's classic book *Zen in the Art of Archery* (1948) echoed. My mind's eye conjured up conflicting images: the grace and femininity of girls on the cusp of womanhood combined with the – typically masculine – physical and mental strength required for an essentially military tradition. That this tradition symbolised a turning point to adulthood, puzzled but fascinated me. My imagination grew wings and I suspect that I idealised and romanticised this ritual.

TARGET PRACTICE

Possibly it is due to the relatively late introduction of firearms that archery in Japan is a popular and well-preserved tradition. The archery competition at the Sanjûsangen-dô temple has a history dating back to mediaeval times. The most famous archer, Wasa Daihachiro of Kishū, set the all-time record at the Kyoto *Tôshiya* competition in 1686, succeeding with the incredible tally of 8,133 hits out of a total 13,053 arrows shot. At that time the competition lasted the entire day and Wasa was, I believe, simply a young farmhand. The Japanese filmmaker Mikio Naruse made a film about this in 1945, of which I have only seen a film still. Although I tried extensively to locate and view this film, all my efforts failed, and I was again left to fill the gap with my own imagination.

Instructing women in archery and sword fighting, as I learned, has a long history. A Samurai wife was expected to defend home and children if her husband was away. She was supplied with an armoured outfit with which she could disguise herself as a man in order to fool hoards of attackers. Her wedding gift was a dagger so she could honourably commit suicide if attacked and her dignity compromised. All this contrasts sharply with the stereotyped image of petite, feminine women and the stories I've heard about the servile position that Japanese women are expected to occupy even today.

There is a Confucian belief that through a person's archery their true character could be determined. The sound of the string being plucked is supposed to strike fear in evil spirits' hearts, and the sound of a master archer shooting is supposed to bring spiritual enlightenment. I find enough to kindle further the flames of inspiration, but there is still much that I do not know nor understand. This work will be as much about my projections onto this ritual as it will be about the event itself.

Through searching the internet I found a Dutch club which practises *kyūdō*, Japanese archery. Together with my camerawoman we have been to their training sessions to practice and to plan the film shoot: the lenses, the camera angles, composition, speed and movement. My only hope is that my estimation of the actual proceedings in Kyoto are correct. The continuing uncertainty regarding permission to film is taking its toll on my peace of mind.

All my work reflects on and relies heavily on documentary principles of filmmaking. To date I have completed two full-length documentary films, *May You Live In Interesting Times* (1997) and *Kingdom of Shadows* (2000). Similarly, nearly all my film and video installations – whether filmed myself or using existing footage – incorporate material of a documentary nature. I am interested in film, video and photography viewed from its recording documentary and anthropological viewpoint rather than material stemming from fictional films, such as Hollywood movies. Whilst originally filmed as an objective record, early footage in particular can be revealing and fascinating.

In video installations such as *Facing Forward* (1999) or *Tuareg* (1999) I have been working with what has been labelled colonial footage. This footage was shot in the early twentieth century by travelling Europeans or Americans and intended for Western audiences. I now am undertaking my own expedition to an unfamiliar foreign country to film what could be seen as an exotic event. After my return I will be curious to compare my rolls of film with this early material. Maybe the same pitfalls and limitations await me. As an outsider to this culture, my touristic gaze cannot be avoided; if anything it will become a part of the piece. Thus, with an open mind in some ways akin to cinéma verité, I want to film the *Tôshiya*.

14 January, Sunday morning

My crew and I were up at half past five to load the camera and check and transport the equipment. Now it's 7 a.m., the temperature is –4°c and it looks like it might start snowing. I'm glad I've brought thermal underwear with me. Shinji and Triennial staff Eric and Naomi are also present to help and translate. A last-minute meeting with the chairman of the archery association has secured us a green light; we can place cameras at all the positions I would like. The men's competition is first, giving us time to set up and test. The women's competition lasts two hours and is our only chance to get the scenes I am looking for.

Mesmerised I gaze at the endless rows of women who appear briefly and then, after the second shot and a short bow, retreat silently from the podium. I lose track of numbers. Their multitude, over 800, overwhelms me. This must be some Japanese idea of heaven I muse, and gaze absent-mindedly at the shapes of girls' ears. In some strange way I am reminded of large flocks of birds. The women perform silently and elegantly as in a choreography; each kimono's more stunning than the last. The gap separating me from this culture becomes even larger.

Appreciatively I watch each movement. The Japanese are said to find the nape of the neck of a woman the most erotic part of the female body. Watching these bustling and restless proceedings from the temple side I can imagine why. I find myself staring at the slight patch of skin that was bared between the collars of their kimonos – it would seem the women wear several kimonos one over the other – and the beginning of the hairline at the base of the head. I imagine – like a man wanting to plant a kiss on such a delicate neck – and draw a deep breath imagining her scent.

After a while I can follow the rhythm of the proceedings. At a nod of the head, in rows of twelve, the women (although in appearance some still seem girls) step forward. Without a pause the preparatory movements are made: a bow in the direction of the target, the careful placement of the feet, the arrow's end slotted in the string. In smooth synchronised motion the bow is raised and, with both arms above the head, the string is drawn. Their concentration draws me in, their faces like masks. Without tension the moment passes. The women bow curtly and step down, their place already taken by the next row waiting behind them.

February

Finally over jet lag, and the flu ...

The shooting of the shooting. I am delighted with the filmed material, to me it's magic and beautiful. Perhaps even too beautiful. The decision to shoot close-up was the right one, the target so far away it seems irrelevant. But for now I need to forget being there – the cold, the crowds, the apprehension and excitement.

I am struck by the little imperfections revealed by the camera: shaking, frowns, the pressing of the cheek against the arrow's shaft, hair tossed by the release of the bow. My readings on the philosophy of *kyūdō* make me dizzy: artless art, directionless direction. (The viewer is the target.)

March

Some distance gained. Still I have the feeling that I am avoiding questions and issues. Making art cannot be an excuse not to think things through. At the same time it is not about content only; the images must be let to speak. The closeness and intimacy of the scenes is for me their most crucial element. So it is a paradox – closeness and distance at the same time.

April

Experimenting with the presentation, I have two sides. They don't have to go side by side, possibly back to back. Forgetting is so important for the work process. Acquiring again the distance of the stranger, but in a different way now.

May

In between travelling. *Saint Sebastian* – as I've decided to call this video installation – seems to be falling into place. And is starting to feel right. I've been showing the edit to a few friends. Now it's on to the practical things. Only I'm not entirely at ease in the necessary alteration between all the modes of working: dreaming, experimenting, organising, producing. I also need to rent a space and the equipment for a trial installation. The last stages – sound, post-production – require the stamina of a long-distance runner.

Just back from opening my first solo exhibition in the US, 'Matrix 144' at the Wadsworth Atheneum Museum of Art in Hartford, Connecticut. I hate jet lag and am glad to be back in Berlin.

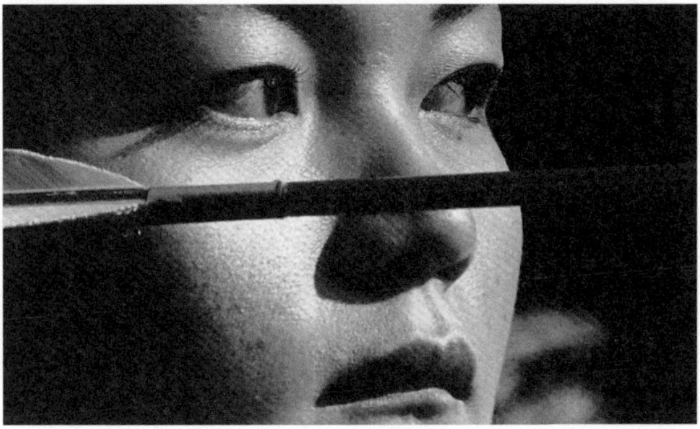

Saint Sebastian (still), 2001

Am reading diaries written by travellers to Japan across various centuries. I compare their reports to my memories. I enjoy the freedom of working backward, and researching all over again. Maybe this will become a work in its own right.

Have spent all day searching in vain for a book I read years ago, name and author of which I cannot remember. I recall from its pages a story about one of the first sinologists who lived in the seventeenth century. He believed that there was such a thing as a key to the Chinese language. A code: crack it and you would instantly be able to understand Chinese. He took a young Japanese man in service to assist him with his research and to compile the first Chinese-French dictionary. The Japanese man, one of only very few Japanese migrants at that time, is reported to have died two years later of tuberculosis and loneliness. The dictionary was never completed.

Do I likewise think that all I need is a code, a recipe by which to complete this piece?

The art of archery and the art of art. The target is so far away that it seems irrelevant. My tools are the camera and the editing table. Viewing things from both sides.

There are two works – the one in my head or in my desires, and the one it will become.

A true shot in kyūdō *is not just one that hits the centre of the target, but one where the arrow can be said to exist in the target before its release.*[1]

Massimiliano Gioni
‘Close Encounters’, on *Facing Forward* and *Saint Sebastian*

Flash Art International, November–December 2001, no. 221, 75–7.

Fiona Tan is an untiring cataloguer of gazes. In *Facing Forward* (1999) and *Smoke Screen* (1997), the artist gathers found footage of old anthropological films to make up an archive of the visual modules with which the West has described and imagined foreign cultures. Born to an Indo-Chinese father and an Australian mother, and now living in Amsterdam, Fiona Tan is exploring the borders of an archaeology of vision. In the very same moment she appropriates the presumably innocent gaze of scientific photography, Fiona Tan aspires to demonstrate its bias: presenting as obsolete, or even archaic, certain ways of seeing and describing, Fiona Tan invites us to question the means with which we represent reality today. She confronts us with the illusion of objectivity. The artist is very discrete in insinuating this scepticism: in *Facing Forward* the simple juxtaposition of various and yet all too similar vintage films shot in different parts of the world immediately evokes the spectrum of a systematic annihilation of differences. When the anthropologist or the tourist holds a video camera, Tan reminds us, their gaze folds back upon itself, annulling all differences. The images captured by the camera tell us nothing about others: photography and the documentary are in reality limited to putting our own gaze on show. Anthropology gives us back nothing but our own self-portrait, reflected in the surface of the objects of our curiosity: we delude ourselves that we can control and categorise others, but we are only trapping ourselves.

For her most recent film, *Saint Sebastian* (2001), the artist herself decided to sit behind the camera. Shot in a temple in Kyoto, Japan, *Saint Sebastian* shows a group of girls involved in a coming of age ceremony called the *Tōshiya*: all the girls, in traditional dress, have just turned twenty, and challenge each other in an archery competition, which has been taking place annually for over 400 years. The camera follows every movement: it scrutinises the texture of the clothes, it loses itself in the folds of the dresses, it investigates the girls' profiles and the curves of the taut bows ready to shoot. The girls' gazes are focussed on the target, which remains off-camera for the duration of the film. The richness of *Saint Sebastian* is to be found specifically in this geometry of gazes: the gaze of the girls and that of the artist chase each other but never meet. The camera approaches the girls' bodies, it brushes past them but is condemned to keep its distance, as though it cannot share in the solemnity of the moment. Fiona Tan is almost writing the choreography for a dance: *Saint Sebastian* describes an endless duel between the desire to be closer to others, to assimilate them, and the necessity of maintaining differences intact, to not annul the diversity that renders this meeting of gazes so enriching, almost sensual.

Fiona Tan
'*Countenance*: A Film Installation'

Documenta XI, exhibition catalogue, ed. Okwui Enwezor, Ostfildern-Ruit: Hatje Cantz, 2002.

SYNOPSIS

For his project *People of the 20th Century*, the photographer August Sander took pictures or more than 500 people from different social milieus and professions in Germany between 1892 and 1954. Divided into seven portfolios, these portraits were intended to reveal the social structure of the time. Today, the idea of making an inventory of an entire nation or even an entire age seems misplaced, overly ambitious and ethically dubious. But the result, besides being of great historical significance, is timeless, fascinating and indeed very beautiful.

Sander's impressive portrait photography is the source of inspiration for my new film installation, *Countenance* (2002). Employing a working method in some respects comparable to Sander's, I hope to record on film the portraits of a couple of hundred citizens of Berlin and its environs. To this end I have compiled a list of categories, occupations, and the like. It is a list based loosely on sociological statistics but determined primarily by individual observations and personal intuition. What I have in mind is by no means an academic undertaking but rather a project driven by visual preoccupations.

My chief motivation is curiosity. I am curious to find out how much society has changed since Sander's time, and I want to see what kind of picture that investigation yields. Perhaps by compiling my own typology, I can attempt to give shape to my own vision of contemporary society. At the same time, however, I call into question this very practice of general characterisation and the way we form our notions of society as a whole. By looking through the camera lens with a frank and open gaze, I want to make a record of how Germany's formerly divided capital and its history reveals itself in the faces, body language and living conditions of its inhabitants.

Each individual is capable of telling apart millions of faces, of recognising thousands, and of observing and interpreting the most infinitesimal facial changes. There is no other object to which our visual faculty reacts in such a nuanced and refined way. What *Countenance* has in mind is a study of the small details: how someone clasps her hands; how the glance of an old man arrests your attention; how a child's pose disarms you.

I am interested in the intermediate region between film and photography. In previous works I have focused on what I call 'photographic moments', scenes in which people pose for the movie camera as if posing for a photograph. Now I want to delve more deeply into such elongated cinematic moments, examining and recording them with precision. *Countenance* is to be shot on 16 mm black-and-white film and presented as a spatial installation.

THE PORTRAIT PHOTOGRAPHS OF AUGUST SANDER

August Sander (1876–1964) set up his own commercial photography studio in Cologne in 1909. To earn a living he started out as a travelling photographer, making portraits of peasants in their homes and on their land in the Westerwald countryside. Sander's style clearly set him apart from the rest of late nineteenth-century studio photography, with its painted background screens, props and kitsch staging. Influenced by the notions of *Sachliche Fotografie* he paid a great deal of attention to the natural surroundings. Later he selected negatives from this work for his portfolio of archetypes, *The Farmer*.

During the 1920s, Sander became friendly with members of the Cologne arts scene. Stimulated by these contacts he developed a plan to construct an 'atlas' of the social landscape. To this end, between 1925 and 1927 he drew up a list of forty-five categories; Sander intended to produce twelve portraits for each category. Although in part aware of the developments taking place in avant-garde photography, Sander's work through the years was characterised by a striking continuity of style. He made his photographs on large negative glass plates, with an exposure time of sometimes 2–4 seconds. He used this technique until the end of his career.

In 1934 Sander's first book, *Face of Our Time* (1929), was declared 'degenerate' and all stocks of the publication were burnt by the Nazis. Sander was unable to continue with his life's work during the war, and he directed most of his energy towards landscape photography. After the war he added to his portfolios the subcategories 'The National Socialist' and 'The persecuted'. The subcategories employed in *People of the 20th Century* – which today seem so peculiar and unscientific – reflect social-scientific notions that were popular in Germany at that time. Sander was never able to finish his project. In the archives he left behind, some occupations are amply represented while others, such as 'Foreign workers', with a mere two photographs, are far from complete.

BERLIN 2001–02: BRIEF STATISTICAL INFORMATION

The population of Berlin is approximately 3.3 million. Two-thirds of the population lives in the western part of the city; one-third in the eastern part (former capital of the GDR). There are approximately 100,000 more women than men living in Berlin. The population is becoming incrementally smaller year on year.

The employed population in Germany has changed drastically in the last eighty years. While approximately 60% of the workforce were labourers in 1925, today the figure is less than 25%. The largest vocational category in 2001 is employees in permanent positions, and civil servants. About 13% of the present population of Berlin are of foreign origin, less than the German national average. The portion of the population with a college or university diploma is 17% in former East Berlin and 11% in former West Berlin. Approximately half of all children are raised by single mothers. The percentage of unemployed among the potential workforce (1.5 million) is 17%, but in the Kreuzberg district, for instance, unemployment has reached 27%.

Group 1: The Farmer Portfolio of archetypes	1. The young farmer 2. The farmer's child and the mother 3. The farmer's family 4. The farmer – his life and work 5. Farming types 6. The small-town dweller 7. Sport
Group II: The Skilled Tradesman	8. The master craftsman 9. The industrial 10. The worker – his life and work 11. Working types – physical and intellectual 12. The technician and inventor
Group III: The Woman	13. Woman and man 14. Woman and child 15. The family 16. The elegant woman 17. The woman in intellectual and practical occupation
Group IV: Classes and Professions	18. The student 19. The scholar 20. The official 21. The doctor and the pharmacist 22. The judge and the attorney 23. The soldier 23a. The National Socialist 24. The aristocrat 25. The clergyman 26. The teacher and educator 27. The businessman 28. The politician

Group V: The Artists	29. The writer 30. The actor 31. The architect 32. The sculptor 33. The painter 34. The composer 35. The performing musician
Group VI: The City	36. The street 37. Travelling people – fair and circus 38. Travelling people – gypsies and transients 39. Festivities 40. City youth 41. Servants 42. Types and figures of the city 43. People who came to my door 44. The persecuted 44a. Political prisoners 44b. Foreign workers
Group VII: The Last People	45. Idiots, the sick, the insane and matter

COUNTENANCE – CATEGORIES (ROUGH LIST), FIONA TAN (2001–2)

Number of filmed portraits: approx. 200. To be filmed on location in all the districts of Berlin at the person's place of work or, when appropriate, at home.

1. Social Groups	Single Newly married couple Couple Mother with child Father with child Family Child Youth Old-person's home resident Flatmates City nomad Sports club
2. Employed People	
Farmer	
Worker/labourer	e.g., construction worker; factory worker
Craftsman	e.g., butcher; baker; painter; brick layer; carpenter
Technical Craftsman	e.g. plumber; metalworker; auto mechanic; engineer
Executive / Civil servant	e.g., tax collector; garbage collector; street sweeper; police officer; teacher; social worker; magistrate

Employee	e.g., cleaning woman; supermarket cashier; cook; computer programmer; financial advisor; office personnel; secretary; receptionist; bank employee
Medical professional	e.g., doctor, nurse, therapist
Self-employed	e.g., taxi driver; estate agent; florist; shop owner; döner kebab seller; greengrocer; gallery owner; barkeeper; sex worker
Freelancer	e.g., writer; journalist; musician; actor; filmmaker; architect; designer
Others	e.g., pensioner; unemployed; beggar; drug addict; student; politician; curator; artist

Mark Godfrey
'Fiona Tan's *Countenance*'

Fiona Tan: Countenance, Modern Art Oxford, 2005, 60–80.

PORTRAIT OF THE ARTIST AS ...

Fiona Tan's *Countenance* (2002) begins with a self-portrait. Her face appears first, in three-quarter pose, on the smallest of the work's four screens, the one that is kept apart in the installation in a kind of annex away from the three main projections. For around ten seconds she looks at the camera confidently, blinks, and blinks again, before her face is replaced by a succession of different head shots, each lasting only a second or two. As she disappears from view, as these other faces begin to beat time, a soundtrack starts to accompany the image. Tan reads aloud a brief diary of her year in Berlin. The narration – which lasts around five minutes – serves as a factual introduction to the project. We hear that Tan was in Berlin temporarily and that she gradually began to assemble an archive of portraits. But we do not get any precise details. We are told neither that she had come from Amsterdam, nor that she was on the DAAD programme,[1] nor that this work developed from earlier concerns, nor that she revisited the work of August Sander. We do not hear why Tan organised her archive of portraits as she did, why she made short black-and-white films of each subject rather than photographs, why she installed the work as she does. All these questions are ones we can explore later, before the three main screens that make up the main body of the work. Tan's narration, meanwhile, should be understood less as a factual introduction and more as an expansion of her own self-portrait; an expansion but also a fragmentation. For many 'Fiona Tans' are presented here, many personas in one. It is a fracturing that stretches to the very heart of her project.

First, we have a portrait of the artist as a traveller. Listening to the narration we gather immediately that Tan is displaced. Having arrived in Berlin, she feels 'lighter, if also set adrift'. Lighter, because she is released from the burdens of her everyday life, the administration and the duties and time pressures which would make a person shut themselves away from strangers in their home city.[2] 'Set adrift', Tan has much more time than usual, time to waste 'staring out the window', gazing at strangers. 'Do I look better at someone's face in a foreign city?' she asks. But what would 'better' mean? As a foreigner, Tan might be more observant; she might have more time to observe, but she might also be prone to see things through her own skewed perspective, failing to understand what she sees. This much she admits, albeit obtusely. '11 May. A map of Berlin hangs on the kitchen wall. It's an older map. The highway routes are coloured blue, and I repeatedly mistake them for waterways.' You can hardly blame her, used, as she is, to a city of canals.

At some point in the year, the project is determined. Tan begins to collect faces. 'I gather together impressions and snapshots like an amateur biologist in the nineteenth century would catch butterflies. Type. Archetype. Stereotype.' A self-portrait of the artist as a scientist, then. But, cutting against the picture of the artist-as-archivist is another facet of the self-portrait, the messy bohemian in the chaotic studio. Towards the end of the narration, we hear of

> *hours spent sorting through my cluttered notes and papers. Hard to choose what to keep and what to discard. I'm a great one for making long lists, even if they are meaningless in the end as if order outside would take care of the disorder inside.*

So, organiser and clutterer, hand awkwardly in hand.

There's also a picture of the artist as fantasist. Tan recalls her childhood facility for recognition. 'I used to think that I never forget a face', she says. *Countenance*, it would seem, sprang as much from Tan's stay in Berlin, her art-historical interests, her analytical tendencies, as from her fondness for physiognomic guessing games. In Berlin, she continues to play: 'Almost automatically I try to guess someone's background and origin.' Yet contrasting the picture of the playful artist-as-imaginative-child, we have yet another persona – that of the knowing, self-aware, self-critical DAAD scholar. This 'Fiona Tan' recognises the blind spots and the biases of the traveller. This 'Fiona Tan' is aware of the dangers of classification, telling the nineteenth-century scientist in her that 'all my attempts at systematical order must be arbitrary, idiosyncratic'. This 'Fiona Tan' reminds the child in her that guessing games are always predetermined, and that there are 'details [of faces] I notice', and others 'I let slip by'. This 'Fiona Tan' recites the children's rhyme 'Tinker, tailor, soldier, sailor', but only to suggest that as the foreign visitor and portraitist she might be 'thief'.

The picture of the artist that emerges from the narration is nuanced and conflicted, and one of its effects is to undercut the authority of the image that opened the reel. In her more conventional visual self-portrait, remember, Tan's countenance seemed confident and calm. In presenting a very different kind of person, her words remind us of the inadequacy of any image to indicate the character of the sitter, that 'countenance' can mean 'mere show'. We leave this introductory screen with some doubt about the very workings of portraiture, but we might also be sceptical about the entire nature of Tan's project. Its ambition is described most precisely towards the end, but hardly with any statement of intent. Where Sander once introduced an exhibition with the confident assurance: 'Nothing seems better suited than photography to give an absolutely faithful historical picture of our time',[3] Tan instead poses a question: 'Could I possibly collect, collate a time in history? Whose history?' And so we enter the rest of the installation, wondering whether she is, as she says, 'doomed to fail', teeming with Tan's doubt.

CAUSES FOR CONCERN

We can ask later if and how Tan infects her archive with this doubt, but for the moment, let us pause as if between the two parts of the installation of *Countenance*, between the introductory 'self-portrait' screen and the three main ones to come. What we know so far is that Tan set out to photograph the citizens of the city she was visiting, to make an archive of the faces of Berlin, to 'collate a time in history'. We have listened to her scepticism, but just why did she deem this project to be so utterly problematic? What about it caused her concern and necessitated all the self-questioning? To answer this, we can break the project down into three parts, thinking first about its archival nature, then about Tan's engagement with the genre of portraiture, and finally, about her role as a kind of ethnographer, exploring a culture foreign to her own.

During the postwar period, and particularly in Germany, artists employed archival forms for many different reasons. When, in the 1950s, Bernd and Hilla Becher began to create an archive of photographs of industrial architecture, they were not only commemorating forms on the verge of obsolescence and disappearance. They were also employing an extremely objective form of photography,

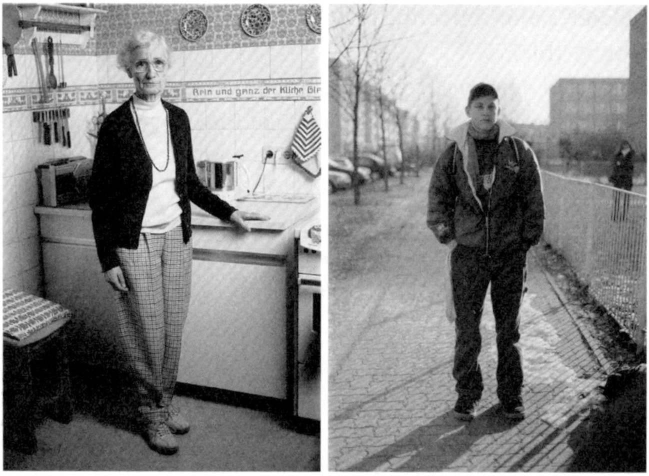

Countenance (stills), 2002

countering the kind of 'subjective' humanist photography championed by Otto Steinert.[4] Gerhard Richter, meanwhile, gathered together on the panels of his monumental compendium *Atlas* thousands of photographs – some taken from found family albums, some taken himself, and many cut out of magazines or newspapers. The compendium has been called an 'anomic archive' because of the way it resists precise forms of organisation. The different kinds of photography collected in *Atlas* dramatise both the necessity of memory in an amnesiac society (for instance, Richter included photographs of concentration camps when they were hardly negotiated in German culture), and the impossibility of memory in a rapidly developing consumer culture where each new day brought new images of new products. Tan's approach to the archive is certainly informed by these artistic confrontations, but it is also informed by the operations of stricter archives outside of the art context.

What, in its strictest sense, is an archive? To form an archive is to attempt to impose order on experience and on the contents of the world. The archivist constructs categories, which, appearing objective, often only reflect their biases. Whether it is an object, a person or a photograph, the complexity of a given piece of data is reduced by the archivist so that it can be placed into its given category. The archive flattens out peculiarity, its organisation only allowing for equivalences and basic differences to be drawn between its contents. As much as they are formed by the desire to organise information, so too in turn archives determine and limit the possibilities of knowledge. Operating in this manner, archives become fundamental to those who control and organise a society. The artist Allan Sekula, whose research has paid particular attention to the function of nineteenth-century police and medical archives, writes:

> *Archives are not neutral; they embody the power inherent in accumulation, collection and hoarding as well as that power inherent in the command of the lexicon and rules of a language ... Photographic archives by their very structure maintain a hidden connection between knowledge and power. Any discourse that appeals without scepticism to archival standards of truth might well be viewed with suspicion.*[5]

[...] [T]he question of portraiture [is] the second main device of *Countenance*. As Benjamin Buchloh has argued, the very legitimacy and possibility of portraiture is questionable now; yet time and time again, artists manifest a 'desire to confide [themselves] in the genre'.[6] If each renewal of confidence takes place in different conditions, the reasons for doubts about its legitimacy are not difficult to fathom. Portraiture, at least in its traditional manifestation, shored up a notion of the individual aristocratic or bourgeois subject, self-knowing and self-sufficient.[7] The late nineteenth century brought many changes in the way subjectivity was understood: Marxism insisted on a conception of the subject inseparable from its class and economic determinants; psychoanalysis posited a model of the subject as internally split, driven by unconscious fantasies and desires. With its faith in mimetic resemblance alone as a guarantor of the subject's representation, with its insistence on the very idea of the individual, how could portraiture survive with any authenticity into the twentieth century?

One way would be for artists to insist on the social and economic positioning of the portrayed subject, and to submit portraiture to the logic of the archive, exchanging the single image for a compendium. This brings us to August Sander, the bedrock of *Countenance*. Sander's *Citizens of the Twentieth Century* was by far the most impressive and ambitious photographic portraiture project of its time. Begun in 1910, yet incomplete at the time of Sander's death in 1964, the project had been distilled in 1929 in the publication *Antlitz der Zeit* (differently translated as *The Physiognomy of Present Time*, or *Face of Our Time*). Believing in photography as a 'universal language', in physiognomy as a means to understand character,[8] and in the possibility that one portrayed subject could stand for whole type (be it a profession, or social group), Sander felt confident that his project would provide an accurate document of German society and would assist others in the study of physiognomy.[9] The completed work would be divided into forty-five portfolios, each containing twelve photographs, spread across seven sections: The Farmer, The Skilled Tradesman, The Woman, Classes and Professions, The Artists, The City, and The Last People. Society was represented in a cycle, starting with farmers, 'ascending' through workers to skilled professions, to artists, and then 'down', to vagrants, prisoners, the oppressed, and the disabled. The organisation of the work would reflect Sander's 'assumption that history follows a cyclical pattern, that society is made up of a guild hierarchy, and that the world of work and the private world are distinct.'[10] [...]

TAN'S ARCHIVE

In 'The Artist as Ethnographer', an essay which explores the relationship of recent art and ethnography, Hal Foster articulates a double problem. The artist might pursue a project with all the biases and naivety of an unself-critical ethnographer, but they might also develop work in which 'the deconstructive-ethnographic approach can become a gambit' – work so very self-questioning that it ends up 'hermetic and narcissistic'. 'Criticality' becomes 'contemptuous', the humility of self-scrutiny flips over into the hubris of self-congratulation, and, far from negating their authority, the artist once again enforces their superiority over the objects of their survey.[11] This articulation, I think, helps to describe one of the key dangers that might have faced Tan as she set about making *Countenance*. Yes, there were problems in building an archive, in confiding in portraiture, and in mapping a culture foreign to her own, but had her work been merely a deconstruction of these three methods, had the self-questioning of the first reel been amplified, she would have risked the hermeticism that Foster describes. To see how she avoided this, let us return to the scene of the installation, and proceed into the main room, where we find before us three screens, each hung vertically, each containing a succession of portrait films. All in all, there is around an hour and a half of material, some 220 faces. As the viewer sits down to watch, it is not long before they sense that the self-scrutiny of the work is matched by its generosity. [...]

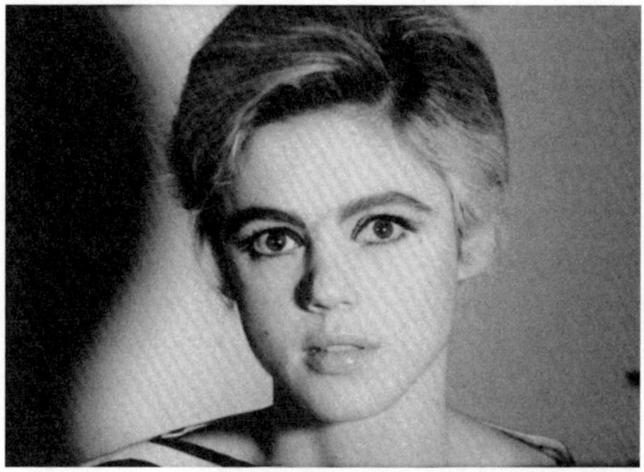

Andy Warhol, *Screen Test: Edie Sedgwick* [ST308], 1965

MOVING PORTRAITS

The most obvious difference between Tan's and Sander's projects is of course that Tan's is not made up of photographs but of short films. These were shot on 16 mm, which meant that before filming, considerable time had been spent setting up lighting, selecting lenses, and adjusting focus. Tan would get to know the subject during this setting-up period, or rather, resume their acquaintance. For some weeks before the shoot, each subject had been contacted and introduced to the project, being told both how they would be categorised in the final work, and about the precedent of August Sander. On the shoot, each subject was filmed twice, each time for around a minute.

In selecting the medium of film, Tan was extending what can increasingly be seen as a sub-genre of portraiture, whose origins lie most obviously in Andy Warhol's *Screen Tests* (1964–6). These were close-up headshot films of visitors to the Factory, often dramatically lit, each filmed for the length of a reel (around 3 minutes), but projected slightly slower than they were recorded. In the last few years, the genre of the moving-image portrait has swollen to accommodate James Coleman's *Untitled: Philippe VACHER* (1990), Gillian Wearing's *Sixty Minutes Silence* (1996), Rineke Dijkstra's *Annemiek (I wanna be with you)* (1997), Thomas Struth's one-hour-long video portraits (1996–7), Catherine Yass' *Town* series (2000), Tacita Dean's *Merz* (2002), and Sam Taylor-Wood's film of David Beckham (2004), to name some of the most disparate examples. What is the effect of the moving

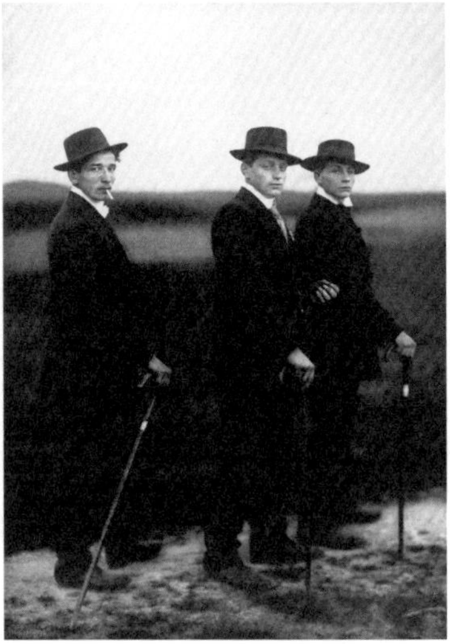

August Sander, *Young Farmers*, 1914

image on portraiture? When he had his photograph taken, Roland Barthes commented that, 'I am neither subject nor object but a subject who feels he is becoming an object'.[12] One facility of the moving image (at least where the subject is awake) is to challenge what might be the objectifying power of photography. No longer frozen in time, the subject is living and breathing. Tan had explored the dynamic of the still and moving image before she came to make *Countenance* in the work *Tuareg* (1999), made using a fragment of archival footage of North African children lining up to have a photograph taken. The film is successively run and frozen, re-played and re-frozen. In its still state, the image asks to be read as an objectification of the colonised 'other'; but as it runs, the figures break out into play, squabbling as would naughty children anywhere, so the ocean between twenty-first century viewer and these subjects evaporates.

One way to explain the use of film in *Countenance*, then, would be that it acts against the objectifying force of photography and allows the subjects to assert their individuality in the face of the archive's cold classification. However, this argument relies on two somewhat simplistic and misguided premises: that a subject of a still portrait is simply objectified, and that a subject of a moving-image portrait is necessarily 'liberated'. Things, of course, are more complicated. To start with the first half of this assumption, one of the ways in which subjects of static portraits assert their authority is the pose. Graham Clarke has shown how this works throughout Sander's project in order to conclude that, 'While [Sander] seeks "types", he celebrates individuals.'[13] Throughout *Countenance* we can see subjects who have very deliberately chosen poses, aiming to present themselves as individuals.[14] One example would be the suite of four 'executives', all of whom know how to present an imposing image of themselves in their office. Another would be the single shot of three 'Garbage Collectors', who impressively recast one of the earliest and most famous of Sander's photographs, *Young Farmers* (1914).

But as much as a pose can indicate the subject's authority, so too it can reveal the anxiety of self-representation. The pose is less a choice made by the subject, but a choice made for them. The first reel of *Countenance* includes a portrait of teenage 'skater boys' who – with their tight grouping, toughened postures and stern expressions – so obviously try to inhabit the image of the hip-hop group, an image they see every day on MTV. The veil of toughness barely hides their fragility. If some poses, even when still, advertise the anxieties of the subjects, the film medium has the effect of emphasising such anxieties, dramatising the difficulty of self-representation (rather than bringing frozen objectified subjects to life).[15] Throughout the archive, we watch people failing to keep still. Sometimes this can be funny, particularly when the subject breaks out into infectious giggles. But more frequently, we see sidewards glances, twitching hands, fidgeting fingers and more unnerving signs of failure.

But to what effect is all this movement? Let us suppose we watch the succession of 'civil servants' and note how some manage to keep still, whilst others are twitchy. Perhaps we can forget their archival classifications as 'judge' or 'social worker' and class them instead as 'confident' or 'nervous'. We are back to the argument that the film medium acts to disrupt the archival categories and to emphasise the character of the subjects. However, this does not seem entirely convincing. I want to suggest instead that by underscoring all the twitches, the film medium is pointing to something more general than any particular person's nervousness – pointing to the way subjectivity itself is technologically determined. What I mean by this is that different new technologies produce new forms of subjectivity. Think, for instance, about the anxiety that is produced by email and 24-hour accessibility as opposed to regular mail. How could a work of art represent the way shifts of technology produce shifts in subjectivity? Only by superimposing two different technologies to examine their misfit. In *Countenance*,

Tan makes film inhabit photography's old clothes and the confusion caused shows up in the fidgets. Subjects pose as if for a photograph. They pose only for a short duration (Tan's films are far shorter than the other examples of moving portraits mentioned above); they pose fully aware of the photographic precedent of Tan's project, but they are tripped up by film, a medium for which they are ill-prepared. All this is to say that by bringing the film medium into what need only be a photographic project, Tan expands the realm of its account of subjectivity. Subjectivity is not only represented in its social and professional determinants, but technological ones too.

COUNTENANCING

[...] Countenancing is a consistent operation in Tan's work. As we have seen in passing, in early works Tan has used material from first-contact ethnographic films and has found a way to redeem this footage despite its often objectifying or patronising character. Just before she lived in Berlin, she travelled to Japan to make *Saint Sebastian* (2001), a film of an archery ceremony involving young Japanese girls. Though initially it might be accused of exoticism, through her edit, Tan found a way to countenance the 'tourist gaze'. In *Correction* (2004), she has countenanced the archive of criminal photographs by subverting the function of the mug shot: confusing the division of prisoners and guards, and reversing in her installation the architectural operation of the panopticon.[16] Considered in this way, Tan's work exemplifies a new direction in critical practice. Where artists in the 1970s such as Allan Sekula or Douglas Huebler had to work hard to deconstruct oppressive forms of organisation and ways of seeing, Tan revisits formerly forbidden practices, never redeeming them casually, nor naively re-accepting them, but thinking again about their facilities as means through which to represent and engage with the world.[17] The move is a brave one, but risks pay off, and the projects are hardly 'doomed to fail'.

Adrian Searle
'Who Are You?', on *Countenance* and *News from the Near Future* at Modern Art Oxford

Exhibition review, *The Guardian*, 12 April 2005.

The curator stands unsmiling beside the museum, as still as a photograph, as though this were a test. A girl stifles her giggles; a waiter, carrying a teapot on a tray, sways slightly; the cook turns his head, uncertain of the camera. Figures appear and disappear on the three free-hanging screens, leaving only a few fleeting, arbitrary impressions.

Countenance (2002) is a flawed portrait of the people of Berlin, and is the centrepiece of Fiona Tan's show at Modern Art Oxford. Tan spent a year in and around the German capital, filming its inhabitants: one by one, group by group, family by family. They posed for her on the streets, in their workplaces and homes. She moves from the farmer in his field to hospital nurses, the homeless, the indigent, city officials, newlyweds. Between the winking lights on the back of a garbage truck, three refuse collectors strike up a grubby chorus line of identical postures. At any moment I expect them to burst into a song-and-dance routine. They don't, but as they take their half-turn to the camera they do remind me of another image, from another time: the three young farmers in their Sunday suits, setting off for the village dance, in August Sander's famous 1914 photograph. Where Sander's subjects turned a wary eye to the camera, this trio of binmen are complicit. They've seen Sander's image and are aping it.

Sander's monumental, lifelong and inevitably incomplete *Citizens of the Twentieth Century*, in which he attempted to photograph and categorise the inhabitants of Germany, was the model for Tan's work. His project began fitfully at the turn of the century and continued until the 1950s; along the way, Sander's photographs were suppressed by the National Socialists, and up to 30,000 images were destroyed by fire in Cologne during the Second World War. What remains, a huge seven-volume collection of images, is categorised according to a taxonomy of Sander's own, quasi-ethnographic invention: a 'portfolio of archetypes' that, under its various headings ('The Skilled Tradesman', 'The Woman', 'Classes and Professions' and, in Sander's final category, 'The Last People' – the sick, the insane), attempted the impossible task of recording and re-creating the broad social mosaic of German life.

We now look at Sander's work more for the vividness of individual photographs, and individual lives, than for his taxonomic pretensions, which were always dubious. His intentions cannot survive critical scrutiny now except as an instance of an outmoded way of seeing the world. Yet his cigarette-smoking secretaries, fat pastry cooks, bailiffs, debt collectors and bureaucrats have become archetypal – and in many cases unforgettable – images of Germans and Germanness in the first half of the last century, a cast list of characters and vignettes.

As in Sander's work, some of Tan's subjects come with what one takes to be the marks of their office: the butcher with his meat and knife, the social worker with a telephone, the homeless man with his can of lager, the shrink standing between her two chairs, a big box of tissues on the floor. But the details – the lump of dough wobbling around the baker's electric mixer, the loud clocks in pensioners' apartments – frequently leave more of a trace than the people themselves. While I'm wondering what comfort the old get from the sound of time passing, I miss entire social groups parading before me.

One grabs hold of fragments, because the totality is overwhelming. I screen-hop as Tan churns through singles and flatmates, sports club members and nuclear families, civil servants, labourers, craftsmen, technicians and the 'Others', among whom she numbers pensioners, the unemployed, drug addicts, politicians, curators and artists. Clearly, this last classification is a kind of wry joke. There are a few people here I recognise, but if it weren't for the captions that appear between shots, I'd have difficulty knowing who was who. And what can labels tell us of the lives behind them? In Kutluğ Ataman's *Küba* (2004), forty subjects tell their stories to his camera and make us feel on familiar terms with them. Tan, in contrast, holds her subjects at arm's length, always out of reach and unknowable to us, barricaded behind the labels that seek to define them.

Tan recognises that her project exemplifies a model social order and classification that is as unsustainable as Sander's. In a way, *Countenance* is a kind of trap. Tan provides her own introduction to this work on a small monitor. Reading from her diary, she asks: 'Do I look better at someone's face in a foreign city?' and 'Almost automatically I try to guess someone's background and origin ... all my attempts at systematic order must be arbitrary, idiosyncratic.' [...]

Countenance, it strikes me, is about how little we know about another's identity. We live with false impressions and dangerous assumptions. Our eyes skid across the surface of appearance like a needle scratching a gramophone record. Nor can we always disentangle what we project from what we deduce when we hear an accent or see a certain kind of face, or notice a smudge on a jacket, a winter suntan, the well-thumbed book poking out of a pocket.

There is something fitting about Tan's pairing of *Countenance* with *News from the Near Future* (2003), a single-screen film created from fragments of old footage from the archives of the Amsterdam Filmmuseum. This is at least the third time she has plundered this resource. Watching old documentary footage, or looking at old photographs, is always an encounter with the dead. It is also invariably affecting: even the scratches on the film, the flickering light and faded colour, add to a sense that time passes and people with it.

News from the Near Future begins with a woman with a parasol and two children standing in a cave's mouth. It is a great opening image to a story that doesn't exist. The sound of the sea is indistinguishable from the white noise of an untuned radio or the roar in your ears before fainting. Most of this film is taken up with boats at sea, strong light slanting on waves, a ketch wallowing in the troughs, the view from the bowsprit of a whaler as it nears its prey. There are ships in trouble, and a flooded Dutch town with the inhabitants punting up the high street; then magenta skies, silhouetted sails, a slow orange sunset. I wonder if, searching out her material, Tan has included footage in which she has searched for her own sense of origin, somewhere in the Indian Ocean.

One repeated image is extremely curious. I am still uncertain what I saw. A man in a hat and smart coat stands on a rock at the water's edge. The tide seems to be coming in, cutting him off from dry land. He peers about, hesitant and uncertain on his little rock, like a man waylaid by water in his town clothes, as though he had made a footling, spontaneous decision which he is about to regret. I wait for him to slip but he doesn't. It made me think of the people Tan filmed in Berlin, and how unreachable and cut off they appear to us.

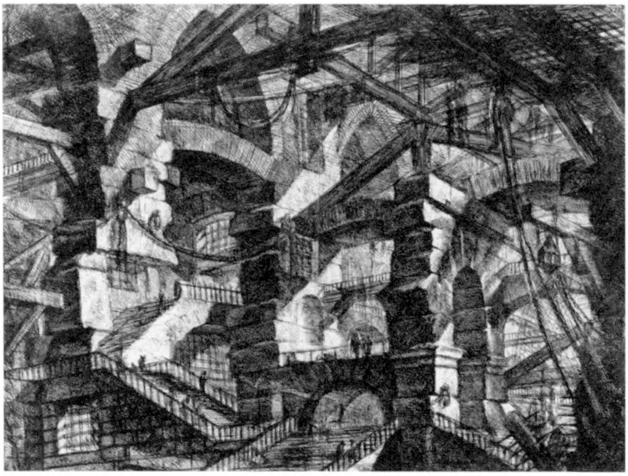

Giovanni Battista Piranesi,
Le Carceri d'Invenzione, 1761

Fiona Tan
'Carceri d'Invenzione' (Imaginary prisons), on *Correction*

Fiona Tan: Correction, Museum of Contemporary Art, Chicago; New Museum of Contemporary Art, New York; Armand Hammer Museum of Art and Cultural Center at UCLA, Los Angeles, 2004, 31.

You cannot meet a prison population; you can only meet persons.
— Pierre Raphaël, *Inside Rikers Island*, 1990

While in the late 1960s the population of inmates in American prisons numbered close to 200,000, this number now exceeds 2.2 million. That is more than any other country and represents a quarter of all prisoners worldwide. In the last decade, more than 350 new prisons have been built and more than half a million beds added to existing facilities.

Correction offers a small survey and sample of the current penal population of America. In four penitentiary institutions in the states of California and Illinois, inmates and officers were approached and took part in the filming of this project entirely voluntarily. More than 300 portraits were filmed in the summer of 2004. All the people seen in the video installation are either prisoners or prison guards.

The misery of gaols is not half their evil ... In a prison the awe of the publick eye is lost, and the power of the law is spent; there are few fears, there are no blushes. The lewd inflame the lewd, the audacious harden the audacious. Everyone fortifies himself as he can against his own sensibility, endeavours to practice on others the arts which are practised upon himself, and gains the kindness of his associated by similitude of manners. Thus some sink amidst their misery, and others survive only to propagate villainy.
— Samuel Johnson, *The Idler*, 1759

Fiona Tan
On *Correction*

From an email correspondence with curator Julie Rodrigues Widholm, July 2004.

This artwork is about invisibility. I wanted to show a sample of this world, which is largely out of sight (and out of mind) and which most people never get to see and would rather not see. By taking portraits I concentrate the project on people, on giving them a face and identity, rather than just more statistics.

I find that looking at a filmed portrait of a person is a very different experience than looking at a photograph. While looking at photographs can be incredibly beautiful and moving, I find it intriguing and challenging to observe someone who has been filmed for a while. I can glance at a photograph – being frozen in time – again and again. I can home in on certain details, parts of the background at my leisure. With a filmed image, I become less aware of the image and more aware of the person as an image, the person within, or even behind, the image. The passage of time emphasises the relationship between subject and camera: the contract/construct, however temporary, that went into making the picture. The tiniest movement made by the person portrayed – a blink, a slight hand movement – is both testimony to this and at the same time involuntary resistance. It is as though I, as a viewer, cannot pocket the image as I could if it were a still photograph hanging on the wall. So I am looking at something that is constantly escaping me.

Joel Snyder
'Setting the Record Straight: Fiona Tan's *Correction*'

Fiona Tan: Correction, Museum of Contemporary Art, Chicago; New Museum of Contemporary Art, New York; Armand Hammer Museum of Art and Cultural Center at UCLA, Los Angeles, 2004.

> *All my work reflects on and relies heavily on documentary principles of filmmaking ... Similarly, nearly all my film and video installations – whether filmed by myself or using existing footage – incorporate material of a documentary nature. I am interested in film, video and photography viewed from its recording, documentary and anthropological viewpoint.*
> — Fiona Tan, 2002

[...] *Correction* (2004) occupies the second-floor south gallery of the Museum of Contemporary Art, a room measuring 76 feet along each wall. Within this space, six screens, each measuring 3.6 feet by 4.9 feet, are suspended from the ceiling, their bottom edges hanging 3.9 feet above the floor, at intervals of roughly 17 feet, providing six points of a circle with a diameter of 40 feet and a circumference of 125 feet. Six digital video projectors, each targeted on a single screen, are mounted to poles and locked into position 7.2 feet above the floor. The projectors stand outside the circle, facing inward. The projected images can be viewed from either side of the screen (a viewer on one side sees a reversed image of what can be seen on the other). A speaker is installed 1.8 feet above each screen. Each projector is fed a unique sequence of video clips and recorded sound contained on one of six DVDs. None of the images projected on any given screen is shown on any of the others. Each shot in the six series is projected for from 20 to 50 seconds: to see every image in the installation requires roughly three hours. The DVD players are not synchronised. Six benches measuring 4 × 1.6 × 1.5 feet are arranged in a hexagon within the circle traced by the screens. Spectators are free to view the installation seated on the benches or while walking outside or within the circle. The room is darkened, with overhead lights washing gently on the external walls.

The 300 video clips of prisoners and guards in four prisons in Illinois and California, filmed in 2004, are presented together with the sounds recorded simultaneously with their production. The installation is frankly political – meaning not only that its substance is drawn from the representation of the uses of power on those who are subjected to it, but also that it provokes analysis of how and against whom that power is marshalled. Fiona Tan reports that the idea for the installation was triggered by reading an article about the rapid growth of the prison population in the United States during the past forty or so years. In her brief remarks she writes: 'While in the late 1960s the population of inmates in American prisons numbered close to 200,000, this number now exceeds 2.2 million. That is more than any other country and represents a quarter of all prisoners worldwide.' These appalling numbers continue to grow. In late 2003 the annual summary report distributed by the Bureau of Justice Statistics of the United States Department of Justice stated that there were an estimated 480 prison inmates per 100,000 U.S. residents – up from 411 at the close of 1995. The report also provided a breakdown of the racial mix of the prison population, noting that by 'midyear 2003 there were 4,834 black male prisoners per 100,000 black males in the United States in prison or jail, compared to 1,778 Hispanic male inmates per 100,000 Hispanic males, and 681 white male inmates per 100,000 white males.'

The title *Correction* is equivocal. It alludes to the way we have, in this country, come to package our thoughts about the goals of imprisonment – not vindictive punishment, but correction; not imprisonment, but corrective treatment. It refers also to the names of the governmental agencies that manage 'houses of correction', state departments of correction. But it is also meant ironically, as a protest – as if the artist was shouting at her audience, 'Correction!' demanding that this policy of ever-expanding imprisonment be subjected to immediate review and change.

Upon entering the installation space, a visitor hears sounds coming from speakers that are arranged in a slightly off-centre circle within the large gallery. The sounds are not noise, or not only noise; they carry distant, muffled, human voices speaking words that are mostly devoid of meaning. These are not, strictly speaking, sounds heard in a prison, but are sounds recorded in jails by a machine that obeys its instructions to amplify all sounds without respect to their origins – the droning hum of ventilation fans, the play of human voices, the thudding

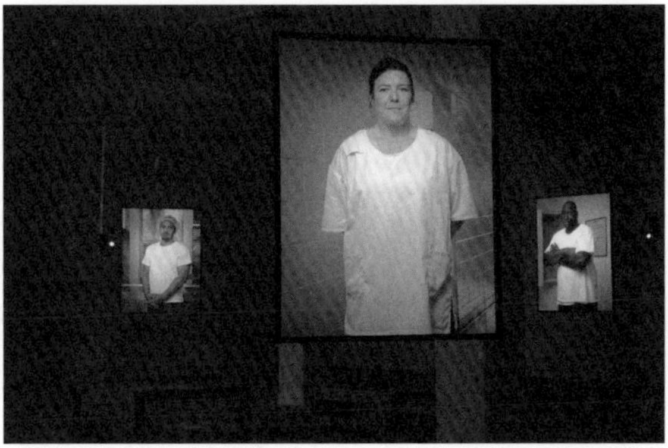

Correction
(installation view), 2004

of footsteps, the slamming of doors – all are given equal weight, all are accorded equal respect by the machine, whether or not they deserve it. These acoustic recordings are also documentary, but they can not provide us with the experience of standing in a prison and listening, straining to make sense of what can be heard; they are the artefacts of electronic recording. And each recording, spilling out of its own speaker, hums, pulsates and hovers at the ear where it merges into five other soundtracks.

Standing at the entryway to the installation it seems that the screens are covered with projected, still, colour photographs that change from time to time, approximating the look of 35 mm transparencies thrown at a screen by a Carousel projector. But as the viewer approaches the screens, it becomes apparent that each picture is not lifeless. The subject moves involuntarily, against his or her own will, or rocks ever so slightly back and forth, performing an ancient photographic ritual (one that dates to the late 1830s) of attempting to become a still life (the French would say *nature morte*) in front of a camera, of straining to suppress all signs of life while sitting or standing for a portrait photograph. Tan entered into an agreement with prisoners and guards who volunteered to stand still for 50 seconds in front of her video camera. She used the camera, which was designed to show people and things in motion, in the service of producing ever so slightly moving pictures. Constrained by the need to stand still for what must feel like an unbearable length of time, her subjects strain to suppress all movement, all signs of life – and because they are human, they fail.

Tan's video clips violate a built-in necessity of moving-picture technology. Film and video cameras are designed to produce pictures in horizontal formats (that is, images that are wider than they are tall), which are intended, in turn, to be projected horizontally. But Tan orients her video camera perpendicularly to the ground, so as to produce filmed portraits that are taller than they are wide and, in turn, uses a vertically aligned projector to exhibit them, producing a format that is foreign to moving pictures. The result is a vertical, moving portrait of a constrained, barely animated human subject – a pictorial metaphor for the inhuman effects of imprisonment. These pictures show what we otherwise could not see: the loss of motility, of animation, of an indispensable condition of life. Why should we expect this loss to result in correction?

Tan's video clips are intermediate pictures, hybrids that in many ways look like magazine illustrations, full-page, frozen photographic portraits made by skilled professional photographers for fashionable, high-end magazines. But unlike magazine portraits, these pictures show undersized signs of life that have been magnified for us by projection. The projectors enlarge these prisoners and guards, presenting them to us literally as bigger than life, so that every small movement they make is exaggerated. We see them as if viewed through a telescope from a few feet away.

Correction relies on auditory and visual intensification achieved through two distinct types of augmentation: amplification of remote, unintelligible human sounds, and magnification of small, involuntary human movements. The tools Tan employs in its production and presentation create a figurative medium for representing the horrifying, dehumanising effects (on both the guarded and the guards) of the equipment and procedures of incarceration. This figuring of incarceration is not meant to give us a vicarious experience of imprisonment (as if anything but being imprisoned could force us to live the life of a prisoner) any more than it is meant to romanticise or aestheticise prisoners or prisons. The installation allows us to look beyond looking, to study, by way of magnification, visualisations of constraint, confinement, suffocating enclosure. *Correction* is a profound meditation on contemporary American values and habits of thought. It is also, not coincidentally, a deeply moving work of art.

Philip Gefter

'Is That Portrait Staring at Me?', on *Correction* at the New Museum of Contemporary Art, New York

Exhibition review, *The New York Times*, 10 April 2005.

Standing face-to-face with prisoners might be a threatening prospect, but that didn't stop Fiona Tan, a film and video artist, from seeking more than 300 felons to pose for her.

First she had to persuade various Departments of Corrections to sign on to her project. It took three months of pleading correspondence, in which she relied only on her credentials as an internationally exhibited artist. One prison in California and three in Illinois finally relented, and Ms. Tan was escorted to the dormitories, day-rooms and workshops where she recruited her subjects last summer for the video portraits in *Correction* (2004).

One female inmate agreed to participate upon learning the work would be shown in Chicago. 'That's great', Ms. Tan said the inmate told her. 'My mom lives there so she can come and see me!' [...]

In Ms. Tan's video portraits, the inmates and guards are stationary, taking our measure as much as we're taking theirs. She posed her subjects as still as possible during the taping sessions, and they stand head-on, staring directly into the camera, centred within the frame. They are displayed on six flat-panel video screens, for 20–50 seconds each; 300 inmates and prison guards appear over the course of three hours. Movement is almost imperceptible as you watch – you're never quite sure you just saw the blink of an eye or the twitch of a muscle.

The screens hang in a circle, with benches for the viewer in the centre. The circular configuration is a deliberate reference to the Panopticon, a spherical prison

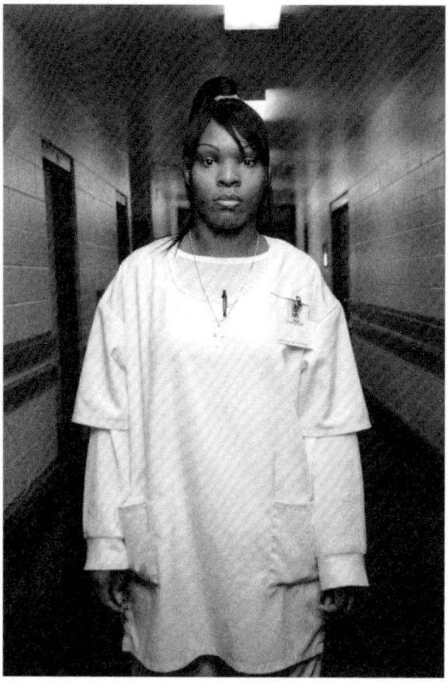

Correction (still), 2004

plan designed by the utopian philosopher Jeremy Bentham in the late eighteenth century as a way to centralise the surveillance of prisoners. (Though the Panopticon was never built, it has lived on as a symbol of ubiquitous Big Brother-esque surveillance.) Each portrait can be viewed in mirror image on both sides of the screen – inside or outside the circle. Recordings of actual sounds heard in prisons – ventilation fans, human voices, slamming doors – play on speakers in the room.

The relationship of subject to viewer is central to Ms. Tan's work, and the title *Correction* applies as much to the viewer's experience as to the subject's: while inmates are in prison to 'correct' their behaviour, the portraits may alter viewers' preconceptions as well. The viewer participates in a kind of stare-down with the subjects. This type of extended eye contact with strangers incites primitive transgressive feelings: it's a dare; it's a threat; it's erotic.

Time is one of the keys to *Correction*: the idea of 'doing time' in prison is emphasised by the video-portrait format. The subjects are standing still, but since time is passing in the portrait, the subjects are trapped in their poses, trapped in the frame. Francesco Bonami, senior curator at the Museum of Contemporary Art

Chicago, said of the work: 'Time passes, but it never passes. Time is wasted; time is never-ending.' In an earlier project, *Facing Forward* (1999), Ms. Tan explored the ways white colonials had viewed natives of Papua New Guinea. The piece was based on archival film material from an early twentieth-century expedition in which groups of locals were asked to stand still before the film camera, as if the filmmakers weren't aware that people could be filmed in motion.

'I am interested in the twilight zone between film and photography, the grey area', Ms. Tan said in a recent telephone interview. The documentary film from Papua New Guinea provides a revealing parallel to nineteenth-century photographic portraiture: technologies like the daguerreotype required the subject to maintain a perfectly still pose for the duration of an exposure, which could take up to a minute. While today's portraits can be taken in fractions of a second, the idea of holding a pose for the video camera over time brings us full circle. [...]

Moving images almost always cross horizontal planes, so Ms. Tan's decision to rotate the frame vertically underscores the photographic foundation of her video portraits. 'I don't consider myself a photographer', she said, 'but I consider photography to be at the base of my work.' To arrive at a format for the standing portraits in *Correction*, she filmed photographs out of the pages of a photography book and projected them on the walls of her studio to see what the proportion would be like. [...]

'A filmed photograph stretches time, and in those often uncomfortable moments a lot happens', Ms. Tan said. 'The viewer can see the embarrassment, the bewilderment and anger, or the curiosity and shyness due to the confrontation with the camera.'

Photography and video both reflect the world as it looks to us, but when it comes to the way we experience the results, the two are different species. A photographic portrait captures a moment in time, and our response to it is shaded by the amount of time passed since it was taken. A video portrait records the passing of time, engaging us in an active, perpetual here and now. Ms. Tan's work insistently blurs that line – and, in the process, sharpens it.

Fiona Tan
Voice-over to *The Changeling*

Fiona Tan: Mirror Maker, Heidelberg: Kehrer Verlag, 2006, 86–9. Spoken by Fiona Shaw. Revised 2020.

I or she.

I write: Her diary she keeps fervently stowed under the pillow every night. Her diary is a faithful friend who never disagrees, who – like a mirror – never contradicts. She writes about herself in the third person, as if she was someone else.

A writer can write herself. Can call the shots. Can paint my picture. I can make a work gleefully disregarding where the photos came from and perhaps distort the image.
My text sets out a tentative line, like a drawing. Carefully negotiating the space in-between the words, feeling out the contours of the character. This slight smirk, this reluctant chin. It would be good if I can get the text, this piece, to a stage where the words are making the image, making it visible. At that point my voice will sink into the image; word and image entwined and impossible to disentangle.
Can I creep into someone else's skin? Can I see behind someone else's picture? And what do I find when there? I would like to make a work which has a feeling of promise. Like a breath held in anticipation, a 'what if'. In moments it could be beautiful, fragile, like the tentative first buds of early spring.

She is at an age where she is changing constantly. However, she is not sure whether she is growing up or just growing old. And is this – this time called a life – is that a be-coming or de-coming? Coming around the corner or coming to a standstill?

She writes in her diary that the chameleon is her favourite animal. So delicate, silently picking its way up a stem or a branch. Its two-toed claws somehow like hands, as they elegantly and with slow precision negotiate each step, each grasp. She admires how the chameleon can move each eye independently of the other.

It is as if the creature can hold two thoughts at once. Its rainbow coat is for her almost secondary to its noiseless presence. The creature moves as if to music, and in this dance winds its tail to form a perfect concentric curl.

When her turn comes, she looks straight into the camera. Its lens like a shiny black bowl. Her chin is set, determined. The camera should see her the way she likes to see herself. She will not let herself be walked upon; she will hold her life securely by the reigns. A woman warrior: courageous and dutiful, tireless, cruel in battle. Crusading into unknown lands. And now she imagines herself her grandmother, looking at old school pictures.

And as her own grandmother she says:

> *Growing plants is like remembering promises. Seeds are secrets. Hidden, waiting. Bulbs are future lovers, full of potential!*
> *Yes, that's me. How pretty I was then, but also how serious! Looking to the future, full of expectation. My eyes may have dimmed but the likeness is still there. Like a cat with nine lives I have lost a few now. Time has taught me to set my sights on a lower horizon. My life has been small. I had first to grow old to know that this is enough. Every morning I take my little stroll around the garden patch to remind myself of this. That was so long ago. The photographer came to take our pictures. We were vain and all brushed our hair at least one hundred times. My hair had been trimmed the day before. My father always said that I have a face round like the moon. Ah, that was so long ago. I look back at my friends and at the stories of their lives. Daphne who flees in great fear from her man but in doing so turns into a tree, frozen to the spot. And Niobe: is it Niobe who, grieved by the loss of her children is turned into stone? These are stories bearing the weight of too much sadness.*

She changes back into her everyday skin – the unwrinkled, slight body of the fourteen year-old. Her diary bears witness: Contrary to what is said about her, she is not gentle but fierce. Trapped inside her is a fiery longing. Not directed yet, but coiled and waiting. At school she does well, but makes sure she is never the top of the class. She is not sure when she ever really feels herself; just that and nothing else. No false front to put up. She reads books – no, she devours them. They feed her hunger for elsewhere. She likes to imagine she was born someone else – another place, another time. Perhaps Cassandra, the young woman whose blind eyes can see all.

Now she slips into the skin of her mother, and she talks to her own portrait as if talking to a daughter, displaying a wisdom which only young teenage girls possess.

And as her own mother she says:

Could this be you? I hardly recognise my little girl in this picture. A stranger. It is unspeakable to not recognise one's own daughter. But there is always so much left unsaid. But this is the way it has always been.

You are for me a volatile mixture of mirror and not. There is too much I recognise. So I, the mother, repeatedly slip up and presume that I know what you think, how you feel. You are the one who likes reading, possessing a quiet inner strength that secretly dismays me. Even as a little girl you were the observer, silently watching all that went on around you. And then, suddenly without warning, you could break into the most heartwarming smile. That smile seems to have left you now. Pride? Yes, I am very proud of you. But you are just embarrassed and rarely want to acknowledge me these days nor give me my place in your life.

Respect, responsibility, yes, your father and I could teach you that. But a sense of fun, joie de vivre, no. These seem to be qualities which cannot be instilled. I feel I have failed in my duties as a mother, I could not save you from pain. We fight about daily chores and you battle my expectations. You seem to hate me and to love me in that order. Will I be able to learn what you demand to teach me?

Girls, she knows, possess a hardness that is never talked about. Mothers know this too. She is the girl who had earned a badge. Who is so good at fitting in, but who nonetheless wants to stand out. In another version of this story she would make sure that her picture is deliberately out of focus. Her story is not sad, nor a failure. She would be successful and happy!

I turn the page. This girl could still be me. There I am but I can hardly recognise myself. Ashamed of ... of what? Ashamed, I guess, in very secret ways of where I am now: of a certain success, and a certain realisation of middle life, of repetition and stagnation. Are the cells simply running out of their ability to renew themselves? My life is secure and careful. I have a house, four walls, a roof and even a garden. Solidity but not much solidarity. So I look at these faces searching for the one in whom I recognise myself. The girl I might have been. To do this the adjustments are small and subtle. Take a deep breath, tense the muscles around the mouth. A slight incline of the head and I straighten my back.

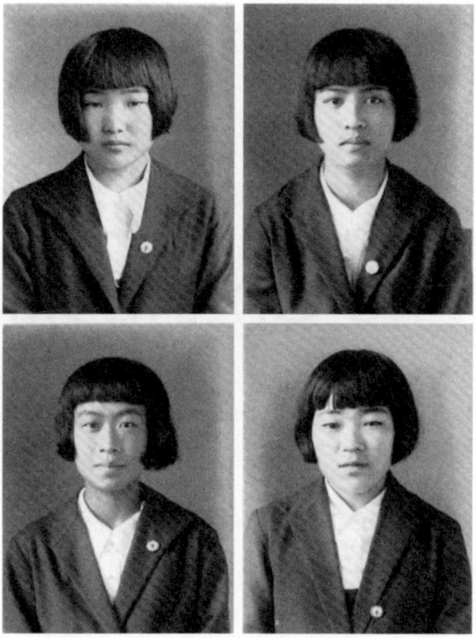

The Changeling (stills), 2006

I remember how often I used to sit at my mother's dressing table. It came from my grandmother and stood against the bedroom wall like an altar. Its mirror is of thick glass and has bevelled edges. There is a reassurance of seeing myself repeated left, right and centre, like the familiarity and comfort of flipping through family photo albums. That's me! Yes, that's me!
This little me, whose whisperings I can hardly hear, surfaces too seldom these days and nights. It is because of this that the work is a self-portrait. It's as simple as that. I feel open and empty – these days, in middle life. And these photos are mirrors, mirroring each other. They are my mirror. This is a portrait in search, once more, of self.

Philip Monk

Excerpt from 'Disassembling the Archive: Fiona Tan', on *The Changeling*

Disassembling the Archive: Fiona Tan, Art Gallery of York University, Toronto; Distributed Art Publishers Inc., New York, 2006, n. p.

... l'ombre enfouie dans la profondeur par cette voile alternative ...
— Mallarmé, *Un Coup de dés jamais n'abolira le hasard*, 1897

Saturday, 2 September 2006

Dear Fiona,

You must think that I've fallen off the edge of the world. Falling, I've recovered topsy-turvy, downside up in some skewed correspondence. To renew our correspondence perhaps means to articulate our lack of response — sorry ... more correctly, *my* lack of response. You've already responded, indeed, corresponded. My response would always be belated.

Perhaps a belated response frees me. At the least, it exempts me from the protocols of correspondence, from following with a proper response, but not as the fiction of an excuse for not corresponding. Fiction is an irresponsible response. I don't excuse myself here. Does it correspond, though, I wonder? That is, correspond to you, to what you do? Oh, I'll always be responding to you belatedly, supplemental to your correspondence with others, however fictional your correspondence with them might be. What would others think of your correspondence if they knew how fictional it is? Your correspondence *and* the other, that is. It might unsettle things if protocol was not respected, not to mention provenance. [...]

Writing this, I have to take care not to presume the fiction of a third-party reader in some future archive: you know, a reader looking over my shoulder while I am looking at the images you were looking at, writing while imagining what you were looking at. I can hardly speak *for* you when I don't know whether I am even speaking *to* you here. I have to assume that my writing is fiction, too. I can hardly presume to say the truth about fiction, correspondence, or the archive, let alone photography. Right off, I have to admit that this is all speculation. Such an admission doesn't annul responsibility.

I imagine you found a collection of old photographs of what was in essence an archive. I *imagine* you found it because I have seen only the end product of your artwork, *The Changeling*. *Your* collection, I imagine, has now been put to a different purpose beyond its original use perhaps where you found it. (That is, if this context did not, in turn, have another context.) You say it is a photographic album, a yearbook, one of many in a series, of 1930s Japanese schoolgirls, each and every girl identically dressed in school uniforms with similarly bobbed haircuts. There are nearly 200 photographs of these generically posed girls. Made within the genre of school portraits, they are pictures without the poise of individuality. As if it was not hard enough for these girls! But I am imagining. Their images are only dated photographs maintained by the chance of your encounter.

Where did this encounter transpire, Fiona? Your response, too, was after the fact of these images and their discovery. Your response to these images is a correspondence, but not, nonetheless, the context of correspondence which preceded you and assembled these likenesses. You write to these images by calling for a response from them that you then fictionalise. You are responsive to these portraits however much you fictionalise them in return, however much you fictionalise your response. Your response is fictional and not; that is, your response is fictional but your responsiveness is real. (Yet, who calls, writes to, or solicits the other in this correspondence between one and the other, self and image?)

I have to admit that I have been secretly sheltering another meaning by my use of 'correspondence'. I've been writing as if 'correspondence' is a communication between the two of us, as in my delayed letter here to you. But now that we have arrived at the photographic image, 'correspondence' takes on the meaning of identity as if it were the very identity of meaning. The photograph is proof of identity in the absence of its referent. Essential to photography, this inaugural divide between the photograph and its referent sets off an abyss of divisions. Yet, critical interrogation always presumes adequacy between image and referent in order to secure a subject, *the* subject: *ourselves*. Photography, it seems, was made for *us*.

You and I, each of us is responsive to the image (your response is fictional, mine is speculative), even if – here is *our* secret – we are irresponsive to traditional thinking on the photographic image. This tradition addresses the image, calls it to the attention of meaning and identity, and regulates it by its own hermeneutic discourse. As *writers*, we look on and write to the image, correspond with it, if not precisely correspond *to* it, that is to say, find our identity within it, if identity, in truth, is to be found in an image, a photographic image, even of ourselves. Take your album. Identity is missing altogether in what you found. Each girl is subsumed within every other within the overall organisation of this archive as if all were produced serially from only one negative. Yet, from the accident of your encounter you saved one image, rescuing all for this one. [...]

Monday, 4 September 2006

It's remarkable how secure the archive is. We secure it. We expect its protective, preservative edifice and protocols of classification to be secure. It's remarkable how secure the archive is in the universal agreement on its function ... and on the contagion it contains. In the Age of the Archive, we expect so. Photography is the name of this contagion. Archives pre-exist photography, but photography represents a crisis for the archive as more than a challenge for classification. For more than 150 years, the span of the modern archive, photography was its crisis. One document among many, it was different. It was different from documents – and not only because, unlike documents, photographs were lodged and lodging at the same time. Documents are older than photographs and, therefore, command more status. They are legal standard. Documents are official record. They record acts and transactions. Of the real, photographs, nevertheless, do not possess the status of an act. They are passive, more reserve than record. The document's archival status is the performance and record of *its* act, which seals a transaction and declares it closed and capable of archiving. No wonder that the passive reserve of photography posed a problem.

Passivity, nonetheless, was an earthquake. It shook structure and ground. Photography's reserve unsettled the accumulated sediment of history's records.

Disaster. The archive's disaster. The disaster of the archive. To what disaster is the archive exposed? What could it not keep secure even though encrypted within its most secret self? [...]

Friday, 15 September 2006

Technology was the event of this earthquake of which still photography was an advent. At that time early in the twentieth century, the photograph did not disturb the archive. The archive was built to house it from a disturbance photography already was. Some commotion secured photography in the archive. The outside commotion motion made, in the technical form and temporal shape of moving pictures, unsettled the archive even through the still photographs it now housed. Technology closed photography behind the archive's door, but not as any archival technique. Motion is the madness the archive contained. (Are we prepared to ask of which madness – photography or archive – we are speaking?) The archive stilled still photographs. Everyone agreed that still photography already was too much commotion.

The fault line of technological change sealed photography's fate to the archive. Technology was no judgement, though, as decisive as it was historically. Its event made others judge. Judgement sealed photography's fate as its own fault. Photography was a threat. It was guilty. It was condemned to the archive as the archive it already was. They were the same: photography and archive. But only one was a threat that the other secured and contained. And since the judgements of these opinions were archived in books, in time they have become our opinions and prejudices. Locked away in an archive, sealed by a book, can a photograph still disturb? Can a still photograph disturb?

I need to digress here, Fiona, and wonder what of the current moment determines photography's meaning for us. What draws the two of us together in a different understanding and use of photography that evades photographic meaning in so far as the archive now determines it?

We accede to the archive, to a belief in the archive, as soon as we believe that from its origins photography was destined to it. Photography's assembly in albums already followed prototype; assembly in the archive was a categorical issue. Photography posed no problem – until some (one) image came to disturb.

Over its short history, photography has been remarkably consistent – remarkable in its consistency to disturb, that is. Indeed, as soon as the first portrait sitters had died and a younger generation then inherited photography's inaugural images in inheriting family albums, all of us always return to the same image, every single generation of writers. We speculate on the same old images (whatever particular one doesn't matter) to ask about the generality of photography, to ask what photography *is* and what it *means*. We return to the same images to ask ourselves why we are disturbed otherwise, that is, disturbed by different details than those writers before us who were equally disturbed by photographs. […]

Christophe Gallois
'On Fiona Tan's "Visual Letters"'

Fiona Tan: Geography of Time, Nasjonalmuseet – Museet for samtidskunst, Oslo; Mudam – Musée d'Art Moderne Grand-Duc Jean, Luxembourg; MMK – Museum für Moderne Kunst, Frankfurt am Main; Tel Aviv Museum of Art, 2015, 39–51. Translated from French by Patrick (Boris) Kremer.

In a 'letter' to Chantal Akerman written on an invitation by the Dutch film magazine *Skrien* in 1998, at the very beginning of her career, Fiona Tan writes:

> *I have been thinking recently about letter-writing and about films. In your films people write and read letters and wait. Waiting is a virtue. As if life is an empty bowl waiting to be filled. Films can be 'visual letters'* [beeldende brief], *epistles posted in the void.*[1]

Although this epistolary dimension is not specifically present in Tan's works from those years – which are mainly articulated around the use of archival footage, questions related to the status of documents and documentaries and the concept of 'real time' – the fact that she perceives it in Akerman's films seems to anticipate the importance it would have on her own practice a few years later, most notably in *The Changeling* (2006), *A Lapse of Memory* (2007) and *Island* (2008), three pivotal works from the second half of the 2000s. In these video installations this dimension manifests itself primarily through the use of an off-screen voice that operates in parallel to the images – a voice that is simultaneously detached from and intimately tied to them. 'I'm interested in the juxtaposition of word and image', explains Tan in an interview from that period, 'in conflicting and contradictory relationships between the two and between fact and fiction, in the displacement of text and image.'[2]

As Tan's statement suggests, the letter as an artistic device in the realm of film or moving images also generates specific forms of time. 'In your films', she writes to Akerman, 'time lasts forever. Your endless scenes confuse my sense of time; I have had to throw my view of "real time" overboard.'[3] In light of the complex relationships between words and images and the singular temporalities they generate, one could say that *The Changeling, A Lapse of Memory* and *Island* present themselves to spectators as visual letters specifically addressed to each individual spectator.

In the opening lines of the narration around which *The Changeling* unfolds, Tan writes:

> *It would be good if I could get the text, this piece, to a stage where the words are making the image, making it visible. At that point my voice will sink into the image; word and image entwined and impossible to disentangle.*[4]

The work as a whole could be considered from the angle of this – utopian – intertwinement of images and words. An installation composed of two identical, vertically hung monitors, and one built-in speaker broadcasting the voice of a woman, *The Changeling* is based on a series of black-and-white photographic portraits of Japanese schoolgirls from 1929, which the artist found at a flea market.[5] On one of the screens more than 200 photographs succeed each other at a slow, regular pace, as though one were leafing through an album. The teenage girls all wear the same uniform, the same badge and the same haircut, and they were all photographed from the same vantage point, frontally, looking straight into the camera. The other screen, in turn, shows a single portrait. Although the image is still, it unfolds in time by virtue of the videographic device. Merging the viewpoints of three generations of women – a main protagonist referred to by the pronoun *she*, her mother and her grandmother – with that of the female narrator, who repeatedly speaks in the first person, the story meanders between several identities, crossing, blurring or intertwining them. As we learn from the final words of the narrator, she tries to sketch 'a portrait in search, once more, of self'.[6] She speaks about photographs, portraits, posing for a photograph, a family album, while never establishing a direct or obvious link between the images in the story and the portraits of schoolgirls. These shifts from one identity to another are summarised by the word used for the title of the work, *changeling*, which, in various European folklores, describes a child who is abducted and replaced by a supernatural creature. As the central subject of the story, the images function as gateways between these different identities. 'Can I creep into someone else's skin? Can I see behind someone else's picture?', asks the voice.[7] In *The Changeling*, the images 'make' the words, spur them, provoke them to the same extent that the words 'make' the images, transform them, shape them.

A similar oscillation of identity lies at the heart of *A Lapse of Memory*, a filmic and oral portrait of a man and the palace in which he lives as a recluse. This work was filmed inside the Royal Pavilion in Brighton – an eccentric seaside palace built in the Anglo-Indian and chinoiserie style between 1787 and 1823 for the prince who acceded to the throne in 1820 as King George IV. It follows a man called Henry, who is described as old, thin, 'worn at the edges' and suffering from senile dementia. In slow, long takes, he is seen making Tai Chi movements, preparing tea according in part to a Japanese ritual, scrutinising a point on a globe by the light of a torch, unfurling and picking up a string of fairy lights in one of the hallways or falling asleep on a thin carpet next to an open umbrella. His gestures seem like fragments of a personal story that ultimately remains obscure and inaccessible to viewers: 'Presumably he travelled extensively in his earlier years.'[8] The off-screen voice, spoken by the artist herself and presented as the scenario of the film unfolding before our eyes – she starts by describing several scenes ('Scene 1: … Scene 2: … Scene 3: …') and continues by presenting the 'main character' – appears to have adopted Henry's memory lapses and confusion. She speaks about his potential pasts: a hypothetical past as a young Asian man called Eng Lie, who followed in the footsteps of his father and grandfather and left for the West; or a more plausible past as a young European who left for the East, where he fell in love with a young woman 'as delicate and fragile as porcelain'.[9] As in *The Changeling*, the voice is timeless and unreels her story in parallel to the images. And as in *The Changeling*, the identity sketched by Tan is hybrid, uncertain, confused:

> *These and other tales Henry recalls to himself night after night. Over the years he has elaborated and embroidered upon them. Restlessly he moves between his various selves.*[10]

Little by little the words impregnate the images and blur them. The portrait of the man eventually merges with that of the building, frozen in time, with its decorations, Chinese and Japanese-inspired miniatures and disproportionate architecture. Henry could be a mere imaginary product of the palace, or, conversely, the palace could be a figment of Henry's imagination.

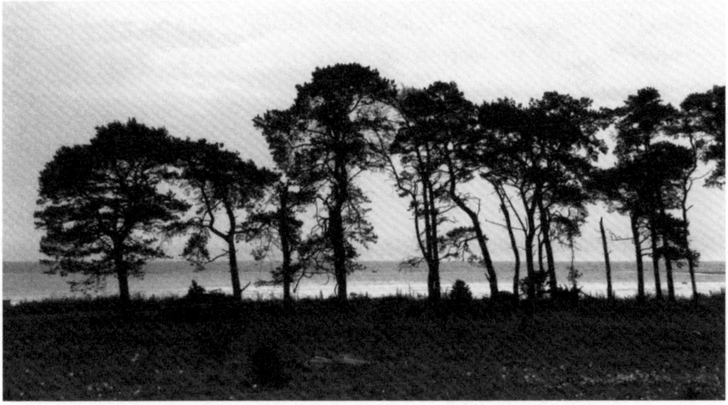

Island (still), 2008

'I was interested in the function of the voice-over. How the reading of a text can charge, imbibe the images with meaning and gravity',[11] says Tan about *Island*, which in a more direct way than any other of her works explores what Marguerite Duras, speaking of *Woman of the Ganges* (1974), described as the superimposition of 'the film of the image' and 'the film of the voices'.[12] Tan's work, filmed in black-and-white on the Swedish island of Gotland in the Baltic sea – the same island used by Andrei Tarkovsky as the backdrop for his last film, *The Sacrifice* (1986) – combines shots of the desert-like island, its wind-shaped trees, heavy skies, lighthouse and scarce houses (the only signs of human presence) with a male off-screen voice describing the presence of a woman who has come to the island for a temporary retreat from the world. We are given no information on this woman – what her story is, where she comes from or where she is heading to, or even what she looks like – except some of the thoughts and impressions that occurred to her on the island. Yet the voice and the images are not synchronous; rather, their overlapping opens up gaps in the film. At some point in the story, for instance, the voice reminisces about another island, an exotic and inhabited island totally unrelated to the one appearing in the images. The film itself is suffused with the characteristic ambiguity, the simultaneously precise and blurred, intimate and ungraspable quality of memories. Tan explains:

> *Memory and its connection to images in our minds is something I wanted to re-examine in this work. Cinema seems to enjoy a special place in this relationship ... Both film*

> *and memories can transport you to a different place, a different time. The experience is like a double projection, of being in two places at once.*[13]

Speaking about the temporalities in Akerman's films, Tan writes in her letter: 'Sicilian storytellers say: time takes no time in a story.'[14] This sentence, which positions film in the tradition of storytelling and the realm of the spoken word, is in fact borrowed from one of Italo Calvino's *Six Memos for the Next Millennium* (1988).[15] It affirms the existence of a story-specific time: 'A story is an operation carried out on the length of time involved, an enchantment that acts on the passing of time, either contracting or dilating it.'[16] It is precisely such an 'enchantment' enacted on the passing of time that Tan seems to use in these three works, in which words and images merge. In an interview with Saskia Bos conducted shortly after they had been completed, she stated: 'Time is both tool with which to shape and chisel and material to fold, distort and configure.'[17] Time, then, as tool and material.

'She is at an age where she is changing constantly. However, she is not sure whether she is growing up or just growing old. And is this – this time called a life – is that a be-coming or de-coming?'[18] It is this working of time that lies at the heart of *The Changeling*, where different temporalities coexist: the regular, cyclical time of the portraits succeeding each other; the still time of the isolated photograph; and, finally, the time of the story and the subjective times within it. As gateways between the different identities, the images are also points where these different times cross or roll backwards, places of projections where past and future come into dialogue with each other to the point of becoming indistinguishable. In the story, these temporal projections start as soon as the image is created. Tan writes,

> *When her turn comes, she looks straight into the camera. Its lens like a shiny black bowl ... [S]he imagines herself her as grandmother, looking at old school pictures ... [S]he slips into the skin of her mother, and she talks to her own portrait as if talking to a daughter.*[19]

What are the portraits of Japanese schoolgirls in the installation looking at? The camera? The future? The past seen from the future, as the narration suggests? The spectators' present? Through this intertwining of words and images, *The Changeling* reaches beyond Barthes' 'that-has-been' to assert that the image is never frozen in time. Rather than belonging to a bygone past, it possesses an intensity that lets various times enter into a dialogue with each other. This allows it to become the place of an experience where, with the help of writing, temporalities unfold: memory becomes presage. This, arguably, is how we must interpret the presence of a chameleon in the story of *The Changeling* – not so much because of its ability to change colours but because it can look in two directions simultaneously, or 'hold two thoughts at once'.[20] Could these be the past and the future? [...]

> *I worked this piece to have a certain timelessness and to operate within a very subjective experience of time. But most of the film could almost be called anti-cinematic, it is as if the images are not moving but are still images but not actual film stills. This paradox is also something which continues to intrigue me.*[21]

Of all her works, *Island* is arguably the one whose temporality is closest to the characteristic time of Akerman's films, itself the result of a camera that operates 'as an unmoving eye that records seemingly insignificant moments'.[22] In her *Autoportrait en cinéaste* (2004), Chantal Akerman asks,

> *What does this street say? Surely, it says something of itself, of its truth, of the truth of its image, but what, and after how much time? We see a street, so what? We are used to seeing a street, so why show a street? Precisely because we are so used to seeing a street that we no longer see it ... This street adds itself to a moment spent in front of another street or to another moment facing a journey in the subway, or facing a man sitting on a chair in the street. And all this past time adds up and creates something, and within this something, sometimes a little bit of truth.*[23]

Perpetuating some of her early works, such as *Tuareg* (1999), which was based on an ethnographic film from the early twentieth century, or her filmed portraits, such as *Countenance* (2002), *Correction* (2004) or *Provenance* (2008), *Island* plays on a certain ambiguity between the moving image and the still photographic image. The long takes of the island's desolate landscapes succeed each other, repetitively, almost still. As for the story, linearity is altogether abandoned in favour of an exploration of other temporal modes: ellipsis, hesitation, projection, time suspended. Far from contradicting each other, these temporalities 'add up'. The instability of memory contrasts with the consistency and solidity of the island's windswept landscapes. The images seem to function as supporting frames, or sensitive plates through which memories emerge on the surface of the present. The spectator's experience oscillates between several times: the photographic time, the filmic time, the time of the landscape, the time of the story and the time, itself plural, of the subjective and temporal experience. Like the palace in *A Lapse of Memory*, the island becomes a metaphorical temporal object, the incarnation, in a place, of time itself: 'This island is like a boat – noiselessly she can sail through an ocean of hours, days, weeks', says the voice at the beginning of the film.[24] The video installation itself presents itself to spectators as an island, 'a temporary retreat, a place out of time and removed from normal everyday life. Not as a place to turn one's back on the world but as a place to rethink one's relation to and position within it.'[25]

> *The film screen is an empty bowl waiting to be filled; filled not so much with the intentions of the filmmaker, but with what the public thinks they see. A personal history 'full of holes' – that is how you describe your biography at the start of* Histoires d'Amérique *(1989). But in your films I think I can see a lot of you: missing scenes, lost images, intimate and personal and yet remarkably anonymous. [...] Never before has the emptiness been so full.*[26]

In the three 'visual letters' Tan went on to create in the following decade, this absence, this white screen, came into its own. In *The Changeling*, it can be perceived in the 'silence' of the portraits of Japanese adolescents, but also in the way Tan's words, far from 'filling' this silence or making up for it, rekindle it and extend it into the present of what we hear – 'what the image says through its silence', as Jean-Christophe Bailly has written on the subject of photography.[27] In *A Lapse of Memory*, this silence infiltrates the work through the void that invades Henry's memory. A void that extends progressively to the entire film and, paradoxically, saves Henry:

> *His forgetfulness is perhaps his greatest virtue. His journey is one yet to be taken. Then he will finally let go of the past and, like a new emperor, he will reset the clocks and restart the calendar at zero.*[28]

In *Island*, the absence is no less absolute, and as Irit Rogoff has rightly pointed out in her essay on this work, it concerns the combined absence of characters, scenario, time and even place.[29]

'Never before has the emptiness been so full.' And yet, these three works are also entirely about presence: the presence of the image, the voice and the memories they bring to the surface of the spectators' experience as much as the temporal projections they trigger. And beyond the gap they explore between words and images, beyond the specific temporalities within them, it might be this singular intertwining of presence and absence that allows us to receive them as though addressed to us. 'Letters are written to distant loved ones but sometimes also to close beloved, to bridge distances and to fill holes', pens Tan to Akerman. 'But in the end, letters are also addressed a bit to yourself as well. You just hope that the recipient understands enough to read between the lines.'[30]

Fiona Tan

'On My Mind ...', on a photograph from *Vox Populi Norway*

Foam magazine #22, the 'Peeping' issue: 'Six well-known figures from the cultural world select an image that has recently been on their minds'. Published by Foam Fotografiemuseum Amsterdam, March–April 2010, 16.

Can I possibly explain why I love this particular photo so much? The child, still a baby almost, is isolated and alone. The linoleum floor would be cool and smooth, maybe even a little cold. The child is wearing stockings. Whether it is a boy or a girl I cannot tell and need not know, but here I will call her a girl. Possibly she cannot yet walk, otherwise she would surely slip over on that shiny surface in her stockinged feet. This is not a home environment but the wide-open interior of somewhere else, perhaps a school, perhaps an office. The composition is instinctively right, with the main figure positioned in the lower half and the background out of focus. This little human figure is a warm and delicate bundle of total unselfconsciousness.

Looking again and again at this image, it feels very private. I am privy and sense a tremendous privilege, a lovely gift. I am sure that the photographer is the parent, or at least feels like a parent at the moment of taking this photo. All of a sudden came the precious chance to take this picture: the child is still, for however long. It is a moment begging to be captured in an image. For me the *punctum* is the child's small and chubby left hand. Her little finger is slightly, unintentionally, folded under. The battery simply conked out on that spot in the middle of the floor. And, bending double, she fell asleep.

Vox Populi Norway (detail), 2004

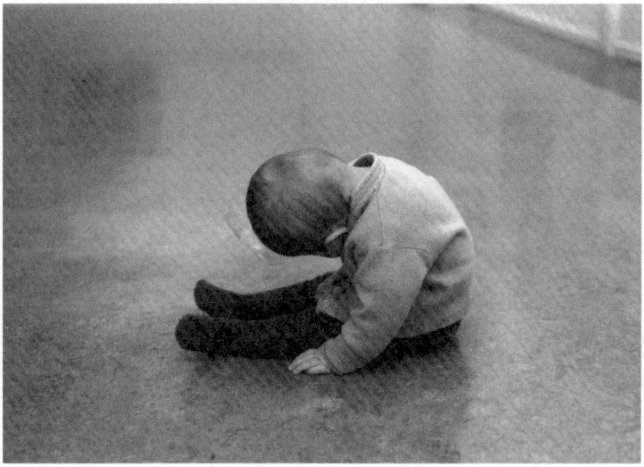

Brian Dillon
'Intimacies', on *Vox Populi London*

Fiona Tan: Vox Populi London, London: Bookworks, 2012, 118–25.

Let us light on a few of these snapshots at first, and see where (or when) they take us. The period, judging by haircuts and short trousers: any time from the late 1960s to the cusp of the 1990s. It is probably late spring: there are daisies on the lawn, the shadows are short, the sun gets in your eyes and a lilac bush is in full flower. In the foreground an upended coffee table, a bentwood chair and a console table have been aligned to mimic a small boat, and three little boys are punting themselves into the future. Or consider this, from the same era, by the looks of the blueing print: a 'middle-aged man' – moustache, spectacles, unzipped cardigan, wide but sober tie – throws back his head while a dishevelled friend or relative pours some exotic liquor (souvenir of a Mediterranean holiday, perhaps) into his wide-open mouth and a third man tipsily grips a paper cup and affects to save that tie from dribbled booze. And again: blazing sunshine (that legendary summer of 1976? the Jubilee holiday a year later?) on a suburban street, and dads in tiny shorts and no shirts are lined up ready for the 100-yard dash.

Among the curious effects of looking at other people's family photographs is a type of nostalgic recognition – I have just felt it here for the era of my childhood – that may have little or nothing to do with the details of place or precise time, let alone milieu in the pictures In fact it may even be true that I've chosen the examples above, clustered in a particular period, rather too knowingly – that is to say, maybe all family photographs of whatever vintage remind me of the 1970s. That is not, I hope, to say something sentimental or solipsistic; rather, this is the paradox of such photographs: taken to remind us of a specific occasion. Not just a day or a date, but the happy accidents of drunkenness, play, togetherness – they end up as mementos of entire historical spans with their customs and their entertainments, degrees of formality and closeness, ways of showing off or hiding ourselves in plain sight. And this sense of the individual snapshot connecting us to a historical past is just as true, just as perplexing, for the persons photographed, for the photographers, for those who know and love the sitters or subjects and peruse their images in after years. Family photographs are estranging objects made out of intimacy, they invoke abstractions.

Fiona Tan's *Vox Populi* (2004–12) broaches the intricate allure of the snapshot in all its historical, geographic and cultural complexity, while remaining alive to the specific, the occasional, the lightness and later mnemonic weight of an individual image made in and of the moment. The project, which concludes with the present selection for *Vox Populi London* (2012), was begun in 2004 with *Vox Populi Norway*, when the artist was commissioned to make a new work for the Norwegian Parliament in Oslo, and responded by canvassing images from family photo albums gathered across the country. Subsequent exhibitions, and the accompanying books, have corralled similar collections of photographs in Tokyo, Switzerland and Sydney. The oscillation between cities and whole countries is not systematic, but it is important: variation blurs the notion of what exactly constitutes a 'people'. That loaded concept might name something civic or national or, as the images themselves attest, a self-definition that's more localised or universal. Much of Tan's work has been concerned with such slippages across the borderlines of identity. [...]

What then of London and its photographic intimacies, its moments of private and personal image-making, drawn again from family albums submitted for the artist's attention? You could plausibly argue that in common with the previous iterations of the project, *Vox Populi London* amasses an inventory of the snapshot, a typology of the times and places, the poses and gatherings, outdoor scenes and flash-lit interiors that go to make up a certain catalogue of convention or even of cliché. And Tan is assuredly aware of that; in fact the project, in each of its geographical instances, has followed an apparently rigorous division of the material into categories that are familiar and also subtly unsettling: Portraits, Home and Nature. (I say unsettling because the categories are not quite in accord with the impetus to grab a snapshot: we don't typically think of photographs of our loved ones as having the formality of portraits, nor of party snapshots as studies of the interiors we inhabit, still less of our weekend excursions as field studies into the abstractions of Nature or Landscape.) Here again, among the London images, the family album expands from photos of individuals, through groups in formal or informal attitudes and happenstance or jokey movement, to outings into the

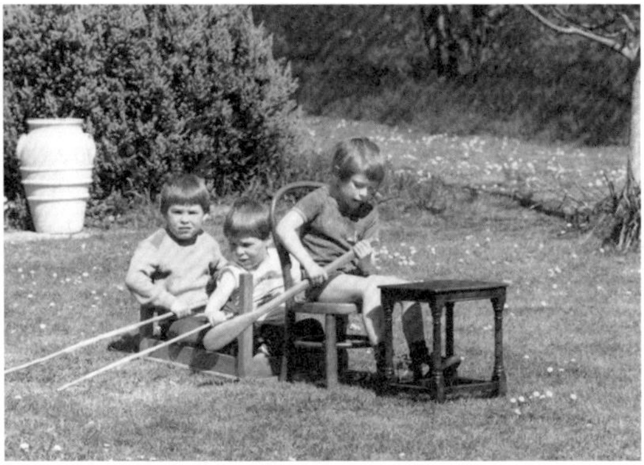

Vox Populi London (detail), 2012

countryside or languid days in the park. Formally speaking, there are predictable naiveties of composition – the subject placed dead centre, or near enough; sometimes lost in the distance among domestic ephemera – and technical accidents or botches: a whole wedding group blurred by the photographer's shaky hand, a bride emerging from a church doorway into the bright rain of a ruinous light leak. And amateurism, of course, allows for the energy of the unexpected: an infant waddles through his or her father's legs, a woman turns her back as if in grief on the remains of a children's party.

One has to assume the albums from which she makes her selections seem to propose various repetitions across nations and cities and cultures: we all want to photograph sleeping grandfathers, bathing toddlers, boisterous groups of pubescent boys and young women in party dresses at the start of the evening But the typologies rub up intriguingly against the evidence of cultural difference. Can we say that there are especially English (before we even get to the city itself) poses and scenes in *Vox Populi London*? For sure, there seems to be a kind of stereotypical reticence or stiffness about some of these family groups, lined up in back gardens that are all lawned and fenced alike, or sitting overdressed at outdoor tables and politely ignoring the fact that one's lunch is being served at the edge of a car park. There are pallid and sunburning bodies by the seaside, sack races and the post-Christmas sofa slump, a royal wedding on the television and a young girl snapped in front of a mountain of flowers at Buckingham Palace in the autumn of 1997. As was certainly the case until very recently, the camera seems to have come

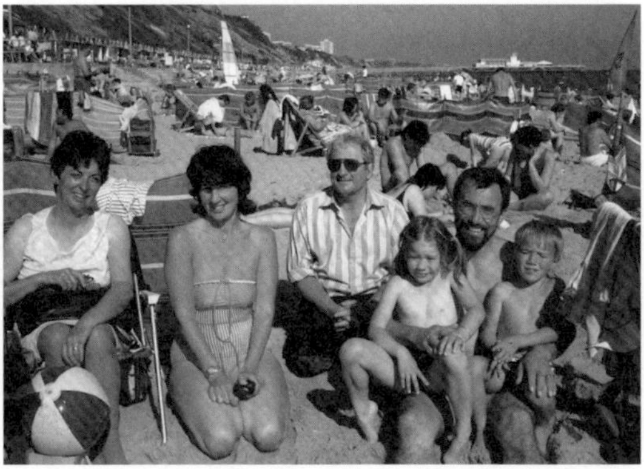

Vox Populi London (detail), 2012

out for 'special occasions', and even the most antic snapshots – a Christmas-day kid in crazy-coloured wig, dancers cutting loose on the front-room carpet – record communal rituals. Though it cannot be true, hardly anybody pictured here looks out of place or like they need to escape, save perhaps for a young man lounging provocatively by flowerbeds, or a teenage girl essaying a smokily distant 1970s glamour: cigarette, lipstick, retro Hollywood hair.

The city itself is hardly in evidence apart from Big Ben, the pigeons in Trafalgar Square, the Thames at night and the view from a snowbound Primrose Hill. And why should it be otherwise? Why should London photograph its public self instead of its private interstices? Though the city (like all cities) is probably the subject now of more photographs than ever, there are hierarchies in terms of what we prize, hold onto and hold back. Because despite the ease and cheapness of domestic photography in the period (the last few decades) that *Vox Populi* covers, quickened by the advent of digital and especially the cameraphone, it is not exactly the case, as media cliché has it, that we live at a moment of total photographic ubiquity and transparence. Our snapshots don't all inhabit the same flat realm of visibility; they tend to organise themselves into albums, for one thing: private and public. One could read *Vox Populi* as an elegy, a work of mourning, for the vanishing intimate realm of the family album, made quaint in the era of social media; but it was never wholly intimate in the first place, nor public. It was always composed of the private and the historical – was in fact, like *Vox Populi*, an eloquent history of privacy.

Dawn Chan

On *Nellie* and *Vox Populi Tokyo* at Wako Works of Art, Tokyo

Exhibition review, *Artforum*, November 2014, 298.

Nicknames, for the most part, arise from familiarity, even intimacy. As such, the pet name 'Nellie', which gives the title to a 2013 video by Fiona Tan, is a wry foil to the work's flaxen-haired cipher of a subject. Loosely based on Rembrandt's illegitimate daughter Cornelia van Rijn, Tan's preteen protagonist remains unknowable throughout the video, her inner life anyone's best guess, as she poses her way through a sequence of successive indoor vignettes, pale-skinned and beatific, her gown a blue-and-white patterned chintz. She moves languidly and sparingly: a model in a tableau vivant, almost, but one unable to hide her ennui. There's Nellie in bed, Nellie slumped on a writing desk, Nellie pacing across a wooden floor. One moment, she's seated against the wainscoting of a water-stained wall, her undone hair brushed into a volumetric frizz; in the next, she's listlessly supine.

The video's inviting visual evocation of Dutch Golden Age portraiture makes its subject's inscrutability, by contrast, seem all the more acute – and it poses an apt question about Cornelia van Rijn: given that her half-brother Titus appears regularly throughout their father's oeuvre, to what extent was patriarchal bias to blame for her eventual obscurity? With its sly ambiguity, *Nellie* (2013) is also perhaps Tan's most humorous work yet: is this a universally resonant portrait of a sullen teenager with nothing to share? Or is Nellie a period-drama heroine created by a screenwriter short on historical fact?

In 1670, the fifteen-year-old Cornelia van Rijn married painter Cornelis Suijthof and followed her husband to Batavia (modern-day Jakarta), where he became a prison warden. Little is known of her life after their move, but she lived out her days in Indonesia – which happens to be the country of Tan's birth. Here again was an instance of the artist's own heritage appearing in the discourse around her work. In 2009, when Tan represented the Netherlands at the Venice Biennale, the catalogue's introduction by Hans Hoogervorst mentioned her Chinese father and Australian mother, and the artist's history in Indonesia, Germany and the Netherlands. 'The almost inevitable consequence', wrote Hoogervorst, 'is that Fiona Tan's work focuses on the hybrid identity of individuals in an era of globalisation.' And yet, in an interview that same year, Tan sought to articulate a shift in her oeuvre: she'd 'left "all that" – meaning my postcolonial roots/routes – behind.' Still, Tan's concurrent show at the Tokyo Metropolitan Museum of Photography this summer featured videos such as *Disorient* (2009) – inspired by Marco Polo – that focus explicitly on cultural confusion and exchange, making her self-coined status as 'professional foreigner' hard to let go. Which raises the question: how are we to understand the elements of cultural dissonance that still crop up in newer works?

One answer lay in the installation of *Vox Populi Tokyo* (2007), the Japanese edition of a project in which Tan hangs, salon style, amateur photos taken by residents of specific locales. Her images of Tokyo's denizens first appeared at the Kunstverein Munich, where they surely conjured anthropological perspectives, as a glimpse into a world nearly 6,000 miles away. Reinstalled at Wako, where most visitors would be seeing photos of compatriots, the work disoriented not by foregrounding chasms between cultures but by revealing specific details about the lives of strangers next door.

Vox Populi Tokyo, like the versions of the project that Tan has done for London, Sydney and other locales, offers little to help viewers get their bearings; absent are wall texts, family trees, names. This seems a reproach to the recent proliferation of archival and data-based art. As so many artists traipse through unknown lands conducting interviews and recording histories, there's an unspoken faith in the artist-as-researcher's powers to extend the boundaries of human knowledge. That stance – call it an epistemic optimism – seems to be Tan's target. In both *Nellie* and *Vox Populi Tokyo*, we see an artist placing all her chips on uncertainty, ambiguity and questions no amount of research can resolve.

Fiona Tan
Voice-over to *A Lapse of Memory*

Scene 1, 'morning':
Long opening shot: Henry lies motionless, asleep on the floor. Some slight background movement. Close-up of feet.

Scene 2, morning exercises:
Warming up for Tai Chi. He practices Qigong.

Scene 3:
Morning tea: he pours and drinks his tea with a few elements from the traditional Japanese tea ceremony.

Description of my main character:
I call him Henry. I imagine him a recluse. He is the only inhabitant of the building – a place he hasn't left in years. He is old, thin and worn at the edges. He suffers from senile dementia. He often dozes off.

Henry's background is unclear. In the voice-over this also remains ambiguous. Presumably he travelled extensively in his earlier years. Now he seems to be living in his own hybrid space. Strangely enough he feels more real to me than the rooms which he occupies.

His story would begin far away across many seas. His real name is not Henry, but Eng Lie. Following in the footsteps of his brothers, his father and his father's father, Eng Lie goes off in search of golden mountains. With little more than the clothes on his back, he leaves his village and travels downstream. The journey would be long and arduous. On the open seas the little boat is battered by storms. Trapped below deck, he is seasick for weeks on end.

Eventually the boat pulls into harbour on the other side of the world.

Here the sea has a careful horizon. Gingerly stepping out on land, he would marvel at the big clean city in the West. He would see many things for the first time: long noses, red hair, huge feet, spotted skin, bushy beards and eyebrows. Fingers would point at him. Feeling lonely he would fantasise and exaggerate his memories of home.

It is more likely, however, that Henry's journey sets out in the opposite direction.

As a young well-to-do European he will travel east. He sees many wonders and learns much about men of various appearances and dispositions. For years he is a restless stone. Behind the mountains, which the locals call the scales of a dragon's back, the villagers stare at him and call him 'white devil' and 'foreign ghost'.

Possibly it is here that he loses his heart to a woman as delicate and fragile as porcelain, whose hair shines as black as night. She offers herself to him like a precious cup. But the next morning he finds her smashed to pieces, a disgrace to the village. He cannot understand why a phoenix may only be glimpsed in parts and never as a whole.

Henry would pack his bags and leave the next day. His untimely arrival and swift departure soon little more than part of a fairytale the villagers tell their children.

These and other tales Henry recalls to himself night after night. Over the years he has elaborated and embroidered upon them. Restlessly he moves between his various selves.

He feels lost within his various selves, his possible biographies. They trap him into a scenario which he does not want to live. And this place can only serve him as a halfway hotel. Henry is waiting for a story he can make his home.

Patiently Henry is waiting for a story which he can make his home.

His forgetfulness is perhaps his greatest virtue. His journey is one yet to be taken.

Then he will finally let go of the past and, like a new emperor, he will reset the clocks and restart the calendar at zero.

Fiona Tan and Saskia Bos
'Other Facets of the Same Globe: A Conversation'

Fiona Tan: Disorient, catalogue for the Dutch Pavilion, 53rd Venice Biennale, Heidelberg: Kehrer Verlag, 2009, 1.22–1.27.

SASKIA BOS: Fiona, you told me you stopped making works that could be characterised as 'postcolonial' about three years ago, after having touched on such issues for ten years or so. Many people still view your work in terms of a search for identity, of finding cultural roots, and although your recent works are not that far removed from this, the search for identity seems to have shifted towards an unravelling of memory. In *A Lapse of Memory* (2007), you seem to be in pursuit of what is recollection, as it determines and influences our fleeting identity. How do you see the connection with earlier works?

FIONA TAN: *A Lapse of Memory* was born out of a chance encounter with a highly unusual building – the Royal Pavilion in Brighton. As one of the finest examples of eastern-style architecture in the West, this building and its interior are a wonderful homage to fantasy. It was an unexpected feeling – I felt that I just had to do something with that place. My own hybrid background straddling East and West and my personal questions relating to 'Chineseness' were for me personally linked to that building. It was over ten years since I had made *May You Live In Interesting Times* (1997), and I felt I had left 'all that' – meaning my postcolonial roots/routes – behind me. But here, all of a sudden, was this building, which refused to go away. It felt like full circle, like a way of completing a sentence. Ten years later, I felt that a conclusive explanation was required of me. And I felt a need for closure. For once and for all, or so I liked to pretend, I would deal with these matters and then put them behind me.

It was only after I completed the piece that I could see that in some ways the character I created to inhabit this empty building was not only a certain personification of the building itself, but also had links with me personally. Identity and memory are undeniably linked. That is the great tragedy for patients with Alzheimer's disease or senile dementia. By losing their memory, they lose themselves and their family, and loved ones lose them too.

BOS: Does the work deal more with cultural recollection as a part of collective memory than with individual memory?

TAN: That I was in pursuit of cultural recollection is a nice way of putting it. Although it felt like an impossible undertaking, I was attempting to look at things on a larger scale. Not just my personal history or identity confusion. I wanted to tackle the persistent paradigms of 'East' and 'West'. It will not surprise you to hear that whilst I was working on the script for *A Lapse of Memory* I read not only Edward Said's *Orientalism* (1978), but also Ian Buruma and Avishai Margalit's *Occidentalism* (2004).

I see clear connections between *A Lapse of Memory* and earlier works like *May You Live In Interesting Times* and *Linnaeus' Flower Clock* (1998). Because the piece required this, I worked with an actor in front of the camera for the first time. This perhaps seems unexpected, but it grew out of a natural progression of works. For *The Changeling* (2006), I worked intensely with several actresses to record the voice-over and it was this experience that made me feel that this was the right way to go.

Looking back at my development, I see a steady progression, in formal terms, from initially a documentary mode of working towards an increasingly controlled and staged representation. This is a development I see continuing on into the piece I am working on now for Venice – a piece called *Disorient* (2009).

BOS: Your new work is inspired by the geo-strategic position Venice once had through its connections to the Middle East and Asia.

TAN: I intend the piece to have a specific in-situ character – both geographically and temporally speaking.

For this work, Venice is my point of departure and of return, literally and figuratively speaking. Venice was a lively and wealthy trading port in mediaeval times. Its wealth came mainly from goods brought back from the Middle East and Asia, which is why the city was traditionally portrayed as 'The Bride of the Sea'.

I have been researching the subject and have focused particularly on a book that was written over 700 years ago. The author was a Venetian merchant who left home at the tender age of seventeen and travelled extensively for the next twenty-four years. His name is Marco Polo. Arguably, Marco Polo undertook his epic journey twice. The second time, he journeyed through his memories – languishing in prison, recalling and remembering with as much detail and accuracy as he could muster every memorable episode from a quarter of a century of travel.

BOS: The search for the self in *A Lapse of Memory* was a psychological journey into the construction of identity. This time you seem to be taking a more sociological approach, as you focus on Venice and how people relate to its cultural history.

TAN: The tenuous relationship between sight, memory and knowledge, the unreliability of visual memories, is something I have been concentrating on in recent works. I am still exploring these ideas in this new work, as I continue to experiment and develop a filmic language that could perhaps be described as simultaneously constructing and deconstructing – employing the tricks of the trade and at the same time exposing them, laying them bare. I am interested in the juxtaposition of word and image, in conflicting and contradictory relationships between the two and between fact and fiction, in the displacement of text and image. I am also interested in the slipperiness of truth or truths and the many versions of Marco's account.

I have always tried to imagine what the world would look like without this dominating paradigm of East and West (which all too often implies East versus West), without the traditional dichotomies of dialectical thought.

One of the things that bothered me about the whole multicultural/postcolonial discussion in art is that it became a discussion only about politics and political positions, particularly during the last decade of the last century. The visual side of things was too often neglected. Images (and as an artist I consider myself an image-maker), their role, their importance, their ambiguities seemed to play too minor a role. It is easier to write and talk about ideas than it is to talk and write about images, I guess. But ultimately that is what visual art is hinged on: images – whether they are three-dimensional, figurative or abstract, multi-dimensional, time-based or even invisible.

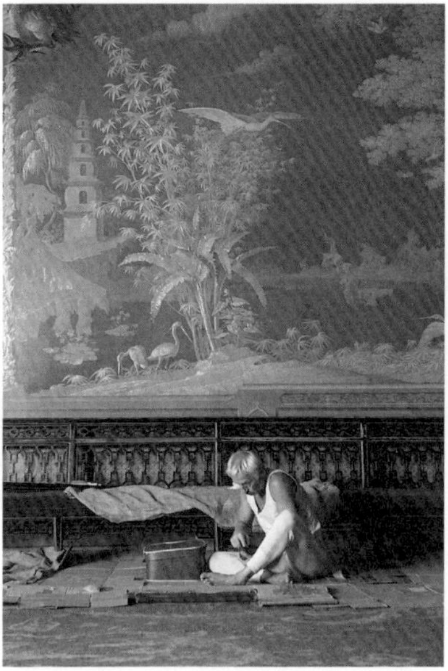

A Lapse of Memory (production photo), 2007

I also find it ironic that my work as an artist is still pigeonholed, filed away in the postcolonial box, whilst the idea of the whole debate was to do away with such categorisations and the need to categorise at all. [...]

BOS: Some films you make seem to exist in a suspended realm: figures are stylised and framed, movements are slowed down or people are asked to pose or sit, which creates anticipation both in the eyes of the beholders and in those of the sitters, who seem to be staring straight back.

TAN: Empowerment is a key word. Cinema and photography have a lot to do with manipulation: framing automatically means that the gaze is confined and there are things off-screen that are left out. With montage, the editing and cutting of a film, the director not only dictates the order in which scenes are presented, but also their exact length. The impact of sound, be it spoken word, music or ambient sound, is much greater than many people realise. I am interested in exposing and exploring all of these mechanisms. I want to empower the subject, empower the viewer, and to bring aspects to the surface, to create a certain visibility, if you like, to foster awareness of our interpretation of the images that surround us.

BOS: Many shows have been based upon notions of archive, where art questions the document as a fragment of collective memory and the manipulation thereof. Is the meta-language of your use of found footage 'true life'?

TAN: Document is for me inextricably linked to documentary film. I am really happy that I ended up living in a country where the tradition of documentary film is much stronger and better than that of moviemaking. The grandfathers of Dutch documentary film, like Joris Ivens, Bert Haanstra and Johan van der Keuken, were my 'teachers'; I learnt so much from studying them, as I did from my extended encounters with the wonderful archives of early film from the Nederlands Filmmuseum. The Dutch national film archives are, in my opinion, more interesting because of the early documentary footage that they have kept and have thankfully preserved and restored than for any movies they might contain.

There is of course a lively, if at times tedious, discussion in the film world about where (artificial, staged) film stops and where documentary film starts. There are actually quite a few renowned documentary filmmakers who rehearse with the people they film, who instruct their real-life subjects and who happily film multiple takes of so-called spontaneous scenes. The idea of the fly-on-the-wall, of cinéma vérité, is arguably impossible. Whatever action or scene a camera lens points at is changed by the presence of the camera and camera operator, however subtly. Similarly, the boundaries of cinema have blurred, even if only on the surface. The handheld rough camera work that smells of true-to-life documentary has become very popular in recent movies.

And then there is the document as it is found in the archive. Whether or not documents are accessible hinges upon the system of the archive, on how and why an archive came into existence and the way it is structured and organised. I do not think that documentary, archival footage is 'true life'. It is, as any image is, a 'take' on life, a subjective view, a limited and manipulating viewpoint. Nevertheless, like any viewer, I make snap judgements as to the truth of a film or a photograph, as to how realistic a representation we sense it to be. I am all for the stimulation of creative archival techniques – I mean this also in a poetic way. For fresh approaches to where and how we file away the images in our memory, in our mind, in our view of the world.

BOS: Your titles are often about time, time lapses, repetition and transformation, while the works themselves play with time by slowing it down, speeding up movement, or suspending it. In *Provenance* (2008), a woman swings back and forth like a pendulum. What is time for you: a friend or a foe?

TAN: Time is most definitely a friend. In many works I overtly deal with this – in *Rain* (2001), in *n.t. (Leidsestr.)* (1997), in *Linnaeus' Flower Clock*. Time, history, memory, they are all connected; they are facets of the same globe. As an artist working almost exclusively with time-based and lens-based media, time is one of my major tools. No, perhaps I can be more precise than that – time is both tool with which to shape and chisel and material to fold, distort and configure. I am thinking here in particular of my most recent work, *Rise and Fall* (2009); a memory is a fold in the fabric of time. [...]

BOS: Some of the early works you made were very physical, like *Roll I & II* (1997), where you are the performer and use your body as material. Some black-and-white portraits seem more conceptual, or seem to have a more graphic quality. Do these distinctions make sense to you? And, if so, do both extremes come together in a work like *A Lapse of Memory*, where the protagonist is the visceral element and the filmic eye seems to be more detached, attentive to pattern and detail?

TAN: It is certainly true – my early works often had a performative and physical character. As a young artist, I employed myself and my own body as material – not an uncommon practice. It was partially, I feel now, a search for my own identity, but also a way to appropriate and get closer to the medium with which I was working. Besides, I was always available and so putting myself in front of the camera cost me nothing, except for the occasional bruise or headache. But I became increasingly tired of looking at myself and dealing with myself in editing and so I started to work more and more with other people. My latest work, *Rise and Fall*, is, I feel, once more a very physical and haptic work. This struck me when I projected it large on my studio wall a few days ago.

BOS: When do you write your texts? Before you start a film, as a sort of storyboard ('My text sets out as a tentative line, like a drawing') or afterwards, when you have filmed the scenes ('Henry is waiting for a story he can make his home')?

TAN: Before, during and after. Writing is a sort of sketching, a way of getting my thoughts and ideas clear in my head. And then, both during and after the process of film editing, I find myself writing again. Often this is the writing of the voice-over or the text in the film. Whether a text is spoken or written can make such a difference, as can which voice reads it and how the words and the image combine. I quite often think of this writing in terms of sculpting. Patience is necessary. In the case of *A Lapse of Memory*, I had written the voice-over text before filming the work, but I ended up rewriting it completely during and after the film editing and the sound editing. I think I must have written at least twenty versions before it finally fell into place.

And, right now, I realise once more that my work does not develop as a linear progression. The works follow on from one another organically, but not in a rigid framework. It is more as with a cloud or a spiral that new works link up with earlier works. [...]

Stéphane Carrayrou

‘Images Murmuring: A Meditation on the Space-Time Construction of the Film *A Lapse of Memory*’

Fiona Tan: Images Murmuring, Le Carré, Château Gontier, 2007, 23–31.
Translated from French by Hervé Couvert.

[...]

BETWEEN IMAGE, SOUNDTRACK AND VOICE-OVER

A Lapse of Memory (2007) is largely built on the subtle connections between image and soundtrack. Image sets the scenery, which evolves independently through time and space. The soundtrack sometimes sticks to the image by giving it depth and providing some scenes with a sensitive incarnation, and sometimes moves through its own time, away from the image. This metaphysical level is the right setting for the meeting of the actual present-time and another present-time that is the reappearance of memory, or the recovering of time.

Image, sound and speech are layered in a space-time ramification. The film's poetic imagery slowly emerges from the crossing over between image-built and text-built narrations, between tactile images and the touch of the narrator's voice. Acute sounds and rustling, far from harming the silence induced by the images, come as an incentive to it – a silence that gives way to their musical quality.

The development of this relation between image, sound and voice-over speech is to a large extent the result of an artistic complicity between Fiona Tan and her sound engineer, Hugo Dijkstal. All happens with clockwork-like precision. The key is in a subtle alternation between moments of sound and/or visual flow and moments of freeze frame and/or sound suppression. This can be noticed as much in *A Lapse of Memory* as in other Fiona Tan films, such as *Linnaeus' Flower Clock* (1998), *Facing Forward* (1999), *Saint Sebastian* (2001), *Rain* (2001), *News from the Near Future* (2003) or *Island* (2008). Fiona Tan has long since integrated what Saint Bernard de Clairvaux already stated in the twelfth century: 'If you wish to see, listen. Hearing is a step toward vision.' Calderón gave his own of this notion five centuries later when he wrote: 'The music of the voice one listens to, now silent, is not the only music, all that makes consonance is music.'[1]

UNDIFFERENTIATED TIMES AND PLACES

In *A Lapse of Memory*, times and places are undifferentiated on various levels: in the voice-over scenario description, that goes beyond the image's temporal dimension by announcing scenes to come or getting back to past ones; in the alleged biographies enunciated by Fiona Tan for her character, in turn Henry and Eng Lie; in the cracks of shade and uncertainty within those alleged biographies; and last but not least in the feeling of time stasis throughout the film. Of course, *A Lapse of Memory* – as well as a more recent film of Fiona Tan's, *Island* – opens on a vision of dawn and ends with the twilight, our 'natural' time cycle. Yet what occurs within this lapse? We see Henry wake up and go to sleep, we watch him as he rolls and unrolls some fairy lights that not only serve as a makeshift lighting but also is a beautiful metaphor of the circularity of time. We follow Henry in his somnambulist peregrinations through thresholds and doors, rooms and corridors, up and down flights of stairs. And every time the film loops back to its starting point, the chorus comes back to itself, all the more indefinitely as this film can be seen and re-examined many times without losing an ounce of its powerful poetic evocation.

THE SUSPENDED TIME OF RAIN

In the exhibition at the Genêteil Chapel, in Château-Gontier, the feeling of time suspension, even of time stasis, was reinforced by the discrete yet very efficient presence of *Rain*. When entering the chapel one's attention focused entirely on the film *A Lapse of Memory*. It was projected down the length of the chapel, on a monumental panoramic screen, with high-definition image and sound as well as a bench to view it comfortably from. Only then would you notice the continuous sound of *Rain* and the two modest TV sets against the right wall, behind the bench.

This work represents on two TV sets the duplication of a virtually identical image: a blue plastic bucket getting filled with water under a pouring rain, and a dog drowsing in the interstice of a wall; the only appreciable differences are the levels of water and a closer view. Minutes pass by, yet the noise level of the rain remains the same and the water levels never change. A moment of sound vision, going on and on without beginning or end ... a single note, indefinitely stretched, like a clepsydra never filling up; time without end, in counterpoint to the ramified time of *A Lapse of Memory*.[2]

A TIME RAMIFICATION ON AN INTERROGATIVE YET NEGATIVE BASIS

For quite some time already – since the late 1990s with *Linnaeus' Flower Clock* and *Facing Forward* – Fiona Tan has been fond of this kind of time ramification, on an interrogative yet paradoxically negative basis. Having read Italo Calvino's *Invisible Cities* (1972) surely contributed to it ... Italo Calvino 'knits' imaginary dialogues between Marco Polo and Kublai Khan, constantly scrambling the borders between reality and fiction, between one's imagination and the other's expectations. Marco Polo rummages through his own past, hoping to find a memory for his future.

Even though I do not know how far Fiona Tan may have been influenced by his short stories, the world of Jorge Luis Borges also comes to mind. A master in the theme of The Double in fiction, particularly so in 'El Sur' (1953, 'The South', the last short story from the collection *Fictions* [1956]), Jorge Luis Borges knows like no other how to put the reader in the position of being the double of the characters fooled by the fiction. In 'El jardin de los senderos que se bifurcan' ('The Garden of Forking Paths' [1941], also in *Fictions*), Jorge Luis Borges uses time in its various forms – punctual time: events occur only in the present; plural and ramified time: any present event forks into two futures – so as to form 'a growing and staggering network of diverging, converging and parallel times'.[3]

This anachronistic approach to time also resembles much of what appears in dreams. A dream has 'little to do with the idea of an orderly succession according to the tripartite division of past/present/future. All in the dream is pure present'.[4]

In the filming structure of *A Lapse of Memory*, and *Island* as well, the dream's sensation of pure present and the bursting of time do indeed coexist. Besides, in the text of *Island* (read in voice-over by the actor Heathcote Williams), Fiona Tan herself compares the mechanics of dreams to the structure of her film:

> *As if dozing off while watching, she remembers the scenes only vaguely. It had a lost, timeless feeling. Disconsolate, desolate and weighted with unspeakable melancholy. It was a film like a dream; too heavy and slipping under, something her memory could not hold onto [...] 'Why is it', she wonders, 'that dreams so often have a film-like quality? Or is it the other way round?' She once heard a theory that dreams are not dreamt, but are created upon the very instant of recall. There is some truth in this notion, she thinks: we do not remember dreams, we reconstruct them.*

SLEEP, 'A STATE WHICH PUTS LANGUAGE TO REST'

Every time I watch *A Lapse of Memory* and *Island*, their dream-like specificities become more obvious. Maybe the language gains in musicality what it loses in mystery; I do then tend to let in a certain amount of sweet drowsiness, somehow reaching Henry's state the whole film long. As Jean-Christophe Bailly said, 'seeing other people sleep makes you also lower your internal voice.'[5] And sleep is 'a state that puts language to rest', a state in which the conscious self melts away, only to precipitate anew in the twists and turns of dreams. In that state of unbinding into which 'I slide inwards and outwards at the same, erasing the division between these putative regions', I find myself perfectly prepared to perceive, from both ends of perception (conscious and unconscious), the occurrences of simultaneity as revealed in the film. By blinking – my eyes shut for one moment – and opening again on the splendour of the images and their concealed secrets, I rediscovered without noticing Henry's gesture of observing the hangings with his torch. This precise moment partly inspired me in the writing of this text, especially after re-reading a passage from Jean-Christophe Bailly's book, *Regarder la peinture* (1992) in which he assigns to the art critic the aim of enlightening the works 'through successive stages, like using a torch to examine fragment after fragment by its light'.

I am not quite sure that I managed to instil the right amount of subtlety required with the work of Fiona Tan, but at least I tended to it in my approach of one of its major characteristics – this way of 'playing at hiding the very meaning it induces'.[6]

FLOATING MEANING, A LANGUAGE HEMMED WITH SILENCE

In conclusion, in *A Lapse of Memory* a certain form of indecisiveness prevails on several levels: in the skilfully blurred, indistinct limit between Henry / Eng Lie's real life in his Brighton palace and his dreamed life all over the world, as in his mental state, described as an oscillation between wake, sleep and senile confusion. The viewers themselves find themselves in a scarcely describable state between awareness and drowsiness, between sensorial immersion and meditation.

Words are hemmed with silence, indeed they 'wear holes' of silence. The narrator's speech fluctuates; it lets you hear things rather than hear about them. The camera reflects both vision and thought, by which Fiona Tan gives scope to our reflection about image as a mirror for ourselves and for the world around us.

Without ever demonstrating anything, by mere suggestion, Fiona Tan's films point to a horizon of meaning 'lying in the distance like a mirage'.[7] They hold the meaning inside, they have you sense or foreshadow it, as it were, while keeping some of it unsaid; they induce us to an interrogative comprehension, trying to catch a poetic fragrance rather than an intellectual hold.

The artwork resists being seized, it resists clear-cut understanding. Something flows, out from afar and passes through time.

Okwui Enwezor
'Allegory in Fiona Tan's *A Lapse of Memory*'

Fiona Tan: Rise and Fall, Vancouver Art Gallery; Aargauer Kunsthaus, 2010, 79–89.

I am sitting on a terrace overlooking the Grand Canal in Venice, a city which in its heyday from the mediaeval period to late Renaissance emblematised the crossroads of trade and peoples. I am chatting with the eminent literary critic and postcolonial theorist Homi Bhabha, discussing the comings and goings of artists who are showing their work in the various exhibition spaces during the early days of the preview of the 53rd Venice Biennale. Bhabha is member of the jury who would select the luminaries of this edition for the obligatory prizes that are less accolades of deep cultural achievement and more a reflection of the consensus of the time. As we talked about the relation of artistic practices to cultural traditions, he tells me that in the present circumstance in which the coordinates of culture points, not in one continuous direction, but in multiple directions, with numerous breaks, and stopovers in the itineraries of artists, that we must learn to favour the idea of cultural archives over those of cultural traditions, because the recourse to archives rather than traditions better describes the modalities in which contemporary artists are today operating, in the postcolonial age. Bhabha's insight is telling, because it poses the question of how to reconcile such archives to the traditions which the inhabitation of the national pavilions in the Giardini in Venice during the Biennale suggests.

As I set out to commence my visit of the various national pavilions my earliest stop was the Dutch Pavilion taken over by the work of Fiona Tan. Upon entering the large central gallery of the Pavilion, what the viewer sees is an almost hallucinatory stream of visual vignettes, like an intricately woven Persian carpet, projected on two cinemascope screens positioned off-centre, across each other on opposite walls. The images of the film, shot in high-definition video, have a lush, exquisitely constructed delicacy, unfurling in slow motion, a rush of scenes traversing cities, villages, ancient trade routes, cosmopolitan crossroads, war zones, tea plantations, poppy fields, warehouses full of goods from global manufactories, a barrack of listless sleeping labourers lying in rows on low camp beds in sweltering heat, temples, traditional pharmacies, sea ports and the like. The double projected film is inspired by the travels of the intrepid thirteenth-century Venetian explorer Marco Polo, who for twenty-four years wandered across Asia, through cities of the old Silk Road such as Samarkand, Bukhara, Urumqi, Damascus, Kashgar, Ahmedabad, Herat, etc. In fact, excerpts of Marco Polo's accounts of these years of wandering are the basis of a voice-over by the narrator of the film, introducing us to a time when global trade inexorably pointed East. Each visual vignette is like the fragment of a world excavated from an archaeological site; or rescued from some dusty cupboards filled with tea-stained documents; or from camphor chests full of folded silk garments and pressed flowers. Or else the scenes remind us, in the long lingering shots of empty fields and fleeting close-ups of gilded religious shrines, of a natural-history shop lined with glass cabinets filled with a stuffed menagerie of tigers, snakes, etc. The scenes, one after the other, are like quixotic notations on the margins of the smudged ledger of an archival entry long ago disremembered by official keepers of memory.

Incidents: a line of trucks rumbling through the rutted streets of a town as a young girl dressed in a crimson outfit sprinkles water (a sign of benediction?) along the path of the passing trucks. In another a textile worker, stained indigo, is stamping cotton fabrics inside plastic drums where the dye makes all that it touches (including a scrawny, white dog now wearing a habit of the dye as it slithers by across the screen) look like acolytes of the Hindu god Vishnu. Melancholy is the ruling mood in the ambience of a temple-like shop and its desultory chiming bells. To rescue us from the sense that we are submerged in some inkwell, the steady, continuous hum of the voice-over helps keep pace over these incongruous scenes of devastation and loss. We are caught in the spell of Fiona Tan's richly woven allegory of ancient encounters and the idea of globalisation as almost synonymous with the East. That East, which Edward Said in his epic *Orientalism* (1978) refers to as a career, has been a recurring theme in many of Tan's films and videos which deploy the archival image and the archival object as two epistemological regimes in the conception of the image and its relationship to photography, film, modernity and memory.

The work in the pavilion is appropriately titled *Disorient* (2009), a notion that unfolds and reveals Tan's philosophical ambivalence towards the common stereotype of the East. But she also employs it as a structure of involution to precisely describe and counteract that stereotype and wrest from it, the sense of place (Orient), and the mark of placement (orientation), as a topographic, as well as mnemonic recall. A reversal of the meaning of the word 'disorient' (a transitive verb and an adjective) would seem to suggest a form of double negation that challenges the patterns of the orientalist imagination. For 'to disorient' is to cut us away from the patterns of familiar thinking about the East. It is to show us the confusion of lines and trajectories that discomfit as the East falls away and spreads into exile, migration, displacement and, well, disorientation.

The wanderings that the male narrator in *Disorient* recounts in a quickening voice and an accent difficult to locate engenders a reflection on what it is we know about the world, and how we have come to know it. In the end what matters most in this rush of pensive images is not the images at all, but the telling that accompanies the movement from one outpost to another: Gujarat, Zanzibar, Baghdad, Socotra, Dhofar, Khotan, Kashmir, Paktia, Tibet, Xian, Sumatra, Madagascar, Aden, Bukhara, Hormuz and a trail of other cities. The words taken from the biography of Marco Polo detailing his years of travel across this region juxtaposes the incongruous with the exotic, as we watch a fleeting footage of American soldiers driving through a mountain pass in Afghanistan and women garbed in brightly coloured saris or wearing silken veils. The East was certainly a career, and the detailing of Marco Polo's travels through the Orient reveals the extent to which the journeys he undertook was a career and an invention of the Western idea of the East. Marco Polo's journey is a recounting told in runes; it is a story of fantasy, a travelogue of the imagination. And Tan's retracing of these journeys, in the Dutch Pavilion, in the city of Polo's birth and death, is a fitting round trip, which deliberately unravels the paradox of the majesty of the journey, its telling, and the loss of suzerainty of the East, as trade and cultural exchange was transformed into cultural imperialism and colonial domination.

Bhabha's counteraction of archives and traditions is at the heart of Fiona Tan's artistic practice. For those who know Tan's work, the choice of this reflective work in Venice may seem predictable. But it is not at all surprising; since the beginning of her career in the 1990s, she has been tussling with the predicament of her own disorientation, leading her to call herself 'a professional foreigner'.[1] And so she is, not being Dutch by birth but born in a former Dutch colony, here representing the

Netherlands, in that most outmoded of structures: the national pavilion, which points to the idea of tradition now filled with the artist's retinue of archives. We all know by now that Tan is a woman who straddles many worlds and cultures, but does not sufficiently inhabit any of those worlds to the full degree in which many people may seek to take possession of an identity and thus create a usable, authentic past. She was born in Indonesia to Chinese and Australian parents, a decade after the monumental Bandung Conference (1955), hosted by the Indonesian president Sukarno, brought together a gaggle of leaders from mostly former European colonies and ushered in the global ideal of the postcolonial moment, with the creation of the non-aligned movement.

Raised in Melbourne, Australia after her family quit Indonesia owing to anti-Chinese riots that further dispersed her extended family back to China, Europe, America and Australia, Tan travelled West to Europe, where she studied in Germany before ending up in the Netherlands, where she currently resides; hence her occupation of the Dutch Pavilion as the national representative of the country. Tan's journey to the Dutch Pavilion in Venice suggests an autobiographical linkage between the storehouse of her own archival origin in Asia, and the Venetian Marco Polo's own travels in the Orient in the waning days of global trade before the discovery of the sea route to India transformed the relationship between the Occident and the Orient, and the rest of the world for that matter. But if this linkage points in the direction of the artist's own cultural archives, its imaginaries spread their tentacles in multiple directions to other places, other worlds, other times, other stories, other destinies.

In revisiting frequently moments in which the Orient and Occident intersect, and where they veer off into different directions, Tan has resorted to using archives as compasses for a multi-directional tracing of the zigzagging paths of globalisation and the postcolonial turns they have engendered. Not being in full possession of anything that could be fashioned as a cultural tradition bound to the certainties of lineage, her work instead is embedded in those warrens of modernity known as archives. The archive exposes other traditions to each other, rather than embalm them in sealed-off jars. The archive, rather than traditions, are ways of knowing: ways of probing the incommensurable experiences of migration. It is the instrument for resisting the utter failure of memory. Thus, the bit of biography which recurs in Tan's other works such as her seminal works: *May You Live In Interesting Times* (1997), and *Facing Forward* (1999), both of which employ archival documentary photographs and film reels to probe the issue of her hybrid identity, and the entangled familial lines. The Orient, in a sense, has become certainly a career for Tan. But the more she follows it the more its paths trail off, or veer into cul-de-sacs. But in the end biography is not essential to the understanding of Tan's art or its fundamental conceptual, philosophical and hermeneutic anchors.

However, its references, in so far as it points to a common global and postcolonial predicament, the citations of the historical past do plumb a strong discursive predilection that carry weight. In Tan's work, the moving image is like a sovereign device employed not only to track the residues of the past, but also to encapsulate their faint traceries into active temporal machines and mnemonic laboratories. If the epic accumulations of *Disorient* show that memory, history, past and archive are not as actively linkable in a causal flow of the evanescent and the tangible, the spiritual and the material, *A Lapse of Memory* (2007) filmed in the crumbling opulence of the Royal Pavilion in Brighton, offers different species of biography as an allegory of remembering and disremembering, of the fantasies of the East against its loss of suzerainty to the West. The Royal Pavilion, sometimes known as the Brighton Pavilion, is a work of architectural pastiche, and in that sense may well be the first postmodern piece of architecture. As such it is an allegorical object par excellence. The pavilion, like the character Henry who inhabits it, simultaneously mimics and invents a tradition out of a miscellany of archives.

Begun in the late eighteenth century and finished in the first quarter of the nineteenth century, the Royal Pavilion was commissioned by the then Prince Regent, the Prince of Wales who became King George IV in 1820. Only three generations before his family had arrived from Hanover to take over the British crown, after the Protestant dispute with the Catholic Stuarts led to the exile of the Catholic King James II to France. The monarchy, as we will say today, is hybrid, inauthentic. The pavilion commissioned by the would-be King is itself a reflection of this sense of hybridity: the knocking together of diverse parts to fashion an appealing entity and thus give rise to an entirely new species of tradition. The Royal Pavilion at Brighton is just such a structure, composed of diverse cultural archives and thus reflects the unique pastiche which it stands for. The pavilion has an exterior that mimics the grand architecture of Mughal India (including its excesses) and surmounts an earlier neoclassical marine pavilion, a structure now swallowed up by the conical domes and pointed minarets, stone latticework and archways. The interiors were designed according to the refined aesthetics of Japanese and Chinese artistic and decorative traditions. Each of these architectural elements is a fable, an invention. And Henry, the protagonist of Tan's allegory, is a man who is not who he is. In the history of the pavilion anchored in British appropriation of the colonial past, and the imported foreign monarchy which came to stand for an authentic British identity, Tan introduces us to a constant psychic element in all her work, namely the incommensurability of an authentic identity and the slippages of history, memory and past. It also points to the network of postcolonial affiliations that encircle her own fragmented history between Chinese immigration in the early twentieth century, the colonisation of Australia, and Dutch colonialism in Indonesia.

The character Henry, a wizened and seemingly taciturn old man suffering from senile dementia, is the crucial avatar of this condition of incommensurability. Henry lives metaphorically in the iron cage of his failing memory, and physically in the grand frescoed halls of the pavilion. He ekes out an existence as his memory plays tricks of recognition and dis-recognition on him. He must reconcile this physiological condition against its psychic disruption, in the archival backdrop of the orientalist interiors (whose painted scenes of elegant Chinese aristocrats, wallpapers of Japanese cherry blossoms, carved pediments of filigreed serpents and twisted dragons, chinoiserie, swaged curtains, intricately laid tiles, knotted carpets) might just prick his memory and thus lead to a cascade of remembering. But Henry, whom we later learn is really Eng Lie, will stare in aphasic incomprehension at his surroundings.

Despite Henry's disorientation, impoverishment and loneliness, there is something regal about him. His silvery hair is cut just a shade fashionably in its almost calculated dishevelment, and his close-cropped stubble, string-bound suit jacket and sarong reveal a worldly figure who, having taken up residence in the pavilion, is in fact at home. But might Henry or Eng Lie, despite what the narrator tells us about his dementia, be one of those postcolonial mandarins who, in occupying worlds hybridised beyond recognition, has chosen to forget? To leave his past in its pastness, thus blurring his present in the ever-encroaching future? *A Lapse of Memory* relies on Tan's increasing turn towards allegory to deconstruct what a cage memory can be for the dislocated; Henry or Eng Lie represents this condition. As an Eurasian character, his story runs parallel to some of the apocryphal tales that people Marco Polo's story of wandering in the East. In fact, the story of Henry places him, as the narrator recounts in the film, as the 'white devil' haunting the Chinese villages he enters once he crosses the mountain range the villagers call 'scales of the dragon's back'. Or else he is a shape-shifter, whose incommensurable identity marks him out wherever he arrives, such as in the West where his taut, sallow skin makes him stand out amidst the pale complexion of red-haired and bearded figures who float by him, inquisitively on the streets, perhaps, in Antwerp, Amsterdam, Edinburgh or Hamburg.

In treating displacement as a metonymy of memory, the allegorical in Tan's work reaches towards the re-imagining of absence as a condition of re-membering, re-constitution, re-weaving. *A Lapse of Memory* is exile as narrative. It is very much attuned to the point made by Arjun Appadurai in the context of describing the methods of embodying the lapses of globalisation through the structure of the 'image, imagination, imaginary'. These three principles are all at work as *A Lapse of Memory* unfolds in the panning shots trained on the luxurious walls, the minutiae of signs trapped in faded screens, the delicacy of the floor tiles, Henry / Eng Lie wandering between rooms lantern in hand, brushing the floor of dirt, unfurling and gathering a cluster of electric bulbs attached to a lengthy yellow line, climbing and descending worn, creaky staircases, all against the aural backdrop of crashing waves which reminds us that the pavilion is a way station, an interregnum between places, time zones and narratives.

These strands of meaning, and their appeal to unfixedness, incompleteness, are, as Craig Owens writes, certainly allegorical in 'the distance between the present and an irrecoverable past'.[2] In fact, in pointing out that the setting of *A Lapse of Memory*, the Royal Pavilion in Brighton in its pastiche of architectural traditions superimposed over disparately different decorative attitudes, I suggested that the pavilion is steeped in postmodern allegory at a point in contemporary culture when questions of originality were seen to be deeply suspect. Owens wrote that 'allegory first emerged in response to a similar sense of estrangement from tradition.'[3] In his important account of such a return to allegory in contemporary art he states:

> *In order to recognise allegory in its contemporary manifestations, we first require a general idea of what it in fact is, or rather what it* represents *[original emphasis] since allegory is an attitude as well as a technique, a perception as well as a procedure. Let us say for the moment that allegory occurs whenever one text is doubled by another …*[4]

A Lapse of Memory, rather than settle on the bliss of forgetfulness or the nostalgia of wandering, revives in both materialist and aesthetic terms the importance of allegory in the treatment of the incommensurable. Tan shows that her work is never caught up in the act of foreclosure, but in possibilities of open-ended narratives that are deeply informed both by the philosophical and the cinematic.

Fiona Tan
‘On *Provenance*’

Provenance, artist’s book, Rijksmuseum, Amsterdam, 2008. The final section, on Rembrandt’s youngest daughter Cornelia van Rijn, relates to *Nellie* (2013).

Perhaps I should briefly explain this project’s point of departure. My name is Fiona Tan. I was born in Indonesia and grew up in Australia. In 1988 I moved to the Netherlands to continue my fine arts studies and have been living and working in Amsterdam ever since. Amsterdam is very much my home now, even though I travel extensively for my work as an artist.

Images of people nearly always play a central role in my films, photographs and audiovisual installations. I am interested in how images affect and inform the internal picture we have of ourselves, of others and of the world around us. Over the years, a considerable collection of faces has accumulated within the body of work I have created, for the most part faces of people I hardly know. And although this dawned on me only recently, it is clear I have become more and more interested in portraiture. I ask myself, why bother to look at images of other people’s faces? What value, pleasure and insight can be had from this? I work with contemporary, time-based media. Film, video and photography are still newcomers compared to the long and time-honoured traditions of painting, drawing and sculpture. As such, I have never spent much time looking at old paintings and felt them to be far removed from my daily life and artistic practice. But now I feel drawn to the old paintings and drawings, and want to delve into history for this project.

I went to the Rijksmuseum’s depot in Lelystad. Until seventy-five years ago, Lelystad was part of the ocean floor and lay submerged under the waters of what was then called the Zuiderzee (‘Southern Sea’). As a storage place for important historical objects and artworks, this location feels to me somehow strangely symbolic. Here I found myself looking at Dutch paintings from the Golden Age, in particular at portraits from the first half of the seventeenth century. I had the uncanny feeling of being a time traveller, and the faces I saw looked very familiar.

Although I wanted to create an artwork based on this experience, I first wanted to read up on my chosen subject matter and research it more thoroughly.

Before I knew it, I had embarked on a long and sometimes wonderful journey to see whether and in what way my work as an artist is linked to this art that dates from a much earlier period. Like driftwood floating out at sea, I allowed myself the liberty of seeing where my unacademic and associative research method would take me. This journey took me not only to archives, libraries and museums, but also to unexpected places and moments in time. 'Provenance' is an art-history term denoting an artwork's origins. I attempt here to unravel this project's heritage, in a broader sense and with a degree of poetic license.

Without a doubt, Dutch art history is best known for the oil paintings by the famous old masters of the Golden Age. But as an immigrant to this country, I am ignorant though curious about this period in Dutch history. Also, on a personal level, I want to know more about the city I live in. Amsterdam is famed for its historical centre, but I want to see what connections I can discover between the past tense and the present.

AMSTERDAM

Amsterdam – or *Amsterdamøya*, as it is known in Norwegian – is a small, uninhabited island northwest of Spitsbergen. It is located in the far north, inside the Arctic Circle. Surrounded most of the time by pack ice, it is a barren and isolated place. In the winter the days are grim and dark: between November and mid-February, the sun never rises above the horizon. In the summer months between mid-April and mid-August it is always light, and the treeless island becomes host to breeding migratory birds and perhaps the occasional polar bear or walrus.

Willem Barentz stumbled across this group of islands in 1596 whilst searching for an arctic route to Asia. Shortly thereafter, Dutch vessels set out on voyages that followed Barentz's route, in pursuit of bearskins and walrus tusks. It was whaling, however, that swiftly proved to be more profitable. It would be another 200 years before the exploitation of oil and gas fields would get underway and the petroleum industry would be developed. Whale oil – called train or sperm oil – was extremely valuable. It was used in lamps and candles, was a key ingredient in soap and ointments, and was used as a lubricant and to keep leather supple. Whales were the gold mines of the sea. They were culled not only for their blubber but also for baleen, which up until the early twentieth century was used for a wide variety of objects including umbrellas, walking sticks, corsets and even picture frames.

From 1614 to 1642, the Dutch Nordic Company ran a whaling operation in the Arctic Ocean. During the summer months, sailors, fishermen and seasonal workers – many of whom came from the West Frisian Islands – undertook the three-week voyage to Spitsbergen. At its peak there were seven tryworks – furnaces that melted the blubber into oil – operating on the island of Amsterdam. Life was hard. Even in the summer temperatures did not often rise above 6° C, and scurvy was common. This small whaling settlement was called 'Smeerenburg'. Train oil was known in Dutch as *smeer*, which means 'grease'. Herman Melville mentions Smeerenburg as being a particularly smelly place. The settlement's name can be translated literally as 'Mount Fat' or 'Fort Grease'. [...]

In addition to the Nordic Company, there were also more and more business opportunities to the East and to the West, courtesy of the Dutch East India Company (the VOC) and the Dutch West India Company (the WIC) respectively. On 6 June 1636, a paper document had been signed; according to the document, a group of Lenape American Indians had sold 36,000 acres of their land to two Dutch colonists. The deed, written in Dutch, described the area as being the western flatlands between the North River and the East River of New Netherland, and today comprises multiple boroughs of New York City and extends into New York State. Here the Dutch bought otter and beaver skins, supplied for the most part by local Native American hunters, and shipped them back to Holland. Beaver fur could be pressed into felt and made into hats, being not only warm but also waterproof. Fur was in great demand in Europe and the fur trade was lucrative. Later it would be taken over by the French and the British.

There is a portrait of an unknown old man, a copy of a painting by Michiel van Mierevelt. His coat is lined and edged with fur. Even in those days, fur was worn not only for its warmth, but also as a fashion accessory. I enjoy looking at this picture: the man has an interesting face and van Mierevelt was a celebrated portrait painter. However, I am particularly happy I have no idea who the sitter was. Serendipitously ignorant, I know nothing of his wealth or importance and can simply look at his face. I see an old countenance, wrinkled and worn, an intense, perhaps sad gaze, the left side of his face cast in shadow. This man's biography does not get in the way when I look at him.

As I write this it occurs to me that in contemporary art, many of the portraits and pictures of people we see are anonymous. In contrast to the old portrait paintings, these modern-day pictures are not made and valued because of who is in them. This is true irrespective of the medium, be it drawing, painting or photography. In the seventeenth century, portraits were painted only of people of some renown or wealth. Perhaps what also appeals to me is the enigma, the mystery of not knowing. I am free to project onto this old man with his fur-lined coat whatever life story and character development I wish. He becomes the lead in a fragmentary personal film, a film that exists only in my mind.

These days, complaints are being voiced about what I suppose could best be termed 'visual inflation'. Celebrity photographs in particular dominate the media and surround us constantly. Because we see them so often, famous people's faces become iconic, and in doing so increasingly empty. The result is a superficiality that the artist Andy Warhol was drawn to and successfully employed. In my work I have always been drawn to the other end of the spectrum – to anonymous pictures of people, to found footage, whether it comes from archives or through circumstance. I prefer images that are free of the baggage of the media, public relations, the film industry and big business. Here again, I am free of information and presumptions that can get in the way of looking. This explains why I am more interested in the lesser-known artists and works from the seventeenth century. The celebrated masterpieces by the likes of Rembrandt and Vermeer are currently subject to such heavy marketing that I feel I am barely capable of looking at these works with a fresh, open and unprejudiced gaze.

Hanging in the rack next to the 'unknown old man' at the depot in Lelystad I noticed a medium-sized portrait of an elderly woman. Her name, so I was told, is Margaretha de Geer. Initially I found out much more about Margaretha's sons than about herself. As a young man, Margaretha's second son Hendrik Trip dabbled briefly in the fur trade in New Netherland in the 'New World' of America. He later teamed up with his brother Louys, and both became highly successful businessmen and – it goes without saying – incredibly rich. Behind a single impressive façade, these brothers built a stately home for themselves on the Kloveniersburgwal in Amsterdam, making it Amsterdam's largest private building at the time. They moved into this house in 1662, Hendrik in the northern and Louys in the southern half of the house. The Trip brothers' wealth came mostly from dealing in weapons and munitions, and they embellished the chimneys of their house with the rather ironical motto *Ex Bello Pax* – 'weapon dealers of peace' or 'peace as a result of war'.

Painted in 1651, Margaretha de Geer of Dordrecht (married women customarily kept their maiden names) must have been sixty-six years old at the time. This portrait by Jacob Gerritsz. Cuyp could hardly be called becoming. To me she looks slight, unassuming and somewhat severe. It is hard to believe she gave birth to at least twelve children. She faces the viewer cautiously, timidly, and her skin reveals her age. Her mouth is a thin, straight line; her cheeks are red from damaged surface blood vessels. The large white collar around her neck, which the Dutch nicknamed a 'millstone', seems to further constrain and confirm her serious character. Nothing, except the fact that her portrait was painted and that it has survived, reveals to me anything of her very considerable wealth and standing.

Ten years later she was portrayed again, this time not by the local artist Jacob Gerritsz. Cuyp, but by a fifty-five-year-old, highly successful painter from Amsterdam, Rembrandt van Rijn. During the same sitting, Rembrandt painted Margaretha twice and her husband Jacob Trip once. Her clothing is almost identical to that in Cuyp's portrait and even more out of fashion than it already was back then. Her husband, aged eighty-six, appears extremely frail and is wearing a nightcap and tabard, clothing that symbolises wisdom and dignity but that was commonly worn at home as a dressing gown. He would die that same year. Possibly he was already sick, for it is the only portrait I know of where the sitter is portrayed in his nightclothes.

At seventy-six, Margaretha – who was ten years younger than her husband – has aged well. Although she too looks frail and wizened, she also seems to have gained dignity with the years. This time she faces the viewer squarely, calm but commanding. Margaretha was in fact one of the most powerful women in the country and this portrait appears to testify to this. On the other hand, however, I find the look in her eyes strangely vacant, clouded over as if she is already looking beyond this life. It has also been speculated that both Jacob's and Margaretha's portraits were completed after Jacob's death. The white handkerchief Margaretha is clutching in her right hand could be an expression of mourning. Indeed, the frontal positioning does render her a solitary figure, and I am left with the impression that Margaretha is facing the world alone. […]

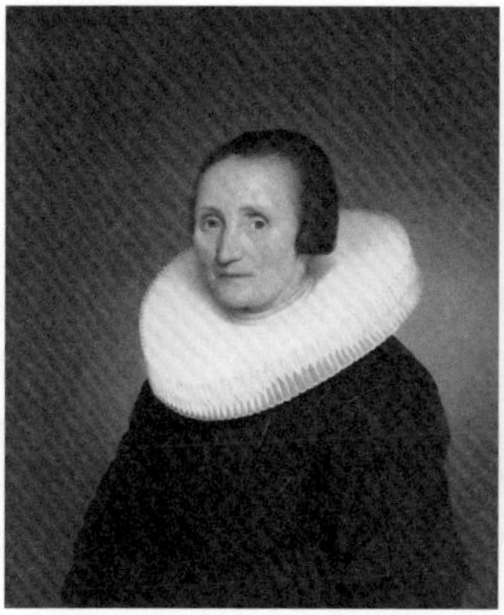

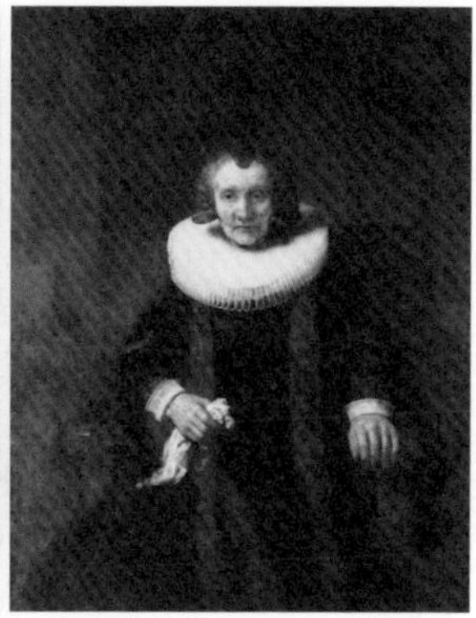

Jacob Gerritsz. Cuyp, *Portrait of Margaretha de Geer (1585–1672)*, 1651
Rembrandt van Rijn, *Portrait of Margaretha de Geer, Wife of Jacob Trip*, c. 1661

FAR EAST

One of my favourite words in the whole of the Dutch language is the word *sinaasappel*, which means 'orange'. Its literal translation is 'Chinese apple', a translation from the French *pomme de Sine*. For years I used the word on a daily basis, but only recently did I stop to think of its origins. I guess this word particularly appeals to me because I have Chinese roots myself, even if I do not look Chinese and can't speak the language. My father is Indonesian Chinese; I made a film about the Chinese side of my family in 1997.

Around 1500, Portuguese missionaries in Asia sent pips from sweet oranges to Europe. In English, the word 'orange', which stems from Sanskrit, also came to describe the colour that had been known as *geoluhread* – yellow-red. Although the orange tree was not suited to the harsh northern climate, this was overcome by building special conservatories for citrus trees to overwinter in. These 'orangeries' were more than just greenhouses – they were symbols of prestige and wealth. The upper class loved to cultivate things that were oriental and exotic.

At the Museum voor Schone Kunsten in Antwerp there hangs an elegant full-size portrait of Maria Stuart, widow of the Prince of Orange, painted by Bartholomeus van der Helst. The young Mary is holding an orange in her hand in reference to her deceased husband. Her hand is resting on her luscious silvery satin dress, the folds of which van der Helst has painted so impressively. The orange appears to have a coarse thick skin, different to the oranges I buy at the local greengrocers' on the Krugerplein close to my home.

I draw my gaze back to the surface, once again studying and admiring the seductive colour, texture and lustre of oil paint. In the Rijksmuseum, a similarly elegant portrait of the young Prince William III of the House of Orange (1654) hangs proudly. With his right hand, the prince is gently pulling an orange off an orange tree. Similarly, in his portrait of Prince Maurice from 1607, Michiel van Mierevelt has given him an orange sash and orange plumage on his helmet. This visual reference to the ruling family's surname is something of a running joke, still in evidence in the bright orange clothing people wear during the annual Queen's Day festivities in the Netherlands.

John Berger has effectively argued that the tradition of oil painting is the manifestation of a new way of seeing the world, one ruled by wealth and possession. As he puts it, 'Oil painting conveyed a vision of total exteriority.' He goes on to say:

> *What distinguishes oil painting from any other form of painting is its special ability to render the tangibility, the texture, the lustre, the solidity of what it depicts. [...] Although its painted images are two-dimensional, its potential of illusionism is far greater than that of sculpture, for it can suggest objects possessing colour, texture and temperature, filling a space and, by implication, filling the entire world.*[1]

The viewer of these paintings is confronted with a vision of materiality. The surface texture of wealth and refinement: shiny pearls, precious jewels, finest porcelain, luscious silks and velvets, gorgeous and delicate lace. The skin of an orange, the feather of a peacock, the opalesque coating of a shell, the fine colouring of fur, the intricate pattern of a tortoise shell. All things that are desirable, oriental or exotic. What went on beneath the surface remains to some extent undisclosed. Perhaps literature, music and other arts addressed this better and were more able to express people's thoughts, fears and desires.

The role of oil painting which John Berger describes has now been taken over by colour photography, although one could argue not as successfully. Photographs used in advertising campaigns may certainly be seductive, and photos of food in cookery books may even cause one's mouth to water, but I have never been tempted to study a 'pack shot', letting my eye wander over every single detail as I have with a still life by Willem Claesz Heda or Francisco Zurbarán. Other writers and artists have also commented on the element of time in paintings like these.

It is as if the time taken to paint them can somehow be transposed into the time required to look at them.

With moving images, another form of perception takes over. As with Jacob Cuyp's portrait of Margaretha de Geer, this results in a gaze that is less preoccupied with 'reading' the image – by that I mean quickly scanning the image's surface as one would tend to do when looking at a photograph. I have developed a strange, anachronistic method of working over the years, one that entails filming people as if for a photograph: they stand still, hardly moving. Paradoxically, this seems to direct the attention away from movement and more into the experience of time passing and into the encounter of spending time with those individuals whom I have filmed. At times it feels like the image looks back. And I would like to think that engaging in this kind of looking also means being confronted and challenged by alternative images of humanity. [...]

Hendrickje Stoffels gave birth to Rembrandt's third and last daughter around the time of the Delft gunpowder disaster in 1654. She is hardly mentioned in the biographical summaries of Rembrandt's life and seems forgotten for the most part – perhaps because Rembrandt and Hendrickje never married (the will of Rembrandt's first wife, Saskia van Uylenburgh, prohibited him from remarrying) and the girl was born out of wedlock. But she was his only daughter who lived to become an adult. Even though she was illegitimate, Rembrandt's daughter was christened in the Oude Kerk ('Old Church') in Amsterdam on Friday 30 October 1654 and given her father's surname. She was named Cornelia, just like Rembrandt's first two daughters, who had both died in infancy. After the deaths of Titus and Hendrickje, Rembrandt named Cornelia in his will as his sole heir.

Not much is known about Cornelia van Rijn and none of Rembrandt's paintings or drawings are considered to be of his daughter. A year after Rembrandt's death, Cornelia, aged fifteen, married a painter named Cornelis Suijthof. The following year the young couple emigrated to Batavia, where they remained for the rest of their lives. I am fascinated with the idea of Rembrandt's daughter living so far away in Asia, in Indonesia – the country of my birth. It must have been an unusual and courageous move, and I wonder for what reasons she and her husband decided to undertake this arduous journey. I myself came on my own to Europe at the tender age of eighteen and am aware I almost automatically empathise with many fellow travellers and immigrants. Perhaps Cornelia, like me, felt the need to get away, to leave the close confines of her home and environment and, in her case, to sail as far away as possible from the stigma of illegitimacy and possibly also from her father's fame.

After settling down in Batavia, Cornelia gave birth to two sons. The boys were named Rembrandt and Hendrik after her deceased parents. Both these children died relatively young, Hendrik at the age of eight and Rembrandt at the age of eighteen in 1691. Cornelia herself was only twenty-four when she died, shortly after giving birth to a third son in 1678. Cornelia's husband Cornelis remarried, and appears several times in the voc records as a 'civilian painter' and also, rather oddly, as a prison guard. In his will from 1690 he bequeathed all his belongings to his second wife, including his gold, his silver and his slaves.

What was life like in seventeenth-century Batavia? I was only two years old when my family left Indonesia and immigrated to Australia, but we revisited Java when I was eleven. My childhood memories of Jakarta revolve around intense smells of rotting fruit, tropical downpours and noisy traffic jams. I remember odd details, like the domestic staff washing our grubby clothes by hand, geckos crawling up living room walls and raucous early-morning calls to prayer broadcast from a nearby mosque. But all this must be a far cry from seventeenth-century Dutch Batavia. Although I once visited the old Dutch fort in Jakarta, I have only vague memories of slightly mouldy white paint on high, chalked walls and an old black disused canon.

Founded in 1619, Dutch Batavia would have been well-established by the time Cornelia and her husband got off the boat in 1671, after a voyage lasting approximately eight months. Bamboo houses were by then forbidden within the walls of the Dutch settlement. Thus, the sizeable city of around 50,000 inhabitants must have had quite a European appearance, even though its population was a rather eclectic mix of Asian minorities as well as white Dutch nationals. The canals that had been built were already silted up with mud, making them the perfect breeding ground for mosquitoes. Thanks to Dutch engineering, the danger of Batavian Fever, as malaria was called, was dangerously close at hand.

It is thought that Cornelia's husband Cornelis painted many portraits in Batavia, although none of his signed paintings have survived. When I try to envisage any of his paintings, I find myself back in the Rijksmuseum depot amidst the many portraits of van Mierevelt, Verspronck and the like. It is a common phenomenon that expatriates fiercely hold on to customs and manners from home. Therefore I imagine that these portraits would have looked very proper and very Dutch. Ironically, typically Asian attributes like shells, porcelain and exotic fruit would figure much more readily in pictures painted back home in Delft, Haarlem or Amsterdam. In the Netherlands the inclusion of exotic objects was considered fashionable. In Batavia I am inclined to think that almost anything exotic would have been automatically censored from any formal portraits. The exotic was, of course, no longer exotic once it became something that could be found in ordinary, everyday surroundings.

Concerning Cornelia's lifestyle in Batavia, I can only make limited guesses. She probably never went outside the city walls, as this was considered unsafe. I presume that she found the heat and humidity almost unbearable, although the rain in the wet season might have reminded her of Holland. Perhaps she loved to eat some of the tropical fruits so abundant in Java: papaya, mango, pineapple, jackfruit and rambutan. I doubt she would have eaten rice – right up to Indonesian independence, the ruling classes always ate potatoes. The tronie Rembrandt painted of himself as an 'oriental' wearing a bulging, misshapen turban embellished with jewels is a far cry from his own daughter's adult life.

Imagine that Cornelia was blessed with her father's talent! What if she was also such a sharp and accurate observer? What if her draughtsmanship was also as accomplished, her hand as swift and her eye as perceptive? I would dearly love to be able to leaf through the pages of her 'East Indian' sketchbook. [...]

David Frankel

On *Provenance*, *Downside Up*, *Projection*, at Peter Freeman, Inc., New York

Exhibition review, *Artforum*, October 2010, 274.

The link between Fiona Tan's *Provenance* (2008) and old master painting is counter-intuitive, for Tan is not a painter but a video artist. In this group of filmic portraits – looped video studies of barely moving figures – she also limits herself to black-and-white, so that her strongest reference is to the photographic tradition. And yet that link is quickly sensed. It's evident partly in the gravity of Tan's process, the unhurried slowness with which she looks at people, her camera standing still or incrementally panning or turning. It's partly the quality of the light, here restrained and even, there glowing from a window as in Vermeer, but always signal in its clarity, allowing a precision of vision that distinguishes and elevates Tan's subjects. Finally, there is the idea that a portrait is built up not just of the features of the sitter's face but of the details of his or her life – objects handled, used, kept close; clothing chosen and bought; environments inhabited and maintained. Just as an artist portraying a seventeenth-century Dutch merchant might have wanted it known that he wore expensive furs, Tan lets us see her subjects' apartments, their books, a child's toys, one woman's japonaiserie, another's laptop.

Tan is established in Europe – *Provenance* began as an installation at the Rijksmuseum Amsterdam (whose collection Tan researched to make it), then represented the Netherlands, with two more of her works, at last year's Venice Biennale – but this was her first solo exhibition in New York. She was born in Indonesia and grew up in Australia before settling in Holland. Strikingly, she begins her exemplary essay in *Provenance*'s catalogue – an artist's book of a kind, both scholarly and personal – with this biography, describing it as the project's 'point of departure'. She is saying, I think, that what she found, what she looked for, in her studies of the Rijksmuseum's old masters was informed by the awareness of global history to which her travels sensitised her, the travels of a postcolonial subject. Among the Amsterdam friends and family included in *Provenance* are a Turkish shopkeeper and his son, their presence referencing patterns of migration through the capitals of the West. And like the Marxist art historian John Berger, whose writing she quotes, she has an impulse to decode the material objects shown in paintings, signs not only of a portrait subject's character but of specific social histories: for Tan, an orange is not just an orange but an index of an economic structure. At the same time, the dignity of her silent images embraces their subjects. Without sympathetic relationships between artist and sitter, *Provenance* would be a very different work.

In a second room, the exhibition included *Downside Up* (2002), a video in which shadows on a city street seem to have more life than the pedestrians who make them, and a new work *Projection* (2009), a self-portrait. Whereas each of the subjects of *Provenance* receives his or her own LCD monitor, which sits on the wall like a painting, *Projection* is shown on a screen that hangs from the ceiling, an altogether flimsier-looking arrangement. And whereas the light in *Provenance* engraves Tan's sitters as clear three-dimensional presences, her treatment of herself is more obscure: having filmed herself standing, she stood behind a hanging sheet on which that sequence was projected, then filmed the sheet as she took hold of and manipulated it from the back, her own body sometimes coming into view. In the end result, the artist comes and goes, the reality of her self-projection in question. It is as if, in *Provenance*, Tan had sought to concretise a sense of individual identity that in this pair of works seems fluid and uncertain.

Fiona Tan
'Introduction to *Disorient*, with excerpt from Marco Polo, *The Travels* (1298)'

Fiona Tan: Disorient, catalogue for the Dutch Pavilion, 53rd Venice Biennale, Heidelberg: Kehrer Verlag, 2009, 1.12–1.17.

Originally written in Old French in prison in 1298 as *The Description of the World*, Marco Polo's *Travels* was also translated under the title *The Book of Wonders* and as *Il Milione*, which translates as 'a million lies' or 'a pack of lies'. The original manuscript, penned by Polo's fellow prisoner Rustichello of Pisa, has been lost. Of the earliest surviving manuscripts over 100 versions of Marco's text still exist, all of which differ considerably from each other and none of which can be considered to be the truly authentic and original text. The credibility of Polo's descriptions have been doubted and rejected from the outset. Nonetheless the manuscript was copied and translated and circulated throughout Europe for hundreds of years and has not been out of print since the discovery of the printing press. For fourteenth-century Europeans the world was flat as a pancake. There were three known continents – Europe, Africa, Asia – and Jerusalem always crowned any map of the world as its centre.

Marco Polo left his hometown of Venice in 1271, aged seventeen. The young Venetian merchant travelled with his father and uncle over land across the Middle East and on through Asia, eventually reaching the Summer Palace of Kublai Kahn in Shang-tu, also known as Xanadu, in Northeast China. As Chinese historical archives confirm, the Polos were received in court and Marco became personally acquainted with the Mongolian Emperor. For seventeen years Marco Polo worked in his service probably as a tax collector but also as storyteller; he travelled the length and breadth of the Mongolian Empire. By the time he managed to return

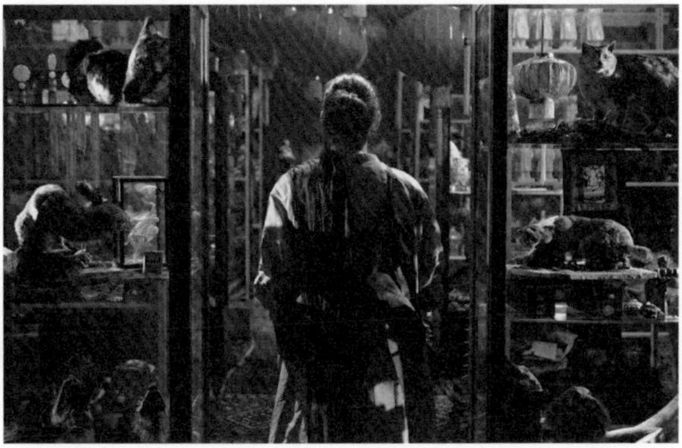

Disorient (production photo), 2009

home to Venice, after a protracted and treacherous sea journey from China via Indonesia and India to Persia, Polo was forty-one years old.

MARCO POLO, EXCERPT FROM *THE TRAVELS*, 1298

> *When they had crossed this desert, they came to a large and splendid city called Bukhara. The province also was called Bukhara, and its ruler's name was Barak. It was the finest city in all of Persia.*
> *Let me begin with Armenia. It is a land of many villages and towns, amply stocked with the means of life. It also affords good sport with all sorts of wild game, both beast and fowl. The climate however is far from healthy; it is, in fact, extremely enervating. Near the Georgian border there is a spring from which gushes a stream of oil, in such abundance that a hundred ships may load there at once. This oil is not good to eat; but it is good for burning and as a salve for men and camels affected with itch or scab. The country looks out over two seas. In this province is a fine city of great size named Tiflis. The inhabitants are Christians besides a few Saracens and Jews, but not many. Silk and many other fabrics are woven here. Let us now turn to the lands lying south and east of it.*
> *Here are made all the cloths silk and gold called mosulin. And from this kingdom hail the great merchants, also called Mosulin, who export vast quantities of spices and other precious wares. In the mountains of this kingdom live the people called Kurds;*

some of them are Christians, others are Saracens who worship Mahomet. They are lusty fighters and lawless men, very fond of robbing merchants.
It is in Baghdad that most of the pearls are pierced that are imported from India. Here too are woven many fabrics, very richly decorated with beasts and birds. It is a great centre for the study of the law of Mahomet and of necromancy, natural science, astronomy, geomancy, and physiognomy. It is the largest and most splendid city in all these parts.
At its southward rim is another downward slope, where the road drops steadily for twenty miles. It is a bad and dangerous road, being infested by robbers.
After two days ride he reaches the Ocean. Here on the coast stands a city called Hormuz, which has an excellent harbour. It is a great centre of commerce. Its king is named Ruemedan Ahmad. The climate is torrid, owing to the heat of the sun, and unhealthy. If a merchant dies here, the king confiscates all his possessions.
The people here are black and worship Mahomet. In summer they do not stay in the cities, or they would all die of the heat; but they go out to their gardens, where there are rivers and sheets of water.
This is a large city. Its inhabitants worship Mahomet. There is iron and steel and ondanique[1] *in plenty, and they make steel mirrors of large size and excellent quality …*
Now let us continue our journey. […]

Juliana Engberg 'Infinite Crossroads', on *Disorient*

Fiona Tan: Coming Home, Sherman Contemporary Art Foundation, Sydney, 2010, 74–9.

Modernist in temperament and style, [the Dutch Pavilion in the Giardini of the Venice Biennale] represents the utopian functionalism of Dutch architect Gerrit Rietveld, who hoped the plain formalism of his buildings would advance openness and a social learning between structure and inhabitants; an architecture, he hoped, in which cognition and the senses would be enhanced and enabled by the lack of obstructive and reductive ornamental eccentricity and bourgeois embellishment.

This is *Olanda*, Holland, the Netherlands. A small parcel of land, gravel and built structure claimed on behalf of its culture in the Giardini, Venice, Italy, which was once a part of Byzantium. The pavilion is a shell space in which different things might dwell, briefly, during the Venice Biennale, where I have come to view Fiona Tan's *Disorient* (2009).

Tan presents two video works in *Disorient*. One is a nomadic account, the other a material gathering. Neither is like the flat, smooth-space lands we have previously encountered in the chinoiserie concoctions of Henry's world in *A Lapse of Memory* (2007). In this instance the images that play on the walls are totally different to the blank illusions that deflect Henry and leave him abandoned in a no-home place, consigning him to a perpetual coming-into-being state.

The first seems almost museological. Artefacts have been gathered and assembled *en masse* like an endless cabinet of curiosities. It reminds me of the National Museum of Vietnamese History in Hanoi, Vietnam, where (prior to the United States trade embargo being lifted in 1994) I saw nineteenth-century wooden cabinets filled with the evidence of culture – a display indebted to the French colonial taxonomy I suppose – and of the Museum Fatahillah (Jakarta History Museum) in Indonesia, where the Dutch embedded themselves.

In Tan's video fresco, everything is round, like the brass bell rotundness of the Buddha's belly: the body of the decorated ceramic vases; the plump folds of the stone Ganesh; beads, bowls, jars and reptilian coiled things. All are spherical, textured and anti-flat. We pan through this assortment of things: bird cages; chests of drawers; Indian idols; wooden textures, woven fabrics, carpets; rich emblems made in dense earth colours of red and terracotta. All a kind of tropical, lush forest of cultural signs and things.

Except for the unexpected appearance of a little ceramic group of figures. I think it's Mao and his Children of the Revolution inside a bottle or some sort of glass cabinet. They are shiny and colourful and not at all like a relic, more akin to a nostalgic collectable. Now that I am alert to this visual intervention, other items seem less secure in their historical, archaeological place. Television and computer monitors are also on shelves; reproduction furniture and collectable icons start to take on the surface of plastic and modern materials. They are given equal position in this increasingly non-hierarchical accumulation of cultural evidence. Some are there as multiples of multiples. Questions of authenticity are useless. One might say all are as authentic as each other.

As if like an object, a male figure dressed somewhat like a Buddhist monk – ubiquitously attired in the orange clothing that has made these men such a favourite with photographers who love colourful regimentations and lines of people in robes with umbrellas – lies napping in a corner. Tan has explained that, 'Actually this figure who very occasionally drifts through the scenes is my representation of Marco Polo; he is wearing a "Asian-like" olden silk robe with Indian clothes underneath.' The television monitor plays a film of Chinese boats punting along another grand canal. The bridge looks similar to the numerous Venetian arches, but is taller, more steeped. The film is early twentieth-century. [...]

Of course, I think of Foucault. This video of artefact and archive is filled with depth and layers, recessed spaces and complicated tunnels. This multiplicity of representations implies the sedimentary archaeology of cultural formations.

A voice murmurs in the space. Well-modulated, worldly: world weary in cadence. A British accent; cultivated, but not aristocratic; imperial, yet not imperious. It fills space. The sound of the voice washes the room; it rolls like a tide around the walls. The voice carries seagulls and albatross in its air, and dips and rises with the waves and wind that push boats through the sea. In ways, it reminds me of the narrator in Chris Marker's 1983 film *Sans Soleil*.

The voice settles in the images of the second video, even while it appears to also narrate the *Wunderkammer* of objects in the first. This video moves between the smooth and striated spaces described by Deleuze.[1] The narrator's voice is even, formulaic. His words, abbreviated from the texts of Venetian explorer Marco Polo, catalogue people and places in a steady predictable list: religion, trade, customs, appearance. The same kind of information now catalogued by the CIA and its database. The colour of the video has been calibrated to resemble the saturations of *National Geographic* magazine photo-journalism. Even though Tan's images are contemporary, they have the hue of historical document.

The traveller lists his ports – Armenia, Madagascar, Cathay, Japan and others – and ticks off his inventory of facts. All the while the camera films terrain, faces, crowds and activity in a smooth taxonomy of Other. Faces stare back at the intrusive gaze of the camera. Where once we were led to believe that the averting of eyes was based on superstition or modesty, we must now believe this steady returned gaze is a refusal to passively participate in this ethnic cataloguing.

Along with the disembodied voice we become one with the eye of the camera, which passes through clouds and travels over mountain ranges to deliver us to scenes in which truck carcasses are carried over rocky ranges, women pray at a wall, opium poppies bob in the wind and are then harvested, fireworks explode. Firecrackers or bombs – I hesitate, in my mind, to confirm which. [...]

A small model of the Dutch Pavilion occupies space on a wooden shelf. Perhaps we are mistaken, but we can imagine from a previous minute of footage that it has been recently manufactured in a reproduction furniture workshop in Asia. The glance of the little pavilion reminds us that we are in a space within a space, within a place that is part of the construction of culture. The voice trails on: cataloguing, generalising; never quite touching its subject.

Upon leaving the Giardini, I pass iron gates with doorknobs fashioned as turbaned heads of Moors. I have noticed these many times over the thirty years I have been visiting this city. I am always struck by the evidence that one is more polished and shiny than its twin because it is used: it is the one twisted during each entry and closure. Other doorknobs demonstrate the persistence of orientalist designs – florette, ziggurat and geometric patterns – utilitarian and incidental objects that hold a history of geopolitical flux and imperial control. Venice is a patina of such ornamentalism.

En route I eat a croissant that the people at Bar da Gino call a *brioche*, and which the people at Brunetti's in Melbourne call a *cornetto*. Some say it was invented by a chef by the name of August Zang in Vienna; others claim it was created much earlier to celebrate the European defeat of a Muslim invasion at the Battle of Tours by the Franks in 732, the shape of the croissant representing the Islamic crescent. Before I board the *vaporetto* I pass the Senegalese street vendors, also known colloquially as the *vu' cumprà*, who peddle knock-off designer bags, belts and artefacts – the Prada brand in particular.

I travel over water and this reminds me of Tan's opening shot in *A Lapse of Memory*. Travelling in Venice always reminds me, too, of Luchino Visconti's film of *Death in Venice* (1971), and the music of Mahler. There are many cultural constructions of place, and this is one of them. Gondolas glide by. I am surprised to have not registered the similarity of Venetian gondolas and Chinese canal vessels. It seems obvious once you think about it. Just as when you think of Italian spaghetti and Chinese noodles, *yum cha* and ravioli.

Fiona Tan
Voice-over to *Brendan's Isle*

I

Let me read to you from a very old Dutch poem.

It tells of the adventures of Brendan, an Irish monk who lived in the sixth century.

Listen! And you can learn
from this wise man of God
how two paradise
there were upon this earth.
He read wonderful things
and of many a large island.
This wise man read also
of another world
underneath this one.
When here turns day,
there always falls night
He read there are three heavens.
Of fish there was described
one with forest and land
growing on its skin.
But Brendan dismissed all this
as too incredible for to be true.

In a fury, the poem continues, Brendan tosses the book into the fire and curses its author. An angel appears. Because of his angry deed truth has been lost. Brendan must undertake a nine-year voyage – to see with his own eyes all that he refuses to believe.

II

For Irish monks of the sixth century, the ocean was their desert.

Together with a handful of monks Brendan sails from Ireland on a long and arduous voyage in a small leather-bottomed boat. They search for an elusive island supposed to lie to the west. This is the *Insula Deliciosa, Terra Repromisionis Sanctorum*, the Island of the Blessed. Here the sun never sets; there are four rivers of paradise, trees are heavy with fruit, birds are always singing. Here one never feels tired, nor is one ever hungry or thirsty. There is no time on this island.

III

I have always loved the sea, but I shiver when I imagine such a long and difficult sea journey. Wet and cold. For weeks on end.

Brendan visits many islands. At Easter he mistakenly lands on the back of a sleeping whale. As with Sinbad the creature stirs when a fire is lit on its beach and Brendan's monks rush back to the safety of their boat. They encounter the Island of Birds, the Island of Sheep, the fearsome Island of Blacksmith. Sometimes the travellers encounter other monks, sometimes angels and other Biblical figures, sometimes dangerous sea creatures. They sail past a mysterious salt-like pillar and become stranded in a thick, leaden, soup-like sea. Perhaps Brendan truly did encounter curious whales, icebergs, a volcanic eruption at sea.

After seven years or so, Brendan finally reaches his destination – his blessed island. According to the poem:

When the travellers with Brendan
went on land there,
both large and small lost
any tiredness or pain
from all that they tasted
of sweet on this island.

But Brendan stays only briefly. After having finally reached heaven on earth, he turns around and sails back home.

IV

The Spanish called it the Not-found or Hidden Island. Much like Ptolemy wrote of one of the *Insulae Fortunatae* that it is never visible and can never be reached. For centuries seafarers continued to search for Brendan's Isle.

There were occasional sightings. Expeditions were mounted in search of it. But none was successful. The earliest maps locate it west of Ireland in the middle of the Atlantic. Later, geographers place the island off the coast of Africa just north of the Canary Islands. Columbus believed it to be located at the most westerly end of the world. Behaim's Globe from 1490–92 shows the island just off the coast of Cathay.

The last sighting was said to be in 1872.

On the internet I found a small black-and-white photograph of the island, taken in 1958 by a Mr. Rodriguez Quintero of La Palma. Somewhat disappointingly it's not much to look at: a small island – bare of vegetation, unassuming and uninteresting.

Just a rocky outcrop sticking up out of the misty sea.

Sabine Maria Schmidt

'Below the Water Line – Associative After-Images Triggered by Fiona Tan's Exhibition "Point of Departure"'

Fiona Tan: Point of Departure, Centro Andaluz de Arte Contemporáneo Sevilla; Koldo Mitxelena, San Sebastian, 2012, 93–8.

> *Before you came here, I knew of your people, who live in a different country, but it never occurred to me to go there.*
> — spoken by a Cuna Indian from Panama to a visiting missionary

When the robot vehicle Curiosity landed on the surface of the planet Mars in August 2012, it reawakened the vision that human beings might one day follow. But critics have reminded us that manned space travel has never brought about any fundamental scientific breakthrough, tending rather to satisfy emotional and patriotic aims or serve power politics. Those wishing to investigate outer space seriously should do so without the nuisance of astro-, cosmo- and talko-nauts. The fact is that human sensory organs can determine very little on the face of Mars – it should be left to machines. The planet may appear hostile to life, but the robot images we received, showing hilly landscapes formed by rivers of water, are all the more astonishing as a result: as if Mars had a past still belonging to the future on Earth.

Even the scientists of antiquity like Ptolemy reported on places that men knew about, which would never be accessible. While we have produced technical images of space and places that we will never be able to see today, the notions of antiquity were based on dreamed, subconscious images and fictions expressed in myths and narratives. The Greeks, more philosophers than geographers, divided the world into three parts enclosing the Mediterranean: Europe, Africa and Asia. The Romans systematically developed the knowledge stored in Alexandria concerning the Earth's spherical form, its main component of water, the size of the Earth's circumference, and methods of mapping. The downfall of the Roman Empire led to an initial loss of ancient knowledge regarding spatial awareness and cartographical ideas; subsequently, it was suppressed or forbidden. Scholars like Isidore of Seville (c. 560–636) devised an image of the Earth as a circular disc surrounded by oceanic currents (see, for example, the world map from the eleventh-century Leipzig Codex). In such maps Paradise, the Garden of Eden planted by God, was located on Earth. Precise exploration of the geography of this landscape of Paradise and the Holy Land, including Jerusalem at its centre, was a key concern of church scholars; their hypothesis remained binding for all cartographers until well into the mediaeval period.

In her audio drama *Brendan's Isle* (2010) Fiona Tan recalls a pre-mediaeval travel report that belongs to the founding myths of Irish history. Brendan's legendary sea voyage, which he is said to have undertaken in the second half of the sixth century – in other words during the period of Ireland's Christian conversion – is a legend that has been passed down to us over centuries as the 'Navigatio Sancti Brendani' via mediaeval manuscripts, including an Old Dutch version.

The exploratory vehicle Curiosity that landed on Mars was most probably bigger than the small boat, a currach made with stretched leather hides (4.8–5.5 metres long and less than a metre wide), which Brendan built and sailed in together with a group of monks. They wanted to search for an island whose existence he had denied for so long. According to tradition, the journey was not the outcome of investigative curiosity or a pilgrimage but an 'expedition of punishment' imposed on the Irish monk, who had previously burnt a piece of writing about two paradises and an island of dreams, cursing their author as a fantasiser. He was told by an angel who appeared to him to undertake a nine-year journey, so that he could see with his own eyes what he did not wish to believe. This means that we could also regard Brendan as the first travel archivist, checking the validity of existing images and collecting new ones.

Brendan set out with a group of monks to search for the island, which was said to lie west of Ireland: the *Insula Deliciosa*, the *Terra Repromisionis Sanctorum*, the Island of the Blessed. Here, it was said, the sun never set; there were four paradisal rivers; trees full of fruit; no weariness, hunger or thirst; and no passage

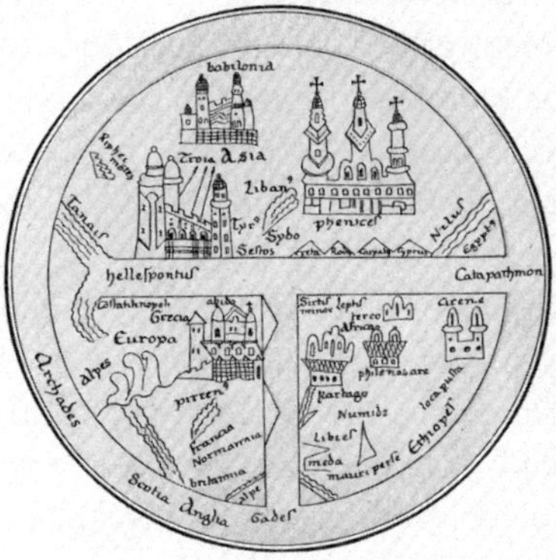

Weltkarte aus einem Leipziger Kodex des 11. Jahrhunderts

World map from one of the Leipzig Codices, 11th c.

of time. The monks experienced numerous adventures and saw strange places. They encountered islands of birds, sheep and smiths. Sometimes they met with monks, angels, Biblical characters, and occasionally they came face-to-face with sea monsters. They travelled past a mysterious pillar of salt and got stuck in a viscid, solidifying ocean. Among the best-known anecdotes is their mistaken landing on the back of a whale, which they only recognised as such when lighting a fire and so triggering a life-threatening quake: a mediaeval travel topos. One of the first black-and-white snapshots from the Curiosity mission, by the way, shows an apparently fantastic photo: the shadow of the flying object approaching a grey mass reminiscent of a fish. It is a mythically charged photo that reminds us of pictures of fantastic sea voyages (e.g., *Moby-Dick*, 1851). Finally, after seven years, the pilgrims arrived at the island. They stayed only for a short time and then returned home.

In Brendan's era (c. 484–577) there were migrations and first pilgrimages, but they were restricted to the continent. Boat travel took place on inland waterways and, above all, in the Mediterranean area; they led to Italy, Asia Minor or Greece. Travel on the 'open sea' was too dangerous and completely unpredictable, since there were no maps or navigation devices. The legendary sea voyages of Greek heroic legend may also be imagined as sailing and rowing from one place on the coast to the next, or as island-hopping at the most. If one lost sight of the coast, the journey became involuntary: an emergency situation. Calm or storm were the only two alternatives. Nonetheless, Brendan's journey, the *navigatio* as a mythical *topos* of faith in God and religious edification, describes one hypothetical success for Irish seamen. When the Vikings arrived in Iceland c. 860, they found Irish hermits living there who obviously had succeeded in reaching the end of the contemporary world in their boats. [...]

In the literature, the principal highlight has been on Tan's interest in images that show what really happened at the moment of taking: not only in front of, but also behind the camera. As a consequence, these images always incorporate the perceptible or conceived counter-perspective of the person recording them. In *News from the Near Future* (2003) there is no counter-perspective or retrospective viewpoint. The predominant treatment of landscape is also new; all the film's sections have in common the motifs of landscape and continually flowing water.

News from the Near Future opens up a panorama of dream-like, sometimes apparently slowed down, dramatically beautiful natural dramas, but also of natural catastrophes such as floods, all of which have developed into collective images and memories. The material can be attributed to the genre of so-called 'actuality film'. By contrast to documentary film, in which the filming itself is generally concealed, 'actuality film' does not hide the presence of the camera, and its position is often static and frontal. It lacks any overarching argumentation or explanatory context within which we are supposed to grasp its images. The structure of 'actuality film' derives from an approach that maintains a neutral distance, representing something visually, defining a standpoint or moving perspective: aesthetics that American film historian Tom Gunning has described simply as the 'view'. The camera imitates viewing per se, for it behaves literally like a tourist, observer or researcher.

Tan's poetic montage links together the autonomous decontextualised film fragments, which resemble postcards set in motion, to create a developing visual narration. And she reveals these images' partial satiation with art-historical examples. Thus, she begins the film with a staged observation of nature by a woman out walking; this is filmed from a grotto with a view out to sea, very much in the style of early landscape painting. It is followed by scenes of various bathing pleasures and swimming competitions, followed by shots of lonely boats out at sea, the play of waves, whale hunting, and fishermen and sailors struggling against the blustering spray of waves in a storm. Tan employs the different colour tones of the film material like a painter, re-staging a 'moving' landscape painting in which water flows over the land with breathtaking beauty. The assembled soundtrack mixes silent sequences, short interspaces of music and historical recordings of radio traffic that resemble incantations. Increasingly, the images are transformed into a magical, yet at the same time threatening, science-fiction scenario of a world that will sink without further trace. Another aspect is characteristic of the work's structure in terms of motif and film technique. The constantly repeated image of 'setting out to sea' is always shown from the perspective of the coast; there is no return, no looking back, no recurrence of the images, only a permanent cycle of departures. The journey's destination remains open. The montage is concluded with a metaphor. It shows the image of a man in a black suit recorded against the light. He is standing helplessly on a rock around which water is swirling: man is an island.

Tan also concludes the audio drama *Brendan's Isle* with a rock. She describes a photo found on the internet, a shot that was taken by an inhabitant of one of the Canary Isles in the 1950s. The photo shows a barren crag in the midst of a foggy sea, supposed evidence of the existence of Brendan's Isle: one of the last failed attempts to locate it to date.

Brendan's journey over the sea progressed slowly; it took so long that it became a piece of life in itself, a phase in life. Historic travel not only corresponded to the conditions of one's form of progress but also to those of a way of life. In addition, Brendan's nine-year journey is a metaphor of life in a world defined by the inhospitality of nature, surrounded by moving water which certainly manifests the mediaeval image of the world, in which water drew its borders. The chance of returning from a sea voyage was minimal for a long time. And those who did return had become different people. And, by the way, it sounds almost like a science-fiction story by J. G. Ballard, but the Mars rover Opportunity (predecessor to Curiosity) – which was actually supposed to explore the planet for only three months – has now been roving the dust of the Red Planet for eight years, continuing to send fascinating images, e.g., of the wandering dunes on Mars, and the so-called Grand Canyon of Mars around Tharsis (a region with a diameter of 4,000 kilometres), images that are explicable only in as much as they are interpreted as a mirror to Earth. [...]

In her exhibition 'Point of Departure', Fiona Tan remains true to some of her major themes: the journey, the construction of identity and memory – but in the process she clearly moves away from the autobiographical approach and her self-definition as a 'professional foreigner'.

Tan has investigated individual and cultural identity in many works, most obviously autobiographically in *May You Live In Interesting Times* (1997), in which she reconstructed and re-assembled the unusual history of her globally scattered family. Her personally experienced conclusion to this film is that identity is characterised mainly by an ability to define what it is not: that despite multilayered historical, cultural and family ties it may be constituted less by belonging and more by difference. As Stuart Hall has written,

> *The subject, previously experienced as having a unified and stable identity, is becoming fragmented; composed not of a single, but of several, sometimes contradictory or unresolved, identities. [...] The very process of identification, through which we project ourselves into our cultural identities, has become more open-ended, variable and problematic. [...] [This subject] is historically, not biologically defined.*[1]

Repeatedly, Tan shifts the focus of her study to the powerful mechanisms of assimilation possessed by both individuals and cultures. The unfamiliar is woven into a zone of overlaps, where culturally defined meanings merge in an indissoluble amalgam. But what happens when the borderlines become invisible? [...] How many spaces – also those on a 'mental map' – can a person deal with before he or she becomes lost in them, without a centre? Or is the protagonist's forgetfulness actually his greatest skill, which permits a new journey? – as the film's name suggests.

Tan not only constructs the individual works in the exhibition, but also creates numerous temporal and narrative cycles with patterns of reciprocal references. Loops, constant returning to the starting point, repetitions of motifs, and extensions of time in films that are slowed down like photographs or portrait images that are speeded up cinematically (*Seven*, 2011) create a structure in which the passage of time can be understood as repetition and a cycle.

The film fragments from a different century, therefore, appear as relevant to us as the latest news from the media or the monk Brendan's existential experiences. They appear as real as they seem fictive, and as a web of references they can also function as an anticipatory view of the world. Tan uses her various sources entirely in the spirit of Walter Benjamin's materialistic understanding of history, whereby the historic object can be torn from its context and embedded into new ones. Here, in her re-use of historic images in these works, Tan links fictive constructions and imaginary images rather than documentary material. The journey on which Tan sends us – with our ears, eyes and sense of touch – leads through different ages of cultural history, when travel signified an act of boldness for good or evil. The viewer is invited to immerse him- or herself in these far distant worlds, which are reflected and reappear simultaneously in the water. These journeys take place in the mind; they consist of memories, rumours, one's own imaginations and traditional ideas, but they are no less full of impressions than real journeys. They have made such a deep impact that they cannot even be touched by time, although everything else falls victim to it. Those wishing to approach these landscapes and mental experiences must encourage people to speak and listen to their stories. They need to collect what is recorded, for without this documentation many events would not exist at all (like Brendan's journey into the blue). Basically, their effect – indeed their very existence – is proven in silent realisation. They are there, as if as a matter of course, and they will make themselves known – but only when we ask for them.

Fiona Tan
'*Inventory* – Some Notes'

Fiona Tan: Inventory, MAXXI, Rome; and Philadelphia Museum of Art, 2013, 27–34.

I

[...]
In English I find 'medium' a difficult term to handle. The word 'medium' suggests the in-between. Is this the interface between me and my audience, between concept and end result? In a nineteenth-century séance a medium was the person who could supposedly intermediate between this world and spirits from the 'other' world. This farfetched connotation to my mind gives the word hints of trickery and falsehood. And the plural term 'media' bears the terrible weight of all the world's current-day, omnipresent press and telecommunications. In Dutch we use the more down-to-earth word *drager*, which literally translated simply means 'carrier'. I prefer this word; it implies both movement and work. An artist's idea and intention is transported across and through the artwork's carrier. The carrier is a trusted ferry boat diligently rowing back and forth from the other side of the river, from my side to yours.

Of course most of the time the medium employed is rendered invisible. We look through it, because we look only at what it portrays. Like a good servant it should never be obtrusive, it must never thrust itself into the foreground of perception. The hierarchy is clear: the carrier underneath supports the image above. But any image is surely dependent upon its carrier; content would be non-existent without its form. And surely this is where art resides. Art is the in-between; suspended, floating or sandwiched in-between the intention and the reception, between the physical and the spiritual, the ubiquitous and the sublime.

There is another Dutch word which aids my thinking in this respect. When we speak of how a medium records or translates the world around us, we speak of the *optekening*: of how it is drawn. This reminds me of the etymology of the words 'photography' and 'cinematography', drawing or writing with light and with movement. I am trying with this piece to point towards the *vluchtigheid van de optekening* – the fleetingness of these filmed registrations. I sometimes feel that in the contemporary it is transitoriness itself which becomes eternalised. In one sense the media are disappearing even whilst we are watching or looking. I am reminded here of a scene from Federico Fellini's *Roma* (1972): digging for the subway has laid bare thousand-year-old murals. But once exposed to air and light, the wall paintings fade from sight before the archaeologists' eyes.

II

Lists or inventories can be tedious or stupid, but they can also be enlightening. I made my first film as a student in 1989. It was a ten-minute film, shot on Super8. Since then I have made works using the following media: U-matic (¾ inch broadband), VHS, S-VHS, Laserdisc, Video8, Hi8, 16 mm, 35 mm, miniDV, DVD, Betacam SP, HDV, Digital Betacam, Super16, HD Betacam, XDCam, HDCam, HD, 2K digital, 4K digital. Most of these moves to a new medium and an even newer camera were not voluntary from my part. Planned redundancy in the technical industries is a powerful thing. Many of these media have almost ceased to exist. I will not bore you with the even longer list of cameras I have used, nor with the list of monitors and projectors used to present the work once it has been completed.

By choosing to make time-based art and to work with audiovisual media, I am condemned, so it would seem, to the transitory. This is endemic of our contemporary life. As Charles Baudelaire wrote in *The Painter of Modern Life* (1863): 'By modernity I mean the transitory, the fugitive, the contingent which make up one half of art, the other being the eternal and the immutable.' I can try to escape into a timeless space, into a less temporary zone. But whether I will succeed only time can tell. [...]

III

The Museum. The Collection. The two are inextricably interwoven and interdependent. In my work as an artist I am also an exhibition-maker, and am indeed dependent upon both. Exactly how I present this new piece is something which will take definite shape when I am installing in the museum, in the space itself. I take

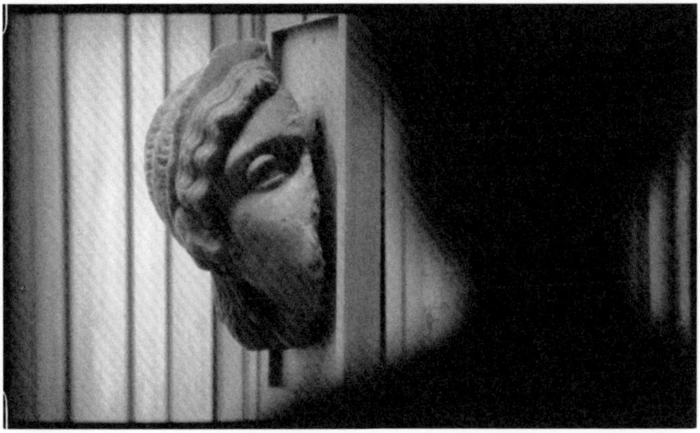

Inventory (still), 2012

pride in my exhibition-making; I like to think that I am good at it. I plan, sketch and devise all my exhibitions. Recently I have been experimenting even more radically with the exhibition as concept and as form, with modes of presentation and exhibition design. And always, right from start, I have been responding to the architectural environment: to the rooms, walls, spaces and constellations I have been asked to work within.

So now, I find myself dreaming about and preparing for a solo exhibition in the most challenging museum architecture I have encountered to date. The MAXXI swings and slopes and slides. The architecture leaves one dizzy and dazed, but as Carlos Basualdo said to me on my first visit to the museum, 'she never crashes you'. I applaud that such a building has been built in Rome of all places. But at times I do feel that I must don boxing gloves and engage in playful combat with Zaha Hadid, the building's esteemed architect.

Of course the public museum is a relatively new invention, it has been with us some 200 years. (Incidentally 'inventory' and 'invention' have the same Latin root 'to find', 'to come upon'.) The Louvre, originally royal palace and then academy, opened its doors in the weekends to the public as the Musée Central des Arts in 1793. Sir John Soane's Museum, the location where I filmed *Inventory*, prides itself as the first-ever public gallery for contemporary paintings. Rooms of Sir John's private house he transformed into a public museum in order to display his extensive private collection. He received visitors to his museum from the early

1820s onwards. A unique time capsule, it is still open to the public and remains essentially unchanged to this day.

Sir John Soane was a architect in the neoclassical age: a time when idealists believed that art could improve mankind. Neoclassicism strived for clear, straight lines and proportions. This clarity of form, so one nobly thought, could rub off on a building's inhabitants. Ironically, Soane's Museum feels to me like its antithesis. These rooms are surprisingly small and tight. The place is narrow and crowded like a rabbit's warren. And the hanging of the collection is very curious and highly debatable. The owner's loneliness and preoccupation with death speak to me from almost every room.

Without exception museums initially started out as private collections. Why collect? Why surround oneself with dead, inanimate objects? This question has occupied me repeatedly and I am not sure that I have found a satisfactory answer. But maybe I should engage in more discussions with living collectors to find out.

IV

> *Except for extremely rare cases of collections that contain all objects of a certain type, a collection is always open and could always be increased with the addition of some other element; especially if the collection is based, as was the case with Roman patricians, medieval lords, or modern galleries and museums, on a taste for accumulation and increase ad infinitum.*
> — Umberto Eco, *The Infinity of Lists*, 2009

All collections must be by nature arbitrary, inconsequent, as idiosyncratic as their owners. As Umberto Eco continues,

> *Save for highly specialised cases, collections always verge on the incongruous. A space traveller unaware of our concept of art would wonder why the Louvre contains trifles in common use such as vases, plates or salt cellars, icons of a goddess such as the Venus de Milo, representations of landscapes, portraits of normal people, grave gods and mummies, portrayals of monstrous creatures, objects of worship, images of human beings suffering torture, accounts of battles, nudes calculated to arouse sexual attraction and even archaeological finds.*

With this summary he could in fact be describing Soane's collection too.

After reading Eco's wonderful and dizzying list of lists, both literary and artistic, I was triggered for the first time to consider and categorise my own works into those consisting of one single image, those with a narrative and those which comprise of a list, a catalogue. Of course Eco too, is a great fan of lists. He taught me also that a painting can be a list, a visible catalogue which sometimes stretches beyond the boundaries of its frame. Although it sounds paradoxical, lists regularly point to the infinite. So a list or an inventory is also a desire to get to the uncharted, to unravel the secrets of the universe, manmade or otherwise. But this all sounds rather high and mighty, even if it is attractive in its ambition. Lists are also a very simple manifestation of one's desire to order and to control, whilst acknowledging all along two universal rules: that whenever possible destiny will take the path of the least resistance, and that chaos is inherent in all that surrounds us.

Adelina Vlas
'Fiona Tan's *Inventory*: Re-imagining the Past'

Fiona Tan: Inventory, MAXXI, Rome; and Philadelphia Museum of Art, 2013, 35–42.

Defined as 'a detailed list in one's view or possession' or 'the process of making such a survey',[1] an inventory is mostly associated with the recording of an accumulation or collection of objects. In her most recent work, titled *Inventory* (2012), Fiona Tan surveys, with six different moving-image camera formats, the rooms dedicated to the antiquities collection in Sir John Soane's Museum in Lincoln's Inn Fields in London. The result is a multiple-projection work that reveals intimate details of one of the most unique private residences to become a public museum while as well as a contemplative visual essay engaging with the universal human struggle over the depredations of time while unsentimentally portraying the creation of a singular Romantic visionary. Structured as a large-scale montage in which the six films are projected on the wall in an uneven grid, with each projection varying in its dimensions, *Inventory* was filmed on-site over a four-day period in September 2012.

Since the 1990s, Fiona Tan has been creating a body of work unified by her interest in memory, history and identity, both individual and collective. With *Inventory* she returns to these themes, as she focuses on the legacy of a historic figure who was himself much concerned with time's passage and human mortality. In its present state, Sir John Soane's collection is as much a meditation on history and life's transience as it is a portrait *in absentia* of one man's passion for a romanticised version of a remote past. The building that houses it, designed and redesigned by Soane from 1792 until his death in 1837, functions as a time capsule in which several centuries coexist side by side in a carefully orchestrated vision that places the collection within a whimsical architectural setting. Today's visitor to the museum encounters not only Egyptian and Greco-Roman antiquities in rooms with names that reference their defining architectural elements

– the Colonnade, the Dome, the Crypt, the Catacombs – but also a collection of eighteenth- and nineteenth-century art and artefacts in domestic rooms called the Breakfast Room, the Drawing Room, the Dining Room and so on. Soane's vision for his multi-purpose building, serving during his lifetime as a residence, a teaching museum, and a theatrical showcase for his collecting passions, endures today even as it challenges the imagination of twenty-first-century visitors with its crowded, idiosyncratic displays and diverse assemblages of objects, from relief and in-the-round sculptures to urns and even an Egyptian sarcophagus.

Tan's filmic approach to this distinctive museum could be seen as a way to slow down the viewing experience, allowing for a closer investigation of the historical materials gathered there. The antiquities densely displayed in the narrow, labyrinthine rooms of the museum are too many to be absorbed in a single visit, when the flow of visitors keeps one moving on to the next room and the next floor. Tan's cameras travel through the rooms more slowly, lingering over the spaces and the objects they contain, granting them a presence otherwise difficult to appreciate. [...]

Soane was a consummate collector, and Tan is particularly interested in how his assembling of objects over time reflected on his life and passions. Her focus on the spaces dedicated to antiquity establishes the connection between Soane and the city whose past most inspired him – Rome. John Soane (1753–1837) was a respected and successful architect who designed, among other notable buildings, the Bank of England (1788–1833) and the Dulwich Picture Gallery (1811–14) in London. Early in his career, he, like many of his peers, embarked on an extensive two-year Grand Tour of Rome, Naples and Sicily, determined to experience the greatness of the past through its ruins. Drawn to an idealised vision of ancient Greece and Rome, the young Soane developed a special attachment to the classical architectural vocabulary of antiquity, which later translated into a style characterised as eclectic neoclassicism. His defining trip to Italy, where he spent time drawing and measuring ruins, visiting the architectural structures still standing, and engaging with the art and artefacts of distant times, remained deeply engraved in his memory. Besides familiarising himself with classical architecture on this trip, Soane met the artist Giovanni Battista Piranesi (1720–78) and acquired some of his etchings. He was to take inspiration from Piranesi throughout his career, influenced in particular by the Italian artist's romanticised *Views of Rome* (c. 1750s) and his atmospheric renderings of *Imaginary Prisons* (c. 1745–50). Soane's architectural vision was definitively shaped by his experiences abroad – not only did he employ the knowledge he had acquired through the observations he made on his trip in his own innovative designs for buildings, but he also infused his structures with romantic details inspired by Piranesi's imaginative renderings.

Nowhere is that vision more eloquently expressed than in his home in Lincoln's Inn Fields. The result of many years of work, its current configuration as Sir John Soane's Museum, although not unchanged from Soane's final design, remains close to his conception, particularly in the rooms housing his antiquities. Collected over many decades after his return from Italy, the various Greek, Roman and Egyptian sculptures and architectural fragments profusely adorn every surface of these rooms. Although Soane arranged some of the objects to form an anthology of antique architecture and decoration as well as a teaching collection, their organisation in the space was deliberately idiosyncratic:

> *His goal was to create a poetic setting, using architecture to evoke the spirit of antiquity. For this reason he eschewed didactic arrangements by periods and different cultures ... Instead he displayed his collections mingled together. The museum was to be not just a repository but an inspirational setting; a springboard for the imagination.*[2]

The architect Helene Furján has observed that over Soane's lifetime the collection of dramatic spaces in the building 'metamorphosed from a museological to a theatrical structure – from a monument to a spectacular space', especially in the section Tan explores in *Inventory*:

> *These spaces manipulated hues, light and shade into glooms, gleams, glowing effulgences and enveloping aerial tints and atmospheres; they constructed, occluded and interiorised vistas that were almost agoraphobic, and dizzyingly vertical shafts that disappeared away in either direction into darkness or light; they produced effects of obscurity, uncertainty and confusion, and confounded spatial understanding.*[3]

Still present in the architecture of the rooms devoted to the display of antiquities, this sense of theatricality and spectacle continues to fulfil its intended function of confusing the visitor.[4] But Tan's use of natural light in filming Soane's antiquities rooms appears to generate a visually precise, objective record. These rooms are a memorial to a vision nurtured by the desire to re-create a time and place that, at its deepest level, only existed in the imagination of an eighteenth-century neoclassical architect. Although the rooms remain spectacular in their unique arrangements, they do not engage the viewer in an entertaining spectacle of light and shadow as Soane intended them. The theatrical experience he hoped to create for his visitors was particularly effective by candlelight. Filmed in daylight, the rooms reveal their contents more mundanely, along with some details that signal the passage of time or contemporaneity with today's viewers – modern light fixtures, cracked windows, peeling paint, museum labels, archival storage boxes – showing that the museum itself is not impervious to the changes brought by time, and making visible a process that, if left unchecked, would inevitably lead to the building's decline and ruin.

In *Inventory*, Tan's camera lingers on busts and figural sculptures represented with their eyes closed, invoking sleep or death. The peaceful expressions of some of the statues and the severe mien of others elicit a solemn, meditative mood perhaps more typical of a mausoleum than a proscenium. In writing about another of Soane's buildings, the Dulwich Picture Gallery, which joins in a single space a mausoleum and an art gallery, the art historian Carol Duncan notes that Soane deliberately constructed a play of light and darkness inside the building that was appropriate for both the art and the tombs, and that was intended 'to prompt visitors to poetic musings and imaginative reveries'. As she notes, this same strategy was deployed in his London residence, where 'the entire setting was meant to prompt meditations on the passage of time and the cycle of life and death'.[5]

As an architect, Soane was very aware of the effect of time on built structures, his own included. His meditations on death and oblivion applied to his personal legacy, as is made clear in a pen-and-watercolour drawing by his close collaborator, Joseph Michael Gandy, known as the English Piranesi. The drawing, a response to the architect's preoccupation with posterity, shows Soane's masterpiece, the Bank of England, in ruins in the future, suggesting that, like all great accomplishments of human civilisation, this building too will be subjected to time's destructive passage. It was in an attempt to counter time's inexorability that Soane decided to donate his residence to the British nation for the benefit of all lovers of painting, sculpture and architecture, stipulating that the interior arrangements be kept in the state in which they were left at his death, a wish that has on the whole been fulfilled by the public administrators.

John Soane was part of the generation of architects that throughout the eighteenth and nineteenth centuries contributed to the dissemination of an international set of standards for the collecting and display of art. This generation shared a knowledge and a passion for the ancient world that were acquired during the

Grand Tour and that were translated into the neoclassical architecture that dominated museum buildings into the early twentieth century. As inventories of the past, museums reflect our collecting impulses, as Soane's unchanged arrangements reflect his. They contribute to shaping how we perceive and interpret our past and in the process rigidly frame certain versions of history in the public imagination. The Greek temple architecture of the Philadelphia Museum of Art, the first North American venue for *Inventory*, indicates its direct connection with the neoclassical tradition. [...]

Inventory is not the first instance in which Tan has attempted to create a visual index of her subject of interest. In *Countenance* (2002), *Correction* (2004) and *Provenance* (2008), the cataloguing impulse is made manifest in a series of portraits of people in particular places: Berlin, the US penal system, Amsterdam. But *Inventory* is more in line with another of Tan's works that is similarly devoid of human presence – *Island* (2008), a black-and-white portrait of the austere landscape of the Swedish island of Gotland that shares the non-narrative, anti-cinematic approach of *Inventory*. Tan's newest work also continues her investigation of film and photography as tools for building a visual index, a concept she further explores in *Inventory* through the use of multiple camera formats. Each of the six projected films was recorded by a different device, and together they represent the artist's technical inventory: Super-8, 16 mm and 35 mm film, analogue video, DVD and HD. The quality of each projection is different: some brighter, some grainier, some sharper. By referencing the time in which each format was in popular use, the variations add another layer of historical detail to a work characterised by a diversity of coexisting timeframes. In other, earlier works Tan similarly sought to negotiate the tension between still and moving images as well as the place of moving-image technology in the lexicon of artistic production. Tan's inclusion of footage recorded by different types of cameras demonstrates the resilience of a medium associated with contemporary practices, a resilience partly due to its unrivalled power to document and represent reality.

In capturing the interior of Sir John Soane's Museum, Tan also makes use of static long takes, a strategy she has previously employed in works such as *Correction*, *Island* and *Provenance* to blur the boundaries between still and moving images, establishing a new visual idiom that has been described as 'filmed photographs'.[6] This strategy emphasises the superiority of the moving image as a medium engaged with temporality – capturing images in time, replaying them as echoes of the past in the present – as the artist continues to investigate and illuminate our responses to the transience of human existence. This related body of works shows Tan's deep concern not only with the search for identity, whether of people or places, but also with the possibility of documenting the world, past and present, in new and thought-provoking ways.

Inventory reminds us of the artist's long-standing preoccupation with time, memory and place, as well as her desire to reveal in poetic ways our various responses to the inevitability of decline and decay and our individual and collective mortality. Although the images captured in *Inventory* lack a living human presence, the history of the place she records and its founder's conception bear eloquent testimony to the human impulse and desire to preserve and immortalise the past and oneself through collecting. Collections, and by extension museums, are repositories of cultural histories shaped by personal as well as shared narratives. Tan's new work literally surveys these collecting impulses, especially as embodied by the incongruous and idiosyncratic assortments of objects in Sir John Soane's Museum, but she remains aware that the desire to categorise, explored in some of her other works through a more analytical approach, is a reflection of the fundamental human yearning for order and control. Tan's concern with the tenuous relationship between sight, memory and knowledge, especially as manifested in *Inventory*, leaves us questioning our memories of a place we may have thought we knew until it was revealed to us through the artist's discerning eye.

Fiona Tan
Voice-over to *Depot*

I

He enters the storage room. In the corner he finds a notebook. He opens it to the first page: Sea star, sea lily, sea biscuit, sea cucumber. Sea horse, sea lion, sea unicorn, sea cow, sea dragon.

Sea urchin. Like blind old warriors they slowly and patiently transgress the ocean floor. As a child he once accidentally stood on one. Just like a hedgehog's, the spines were sharp as needles. But they were also brittle and snapped off after lodging themselves underneath the skin.

II

Glass. He realises that he sees the world through glass. Grimy and mottled and tinted windows. The glass of his reading glasses. The looking glass. The magnifying glass. The lens of the camera. These jars and vials.

The Ancient Greeks called the paper nautilus 'the sailor of the sea'. The female nautilus secretes and shapes a paper-thin shell – a fragile egg case in which she also resides.

The shells are fragile as glass, but he once found a whole one, perfect and glistening white, larger than his own hand.

III

His dreams as a child were always at sea. A night-time journey, the moon reflecting across black ripples. He could swim through air. Underwater he could breathe.

There is something ancient and alien about horseshoe crabs. For the Japanese they are reborn Samurai warriors who sacrificed their lives in battle.

He finds himself surrounded by these sad messages in bottles, which he tries to read and interpret. Like photographs, they speak first of death and, only after that, of what they once were.

He remembers the comical image of encountering his father underwater, who, being shortsighted, always wore glasses. His father had attached an old pair of thick-rimmed spectacles to the inside of his snorkelling mask with a suction cup, giving him the appearance of an underwater professor.

IV

He wonders about the function of dreams. Does a fish or an octopus dream? Memory and dreams are closely related. Can an octopus remember?

He turns the page and reads:

We do not remember, we rewrite memory much as history is rewritten.

In the summer he loved most of all to swim in the sea – snorkelling at low tide, down by the reef at the edge of the bay. Sun on his back, shallow warm water supporting his body, the sound of his own breathing.

Once, he got his legs caught up in the metres-long kelp which grew like a forest beyond the edge of the reef. The waves crashed onto the sharp reef edge; he thought he would drown. Like tentacles, the strands of kelp wrapped around his feet and pulled ever tighter.

V

For some reason this specimen reminds him of unicorns. The horn of a unicorn was worth more than gold. But such a horn was in fact the tusk of a narwhal, the unicorn of the sea. In powdered form the tusk was prized as an antidote for poison and even for melancholy.

In his childhood memories everything stays the same. But, as a grown man, he returned after many years only to find the same reef from his childhood stripped bare and barren. Haunted and deserted like a graveyard. Sadly, he remembers the story of a Russian guide during the Second World War, who would give tours through the empty galleries of the Hermitage in St. Petersburg, offering complete descriptions of paintings which were no longer there.

He reads again from the notebook. To his great surprise it is here that he finds immortality. Jellyfish have roamed the seas for at least 500 million years, but there is more than that. One species is thought to escape death. They are able to grow backwards to infancy, transforming themselves from medusa back to a polyp.

VI

Natural history came of age in the nineteenth century – the golden era of exploration and expedition; a time when maps lost all their blank spaces. Time and space expanded. And, together with all that forward-thinking, swelled the insatiable desire to amass, to collect, to catalogue and collate, to measure and to circumscribe, to describe, to own, to conquer.

He reads:

Memories must make do with their delirium, with their drift.

On the last page he finds a note written in haste:

It is time to abandon hope of a better past.

Long forgotten, a picture resurfaces. He remembers now the ferry crossing, sitting on deck in the wind and sun and looking out across the bay. 'Blowers' they were called – white fountains of water shooting up across the calm waters of the bay – a regular occurrence that no one paid much attention to. Only now he realises that this must have been whales, spouting as they came up for air.

Fiona Tan
Excerpt from 'Depot'

Fiona Tan: Depot, artist's book, BALTIC Centre for Contemporary Art, Gateshead, 2015.

INTRODUCTION

'Whale-road' is an old English word for 'ocean'. I cannot think of a more poetic nor fitting description of the sea. This artist publication has been printed to accompany the art project *Depot* and the resulting exhibition of the same name. Rather than a comprehensive catalogue it aims to provide brief insight into my research leading up to the exhibition and to share with you some of the wonderful and wondrous images and readings I have come across whilst doing so – a tip of the iceberg from an inspiring and at times surprising aquatic voyage.

More than once, the sea and water have featured in my film and video installations. As a child growing up in Australia I was fortunate to spend a considerable amount of time close to the sea. Furthermore, I had parents who showed me how varied, rich and beautiful marine life can be. So this project has a personal point of departure, but it also tries to reflect upon mankind's relationship with animals, particularly those of the sea, and how that has changed over time.

In 1836 a ship ran aground on the rocks of the treacherous Chale Bay on the southern coast of the Isle of Wight. As sightseers flocked to the site, Alexander Dabell, a Victorian entrepreneur, realised that the ravine running down to the shore known as Blackgang Chine had potential as a key tourist destination. Dabell planted gardens, and cut and carved pathways and panoramic views in the ravine, creating the first amusement park in the UK.

A year after the Chine opened to the public, an eight-ton whale was stranded at the Needles, a little further along the coastline. Dabell purchased the whale carcass, sold its blubber, bleached its bones, and built a special hut to house the skeleton. To descend through the Chine, visitors now had to pass through the hut full of souvenirs and knick-knacks, a whale skeleton overhead. Through erosion, the coastal ravine on which the park sat has since been destroyed. But the attraction park, moved further inland to safer ground, has remained open to the public to this day.

As is well known, whales were extensively hunted in the eighteenth and nineteenth centuries. Their blubber and oil was a primary source of energy; only gradually during the twentieth century was whale oil replaced by fossil fuels. It is no longer common knowledge that between 1752 and 1849 Newcastle was one of England's principal whaling ports. Even as late as 1930 Newcastle shipbuilders Armstrong, Whitworth & Co. built the whale factory steamer, the *Tafelberg*, designed to process whale oil and blubber on board at sea.

Up to the 1970s whale oil, bone and meat were industrially used in a variety of products including cosmetics, margarine, fertiliser, pet food and lubricants. In *Moby-Dick* (1851) Melville describes how whale oil was used to anoint royalty, but also, more importantly, as fuel for lamps. Indeed the term for measuring light – the lumen – comes from the brightness of a single pure white spermaceti candle.

Britain only began whaling in earnest in the mid-eighteenth century. As Philip Hoare writes:

> *Once [the industry of whaling began], however, Britain excelled, employing the same efficiency it brought to slavery. On both were built the foundations of empire: the trade in humans for sugar; and in whales, for oil. As a result, London became the best-lit city in the world. By the 1740s, five thousand street lamps were burning whale oil, expunging the primal darkness.*
> — Philip Hoare, *Leviathan, or The Whale*, London: Fourth Estate, 2008

Sedna, in Inuit mythology, is the goddess of the sea and the whale is her most majestic subject. Many versions of the Sedna legend exist. In one she is a voracious giant, in another a beautiful maiden, and in yet another, she is a mistreated orphan. In one rendition, Sedna is a winsome girl who has spurned all of her suitors, choosing instead a bird as her mate. Outraged, her father kills her husband and takes Sedna away in a boat. No matter the reason for arriving there or the shape of her character, once at sea Sedna is thrown overboard. She clings to the edge of the boat, and her father chops off her fingers, one by one. Sedna then turns into a voracious deity of the lower realm, ruling over all the creatures that dwell

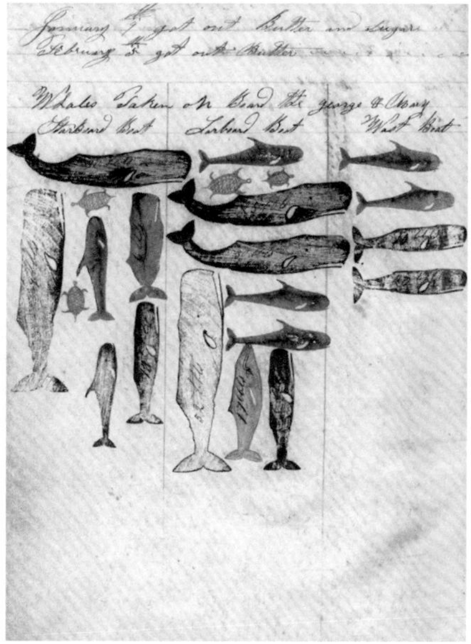

Page from the journal kept by Captain Samuel B. Devoll onboard the bark *George and Mary's* 1855–7 whaling voyage out of Westport (Massachusetts, US), 19th c.

in the sea, and each of her severed fingers turns into an animal: a right whale, a narwhal, a beluga, a seal and so forth.

> *The beached whale was peculiar among a rich array of portents and omens in that it carried in its imposing bulk both associations of riches and reminders of their penitential obliteration. The great leviathans, their sonar scrambled by the North Sea sand, were migrating not only from Atlantic to Arctic, but from the realm of myth and morality to that of matter and commodity, sometimes becoming stranded on the submarine slopes of Dutch cultural contradiction. [...]*
> *The greatest of the Haarlem masters, Hendrick Goltzius, who had made a drawing of a pilot whale stranged at Zaandvoort in 1594, made a more detailed and splendid drawing that was engraved by his pupil, Jacob Matham. Matham followed Goltzius' famous error in supposing a fin to be the whale's ear, but in other respects, the print was anatomically faithful, and became the prototype for a number of versions.*
> — Simon Schama, *The Embarrassment of Riches: An Interpretation of Dutch Culture in the Golden Age*, London: Harper Perennial, 2004

Beached whales have always drawn crowds and attracted considerable attention. In fact the exhibiting of a whale's carcass has been a touring attraction more than once. On the Belgian coast at Ostend a blue whale was stranded in 1827. Its skeleton was preserved and subsequently toured across Belgium, Germany, France and England. In London it was displayed at Charing Cross in 1831 where visitors could enter through the jaws and – like Jonah, but in considerably more comfort – sit inside the ribcage.

It seems that there were three whales which toured Europe from 1953 on – Jonah, Goliath and Hercules. They were caught and killed near Trondheim, off the coast of Norway. Jonah was a 70-tonne fin whale, 23 metres long. Another fin whale, Goliath, was 22 metres long and 68 tonnes. Little is known of Hercules. It appears that he (or she) was disposed of in Spain when a circus went bust. A decade ago, a man from Barnsley began searching for Jonah, which he remembered seeing as a child. He found a handful of people who had a vague early memory of having seen a whale as a sort of circus amusement, but they nearly all presumed that this was only a dream or a figment of their childish imagination.

But after diligent research, stories begin to unfold. Goliath's carcass was purchased from his hunters by Giuseppe Erba of Turin. The whale's carcass was preserved with 7,000 litres of formalin; the hope was that the public would be able to walk into its interior. And so it was. Golia, as he was then known, was installed in the Giardini della Cittadella, a grand manicured park in the centre of Turin. It was summertime, and despite initial excitement, public opinion swayed as the stench emanating from Golia increased. The show lasted only six days, closing on Sunday, 25 July 1954. The details aren't clear but it seems that Golia travelled to other piazzas across Italy, and at some point along the way was bought by a pair from Switzerland, Pierre Siffert and Jean Rezzonico. The carcass was then renamed Goliath, and toured both Eastern and Western Europe before disappearing sometime in the 1980s.

On a divergent path, Jonah travelled to Oslo, to be examined and exhibited at Oslo University. His organs were removed, lungs inflated and a refrigeration unit installed internally. The whale was then loaded onto a specially constructed extended trailer – at the time the biggest lorry in the world. After touring Norway, Jonah's carcass went on a twenty-five-year voyage to towns in Europe, Japan and Africa. Over the years he passed into the hands of circus owners and showmen,

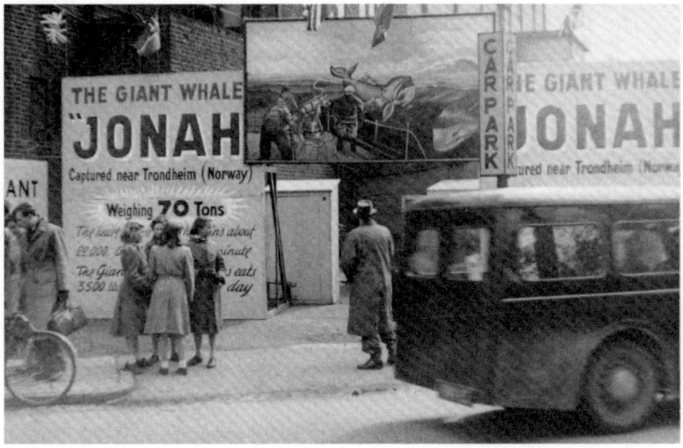

Jack Leeson, *Jonah the Whale Show*, Rugby Fair, GB, front view, March 1954

and finally into those of yet another Swiss businessman. At some point Jonah's appeal waned and the lorry with whale carcass was moved into storage near the Dutch/Belgian border, staying there for thirty-odd years. One report states that Jonah has since been bought by another showman and is now back in the UK undergoing restoration.

In 1997, a newborn grey whale beached on the coast of California by Marina del Rey. Despite concerted efforts, her mother could not be located. Comatose, hypoglycemic and emaciated the whale was given emergency medical care. The infant, a female who was given the name J. J. was then taken to Sea World where she lived in captivity for fourteen months – the only grey whale to ever do so. On 1 April 1998, measuring 31 feet and weighing 19 tonnes, J. J. was returned to the sea. The tracking device with which she was equipped was soon lost and it is not known what became of her.

The Thames River whale met a different fate. On Friday 20 January 2006 a juvenile female northern bottlenose whale was discovered swimming in the River Thames in central London. A photo of her dorsal fin protruding from the water with the Houses of Parliament behind her, went around the world. The whale appeared to have gotten lost – far away from her northerly habitat. The media coverage and public reaction bore testimony to current sentiments towards marine mammals:

The London whale was doomed form the moment it entered the estuary, and from which it was scooped up and carried in a procession back towards the sea, watched by news crews and crowds on the Thames bridges. As it lay on its inflated pontoon, the whale's frantic muscular movements began to flag. At seven o'clock that evening, it finally expired, somewhere near Gravesend, two hours from freedom. Borne on its rubber bier, its tearful attendants asked that the cameras be turned off in respect for its passing.
— Philip Hoare, *Leviathan, or The Whale*, 2008

The Thames River whale's bones were conserved by the Natural History Museum in London and the skeleton was displayed to the public in 2011 at the Natural History Museum in Tring.

Natural history came of age in the nineteenth century – the golden era of exploration and expedition; a time when maps lost all their blank spaces. Time and space expanded. And, together with all that forward-thinking, swelled the insatiable desire to amass, to collect, to catalogue and collate; to measure and to circumscribe, to describe, to own, to conquer.
— Fiona Tan, from the voice-over to *Depot*, 2015

In 1752, Voltaire (1694–1778) wrote the short story *Micromégas*. It is both a seminal work in the development of the genre of science fiction and a satirical commentary. Micromégas, an inhabitant of one of the planets that orbits the star Sirius, stands at 120,000 feet tall. Banished from his court due to heresy, he decides to travel. Along the way, he meets the secretary of the Academy of Saturn, a man less than a twentieth of his size, a 'dwarf' standing only 6,000 feet tall. Upon their arrival on Earth they determine that a planet so preposterously small must be devoid of life. But by chance, the secretary from Saturn spots a tiny speck, and, using a microscope, discovers that it is a whale.

But they struggle to make sense of this:

Finally the Saturnian saw something elusive that moved in the shallow waters of the Baltic sea; it was a whale. He carefully picked it up with his little finger and, resting it on the nail of his thumb, showed it to the Sirian, who began laughing for a second time at the ludicrously small scale of the things on our planet. The Saturnian,

persuaded that our world was inhabited, figured very quickly that it was inhabited only by whales ...
— Voltaire, *Micromégas*, 1752

Leviathan. In ancient Near Eastern, Jewish and Christian literature and iconography, Leviathan was represented as a dangerous sea creature – a monster of the sea.

In 1651 Thomas Hobbes took up 'Leviathan' as the title for his treatise on government and human nature. He argued that civil war and the brute situation of the state of nature ('the war of all against all') can only be avoided through strong undivided government and the rule of an absolute sovereign. Unlike his predecessors and contemporaries, he argued that there is no such thing as the common good, due to the variability and diversity of human desires. Instead community could be organised around a shared fear of a greater evil, the fear of violent death. For him, Leviathan is a necessity.

For me, the word 'Leviathan' illustrates the paradigm shift in our perception both of nature and of humanity. Whereas the whale was once synonymous with the Leviathan, it is now seen as innocent, gentle, intelligent and above all, as an endangered and threatened creature. [...]

Denis Gielen
'Memory, Too, Holds Its Breath'

Fiona Tan: L'Archive des ombres / Shadow Archive, Musée des Arts Contemporains, Grand-Hornu, 2019, 112–7. Translated from French by Emiliano Battista.

Depot (2015) is a film that Fiona Tan shot in the storerooms of the ichthyology collections of two natural history museums, Berlin's Museum für Naturkunde and Leiden's Naturalis Biodiversity Center. Precise and poetic, the film's construction relies on the parallel flow of contemplative shots of marine specimens (preserved in formaldehyde or as skeletons) and of a voice-over that gives the viewer glimpses into the reverie of a fictional male character – probably a curator of the collections and the artist's alter ego. Like the absorbing spectacle of the creatures we see in the film, this reverie is itself a plunge into the sea, placing us among the limuli and nautili. More importantly, it is also, like all reveries, a plunge into an 'inner sea': that of the soul of a poet. Baudelaire writes: 'Man – a free man – always loves the sea / and in its endlessly unrolling surge / will contemplate his soul as in a glass.'[1] Thanks to neuro-imaging technology, science has recently been able to confirm this analogy between the sea and reverie, between the soul's movement and the sea's: scientists aptly describe the activity of the brain when the mind wanders as a 'large wave'. Moreover, when our attention is not aroused by anything in particular, a phenomenon known as 'dark energy' (an electric wave of slow frequency but great amplitude) courses through us like a groundswell; scientists have observed that this process repeats every ten seconds. According to the immunologist and writer Jean-Claude Ameisen:

> *This 'dark energy' of the brain is what feeds our memories, our daydreams, our intuitions, our unconscious deciphering of the meaning of our existence – when we are awake, when we are asleep and thus not in direct contact with the events of the external world, and when our minds wander.*[2]

The two tracks of *Depot*, the visual and the verbal, which unfold and intertwine over the course of the film, create between them a network of associations in which the sighting of a sea urchin, for example, calls to mind the childhood memory of having 'accidentally stood on one'. Following this helical axis, the film evolves to the rhythm of the 'portraits' of sea animals and of fragmented readings taken – says the voice-over – from the notebook that the mysterious character opens at the start of the film. Thus, *Depot* begins with a list of the common names of marine species that owe their poetic sonority to the repetition of the word 'sea': 'Sea star, sea lily, sea biscuit, sea cucumber. Sea horse, sea lion, sea unicorn, sea cow, sea dragon. Sea urchin.'

The immutability of the archetypal museum, the strangeness of the sea creatures, the nostalgia of childhood memories, the slowness of the images, the calm voice: everything in *Depot* converges toward melancholy. This is the case, in the first place, because to plunge into these storerooms is to encounter death. While museums of natural history are supposed to present the panoply of life on Earth, what we see, in fact, are animals or skeletons preserved like so many 'still lifes', embodying the paradox of a scientific vision that must asphyxiate life in order to be able to observe it through optical instruments.

> *Glass. He realises that he sees the world through glass. Grimy and mottled and tinted windows. The glass of his reading glasses. The looking glass. The magnifying glass. The lens of the camera. These jars and vials ... He finds himself surrounded by these sad messages in bottles, which he tries to read and interpret. Like photographs, they speak first of death and, only after that, of what they once were.*

There is as well, beyond the museum and the deadly sciences, the melancholy that is specific to the sea: to the way we see it, to the image we have of it from myths, legends, novels and encyclopaedias. Jules Michelet, a prophet of the vulgarisation of science in the nineteenth century and a marvellous writer, perfectly captured the sadness of the sea in one of his most beautiful books, *The Sea* (1861). He regarded the sea as the 'unfinished' part of the world. For a positivist mind such as his, animated as it was by the utopia of social and scientific progress, the sea had not attained the ideal of 'fixity' toward which natural history strives, the 'fixity' achieved by the terrestrial animals, which superseded their amphibian predecessors: 'If the life of the sea has a dream, a wish, a confused desire, it is that of fixity.' The creatures that reproduce and devour each other in the sea with 'wild fierce joy' and 'marvellous health' suffer, according to Michelet, from the dynamic antagonism between life and death because of their biological inability to escape perpetual movement and thus make the historical leap toward a sedentary life. 'What is melancholy in the sea is not her carelessness to multiply death, but her impotence to reconcile progress with the excess of movement.'[3] A little further on, as he explores the slightly delirious idea of a genealogy of the living in which the unfinished world – the inferior and still chaotic world of the sea – endures like a memory, Michelet concludes:

> *Great mother that hath commenced life, thou canst not perfect it; allow thy daughter, the Earth, to continue the work. You see it, even in your bosom; your children think of Earth and long for its fixity; they approach her, offer her their homage. It is for thee still to commence the series of new beings, by an unexpected prodigy, a grandiose rough draft of the warm amorous life, of blood, of milk, of tenderness which will have its development in the terrestrial races.*[4]

Finally, what gives *Depot* its properly elegiac character is the melancholy provoked by the irruptions, here and there in the flow of images and the unfolding of the narrative, of childhood memories. The feeling of sadness that attaches to those memories is intimately linked to nostalgia, to the painful awareness that we are subject to the irreversibility of time, and to our knowledge that memory is the only place where we will be able to find still intact the cities we once lived in or the homes we have loved:

> *In his childhood memories everything stays the same. But, as a grown man, he returned after many years only to find the same reef from his childhood stripped bare and barren. Haunted and deserted like a graveyard.*

More than a gallery of specimens that bears witness to the immense diversity of marine life, *Depot* is also a bestiary, or even, given the meticulous gaze of Tan's camera, a cabinet of wonders, wherein extraordinary animal figures are permeated by their natural or legendary auras – much like the narwhal, whose tusk, 'in powdered form', the voice-over reminds us, 'was prized as an antidote for poison and indeed for melancholy'. The precursors of the natural history museum were the *studiolo* and the *Wunderkammer*, which started appearing in Italy and northern Europe, respectively, during the Renaissance. Originally, though, as we can

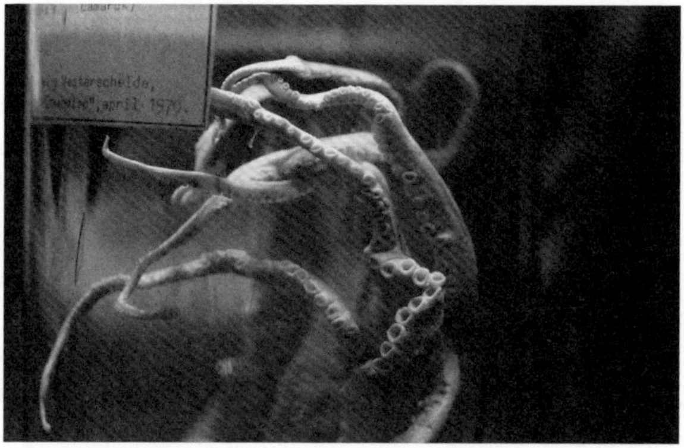

Depot (still), 2015

see from the critique formulated by the French naturalist Jean-Baptiste Lamarck against shellfish collections, they were not so much instruments of scientific knowledge as of aesthetic reverie:

> *In truth, for a long time conchology was nothing more than a vain object of amusement, a subject of ostentation and, even, of luxury. Consequently, conchology collections hardly produced in the mind of their owners or their observers anything more than a sterile admiration – for the multiplicity or singularity of shell formations, for their almost infinite variety, and for the vibrancy of their colours.*[5]

Tan has not erased from *Depot* this culture of 'amusement', founded, as it was, on the taste for 'rarity' that foreshadowed the birth of the natural history museum. On the contrary, her film wants to draw attention to that culture – hence, the installation she conceived for its premiere. Although it has since been shown in darkened rooms, *Depot*'s first showing, at the BALTIC Centre for Contemporary Art in Gateshead, England, in 2015, took place in a space that was charged, haunted even, by the genius of the sea: the North Sea all around it. Indeed, to see the film, viewers had to climb a short flight of stairs that led into the trailer of a semi-truck Tan had transformed into a cabinet of wonders. Besides *Depot*, it contained an extraordinary collection of models of sea molluscs made in the nineteenth century by the famous German glassmakers Leopold and Rudolf Blaschka as well as the twisted tusk of a narwhal. The truck itself was an almost exact replica of the one used in the 1950s to transport 'Jonah', an embalmed whale weighing seventy tons, to various fairgrounds – a truck that bore on its sides in large block letters, as Tan's truck also did, the words 'The Giant Whale "Jonah"'. Lastly, the stairs that led up to the 'trailer-cabinet' were reminiscent of those used by members of the public to visit the comfortable interior of 'The Pavilion of the Whale', a famous nineteenth-century attraction constructed from the skeleton of a whale that had washed ashore in Ostend in 1827 and that, like Jonah, toured Europe.[6]

The whale – whether from mythology, science, collective history or an individual memory – is a central figure of *Depot*, the film and the eponymous exhibition. A significant part of the 2015 exhibition catalogue is devoted to the iconography of this curious animal, from the eighteenth to the end of the twentieth century. It goes without saying that these pages tell us less about the nature of the whale than about cultural representations of whales over time. To human eyes, the whale was, at first, a monster, a freak of nature, a giant, a disproportionate creature; but whales were also – as we can see in the number of seventeenth-century engravings of beached whales – a veritable public attraction. Mostly, though, these scenes of beached whales are striking because the animal, depicted in its monumentality, becomes a landscape: a mountain climbed by Lilliputians, a cave to visit. And this metamorphosis can happen, as we know, even in the open sea. Milton wrote:

> *The fisherman belated at night in the North Sea saw an isle, a shoal, which, like the back of an enormous mountain, lay upon the water, and in that isle or shoal he fastened his anchor. The isle fled and carried him away. That isle was Leviathan.*[7]

From this surreal iconography, Tan selected a single but enormous image for her show at the BALTIC, which featured, in addition to *Depot*, a monumental projection of found footage documenting the flensing of a whale at a whaling port. Entitled *Leviathan* in reference to the Biblical story of a sea monster, this film also referred the visitor to the context of the exhibition space itself: the port of Newcastle, a stone's throw away from the venue, was an important site for industrial whaling from the 1750s to the 1850s.

Whether washed ashore, where they become an object of curiosity, or hunted to supply the lubricants used for machinery during the Industrial Revolution and oil for domestic and urban lighting, whales have long been the sad victims of fate, or of men. For a nineteenth-century evolutionary naturalist such as Michelet, the whale illustrated the pathetic desire to escape the water and live on land: as such, the giant mammal embodied, better than any other marine creature, the 'melancholy of the sea'. Michelet writes:

> *Escaping from his enemy, the water, he found another enemy in the land, and his mighty lungs were overwhelmed, and collapsed. His magnificent blowing apertures throwing up columns of water thirty feet into the air, are, in themselves, proofs of an organisation infantine and rude. In throwing up that column towards the sky the panting blower seems to say, 'Oh, nature, why hast thou made me a serf?'*[8]

Over the final images of *Depot* – in which we see, like the last links of a submarine evolution, gigantic skeletons – the narrator's inner voice evokes, albeit differently, these 'panting blowers':

> *Long forgotten, a picture resurfaces. He remembers now the ferry crossing, sitting on deck in the wind and sun and looking out across the bay. 'Blowers' they were called – white fountains of water shooting up across the calm waters of the bay – a regular occurrence that no one paid much attention to. Only now he realises that this must have been whales, spouting as they came up for air.*[9]

While Michelet had seen melancholy in the whale, the speaker in *Depot* – perhaps unburdened by his lack of knowledge – sees in it an even more universal movement of the soul: the flux of memory. Like the whale that swims in the depths of the sea until it shoots up to the surface for air, memory, too, holds its breath as it rests in the depths of the unconscious, until the moment arrives when it irrupts into consciousness. In contrast to science, which requires previous knowledge, the work of memory recognition is produced unwittingly, as it is propelled by the very movement of the memory that suddenly manifests itself on the surface of the mind. [...]

Laura Cumming

'Mementos from the Deep', on *Depot* at BALTIC Centre for Contemporary Art, Gateshead

Exhibition review, *The Guardian*, 19 July 2015.

In the autumn of 1827, a blue whale was seen swimming off the coast of Belgium. The exact nature of what happened next is debated, but within a matter of weeks its preserved skeleton began a European tour that reached London in 1831. Visitors could enter through the open jaws and sit inside the ribcage, like Jonah. Fascinated by this tale, Fiona Tan has produced a captivating installation that invokes the many whales that have been dragged about the world for our wonder and amusement. A gigantic lorry (a facsimile of the one that ferried dead whales around Britain in the 1950s) is beached in the BALTIC, giving the sheer measure of the creature. Clamber inside and you will certainly see bones, and whales aplenty in astonishing old photographs, but Tan has reversed the historic experience. The skeleton is no longer empty: it contains an ocean of images.

In *Depot* (2015), these come in the form of a classic Tan film – beautiful, slow-moving, so absorbing you could watch it over and again – which balances an interior monologue concerning one man's lifelong passion for the undersea world with an equivalent narrative filmed in the amber twilight of a natural history museum. He remembers the long-ago past, a life spent searching for strange creatures beneath the waves, dreaming that he can breathe in this watery element; and the camera moves pensively among these creatures, suspended in glass vessels of formaldehyde. Two kinds of memory are preserved. Tan's film circles the exhibits as if they were still alive, so animate do they appear in their shining fluid, not so much dead as sleeping, while the narrator's words turn them back into a

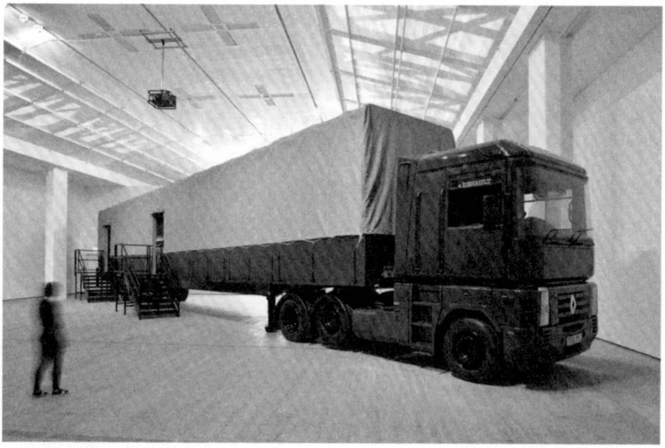

Depot (exhibition view), BALTIC, Gateshead, 2015

shoal of myths. Here is the narwhal, the true unicorn of the waves; here is the swordfish, a Samurai reincarnated in Japanese folklore; here is the sea urchin, an old blind warrior roaming the ocean's floor. Fish, eyeless and lacquered, vector forward like spiky bronze dragons; seahorses ride high in their glass vitrines; nameless serpentine forms turn gold in the museum light. The narrator describes them as sad messages in bottles, turning up in the present long after the writer has gone. Like photographs, they speak of death before they speak of life; and some are now all that remain of memory too. Many of these creatures are now extinct. [...]

As always, Tan's camera seems to see everything as if for the first time, intent with wonder, acutely perceptive, even when she is filming the same object over and again from different angles. As always, her film is delicate and humane. But as the classical strings hover in the air, intensifying the sense of estrangement and melancholy, she seems to be portraying time's depredations as our memories of the dead come and go, shuffling, slipping, fading like dreams. The film is itself an elegy.

Fiona Tan
Excerpts from the voice-over to *Ascent*

Both the victor and the vanquished are but drops of dew,
but bolts of lightning – thus should we view the world.
— Ōuchi Yoshitaka, 1551

[...]

SCENE 4

MARY: I'm sitting in an armchair in the study with my eyes closed. And I think of you, Hiroshi. This is how I like to start each day. I hear your voice. I remember that you like to tell stories.
One day an old bamboo cutter came across a stalk of bamboo which was shining and glowing from inside with a mysterious light. After cutting the stalk open, he rejoiced to find inside the hollow stem an infant the size of his thumb. The cutter, who was childless, took the girl home, where he and his wife raised her as their own. Thereafter the old bamboo cutter found that, whenever he cut down a cane of bamboo, a gold nugget was lodged inside. The girl grew to become a woman of extraordinary beauty.
Emptiness or void, you explained patiently, never has negative connotations in the Japanese language. Just like the shining bamboo, a void has the potential to be filled.
HIROSHI *(speaking in Japanese)*: In Japanese the word for void is *utsuro*. But if you change the last syllable to 'wa', the word becomes *utsuwa*, meaning 'bowl'. A bowl can receive and hold some very important things; a bowl for rice; a bowl for tea. If a 'roi' is added to the end the word then becomes *utsuroi* – 'transience', a word representing a concept of time rather than of space.

But to get back to the story:

MARY: The story continues, like many legends do, with princes and tests (which they all fail) and with even the Emperor of Japan falling in love with this strange and beautiful woman. As it turns out the woman is a visitor from the moon, a guest from the heavens. Homesick, she decides to return from whence she came.

She flies back to the moon, but not before leaving a letter for the lovesick Emperor. This farewell letter she has perfumed with a drop of the elixir for eternal life. But the Emperor gives orders for the letter to be burned at the top of Mount Fuji, whose highest peak is the place which is closest to heaven. He does not desire immortality if that means that he will never see her again. It is said that the smoke from the burning letter can be seen to this day.

I open my eyes. Back here, in the land of the living.

SCENE 5

MARY: A parcel has arrived! After the postman has gone, I'm impatient to open it, tearing off first the brown paper and tape and then removing a dark purple cotton cloth elegantly folded and knotted at the top. The heavy cardboard box is full to the brim.

I recognise your small, neat handwriting, slightly faded but still legible. I lift it up to take it into my study. But it slips from my hands. Photos, notebooks and papers spill and scatter across the floor.

What to bring:

a sun hat or cap;
a warm beanie is also recommended;
light and warm clothing in layers; a change of clothes;
good, sturdy hiking boots;
warm socks, two pairs;
gloves;
backpack;
rain gear;
insulated parka;
backpack rain-cover;

water and other liquids (2–3 litres recommended);
food (one or two meals);
small first-aid kit;
can of compressed oxygen;
lots of cash, in particular 100 yen coins;
garbage bags;
walking stick;
flashlight or headlight;
towel;
toilet paper;
earplugs, if you intend to stay in one of the mountain huts;
health or travel insurance documentation;
sunglasses;
sunscreen;
lip balm.

SCENE 6

MARY: The ascent of Mount Fuji is open only in the summer months of July through to mid-September. The hike from the foot of the mountain is divided into ten stations, and there are paved roads up to the fifth station, which is about 2,300 metres above sea level.
The ascent from the fifth station of the most popular trail on the northern flank can take anywhere between three and eight hours, while the descent can take from two to five hours.

SCENE 7

MARY: Here at the fifth station of the Yoshida Trail ...
HIROSHI: ... we are already quite high up. You wonder, perhaps, what I am hoping to achieve and why I have come here. As you well know, I am not a sporting man, but I am glad to escape the humidity and heat of Tokyo. Sometimes a journey makes itself necessary. I have packed only the minimum. My backpack is light.

I am impatient to get going. All around me there is an infectious atmosphere of nervous excitement.
Seen from close up Mount Fuji is nothing more than one huge heap of volcanic ash and solidified lava. It isn't nearly as attractive close up as from a distance. Involuntarily I think of the goddess of all volcanoes, Kono-hana, who is said to dwell on Mount Fuji. [...]

SCENE 10

MARY: From the top shelf I take down a book of his prints. The first image of Hokusai's series 'Thirty-Six Views of Mount Fuji' is known as *The Great Wave*. Nowadays it is sold on mouse mats, tea towels, coffee mugs. But I had overlooked the small peak of Fuji in the background, to the right of the great wave. Across the centuries the mountain is a silent watchful eye, looking down at all human activity as though we were ants.
But time is my enemy. And these images before me are exercises in certainty, in permanence.

SCENE 11

MARY: Inexpensive and produced in large numbers, these rather nostalgic prints, known as *Ukiyo-e*, became widely available to the ordinary Japanese.
Ukiyo-e means literally 'pictures of a floating world'.

SCENE 12

MARY: Van Gogh bought his first *Ukiyo-e* in Antwerp. Too poor to pay the rent, however, he went to Paris and moved in with his brother Theo, where he stayed for two years. Vincent and Theo soon became avid collectors, amassing over 400 Japanese woodcuts.
You never liked van Gogh. 'The painter of the colour-blind', is how you describe

him. But as a girl, I admired van Gogh enormously. To my mind all of his mature work is founded on Japanese art.
Van Gogh admired the cropped composition, the bright, cheerful colours, the use of outline and of diagonal elements. He wrote: 'It is almost a true religion which we are taught by the so uncomplicated Japanese, who live in nature as though they were flowers themselves.'
Of course, the Japanese are not flowers, nor are they uncomplicated. No more than Westerners are. [...]

SCENE 24

MARY: During the 1930s Japan became in essence a military dictatorship. Annexing Korea, invading Manchuria and China, Japan went to war and stayed at war for several decades. Fighting on several fronts at once continued until the end of the Second World War, or, to be more precise, until Japan surrendered.

SCENE 25

MARY: Your father, your grandfather? Your brother? Pain transgresses more than one generation. I remember you telling me about Japanese death poems, a tradition of Samurai warriors.
A small night storm blows
Saying 'falling is the essence of a flower'
Preceding those who hesitate.

SCENE 26

HE: *You saw nothing in Hiroshima. Nothing.*
SHE: *I saw everything. Everything.*
HE: *No. You saw nothing in Hiroshima.*
SHE: *The hospital for instance. I saw it. I'm sure I did. There is a hospital in Hiroshima. How could I help seeing it?*

SCENE 27

HIROSHI: On behalf of the Allied Forces, the US occupied Japan for seven years. The population was impoverished; Tokyo lay in ruins. The government and constitution was democratised. Factories rebuilt. The economy restored.
Not least amongst the democratic reforms was the freedom of press and banning of censorship. But did you know that the US forces strictly monitored and censored all movies produced and distributed at that time? Considered a symbol for the wrong sort of patriotism, Mount Fuji was removed from all films. An omission, the great irony of which being that this omission itself was carefully omitted from all public mention.

SCENE 28

HIROSHI: Mount Fuji's image was employed, misused and manipulated by both sides. The military government paraded the mountain as a call to arms, a reminder of duty, loyalty, homeland, nation. At the same time pamphlets which were thrown out of US aeroplanes show a mountain evoking homesickness, longing for peacetime and for family.
MARY: But the mountain itself is only and ever mountain. It never speaks in human language.
And all this time, during all this suffering, the mountain looks on.
HIROSHI: Times change, but the mountain never forgets. A silent eye which never blinks. The mountain sees centuries of life roll together into one brief animated scene. An atlas of time.
MARY: Is this what you want me to see? What I need to understand? That all these images are saying just one thing, if only my ears will listen.

SCENE 29

HIROSHI: I suspect you never saw this movie, my favourite Japanese movie, so please allow me to explain. Godzilla is a huge, angry prehistoric monster with the looks of a carnivorous dinosaur and the capabilities of a nuclear bomb. At that time, US-army testing of H-bombs in the Pacific ocean was contaminating tuna sold in Japanese market stalls. And in any case the horrors of the bombing of Hiroshima and Nagasaki were all too fresh in people's minds.

In the final scene of the third Godzilla film from 1962, King Kong and Godzilla engage in a definitive battle on top of Mount Fuji. Eventually they both fall off Mount Fuji, plunging into the sea. Godzilla disappears, leaving Kong to swim back home to the imaginary island of Faro, far away in the Pacific Ocean.

SCENE 30

MARY: Mountains and molehills. Perhaps you are trying to make magic or move mountains for me, or just this one at least.

I am never quite sure just how feelings translate. Even just translating from one language into another feels like groping for a light switch in the dark. And if I am honest with myself this terrifies me. On the skin of the surface all appears smooth and calm but underneath I can feel pressure building and fissures opening. A volcano's eruption cannot be predicted.

When I was a student at university my professor once said that photography is like ice and film is like fire. Film is light and shadow, incessant motion. Film is transience; like flames it flickers and disappears. Photography arrests time. It is motionless and frozen: It can chill and preserve objects through time without decay. Now I see why photos make the perfect memento mori. Photography, like grief, stops time.

SCENE 31

HIROSHI: With difficulty I have pulled myself up out of a shallow and fitful sleep. My body is protesting and wants to do anything but this. But here I am, in the dark, following the narrow light of my headlamp torch. Struggling, cursing and groping, I have forgotten what I came here for.

When I turn and look back down the trail I see an endless line of lights erratically tracing its way. Mankind is a string of glow worms trudging its way up a mountain.

SCENE 32

MARY: Only now do I remember that my professor continued his analogy contrasting photography and film. The two were incompatible, he warned. Fire melts ice into water, which in turn will extinguish the flames.
But I contest incompatibility. Is not Kono-hana goddess of both the volcano and of cherry blossoms? [...]

SCENE 40

MARY: Our world is filled with images and it feels at times like all those images insert themselves between us and the world. I see now, Hiroshi, that this is what you also wanted to show me, what you needed me to figure out.
And there is something I also want to explain, now that I have had more time to think. Film is not fire and photography is not ice, and the two are definitely not opposites nor enemies.
But if photography is ice, then perhaps film can be better likened to steam: dangerously hot, invisible, even volatile.

SCENE 41

HIROSHI: The tale of Akinosuke. Sitting under his favourite cedar tree in his garden with friends, Akinosuke suddenly feels tired and takes a nap. When he awakes his friends are gone but he sees coming towards him a grand procession of royal attendants. They inform him that the King of the Tokoyo requests his presence at his palace. Upon arrival Akinosuke is offered the King's daughter in marriage. Soon he is even appointed governor of an idyllic and bountiful island. His beautiful wife bears him seven bright and happy children.
One day however his wife suddenly falls ill and dies. Akinosuke goes to much trouble to give her a befitting funeral and erects a stone monument in her memory. The King sends for him, telling him not to worry, that his children will be cared for. As Akinosuke sails away and looks back, the island suddenly disappears and he is shocked to find himself under the cedar tree once more with his friends to whom he relays his dream. They, in turn, tell him that he

was only asleep for a few moments and of a yellow butterfly which flew out of his mouth and was grabbed by an ant. They wonder whether the butterfly is Akinosuke's soul.
Digging under the cedar tree Akinosuke finds a kingdom of ants and realises that this is the kingdom of his dream. Digging further he comes across a second nest and a small stone shaped like a monument beneath which he finds, inside a small clay coffin, the body of a female ant.

SCENE 42

MARY: I turn off the lights. Another sleepless night. Hiroshi, you were also an insomniac just like I am.
But if I close my eyes now, there right in front of me I see the mountain – Mount Fuji – patiently waiting, standing guard. Your mountain. My mountain.
You told me once a long time ago that if you can't sleep at night it's because you are awake in someone else's dream.

David Campany

Excerpt from 'Still Point of the Turning World: Fiona Tan and the "Photo Filmic"', on *Ascent*

Fiona Tan: Ascent, Izu Photo Museum, Shizuoka; De Pont Museum, Tilburg; Tokyo: NOHARA, 2016, 5–19.

The screen is dark. Out of the black, small still images emerge. Sound rises ... ambient, crackling, inhabiting the images. It is a very particular designation for a very particular kind of film. Seventy-seven minutes of still photographs appearing, disappearing, dissolving and scrolling across the screen, complemented by sounds, music and two scripted voices – one English, one Japanese.

Ascent (2016) takes as its subject Mount Fuji, or more precisely, the shifting representations by which we think we have come to know Mount Fuji. Fiona Tan has made an imaginative journey around of the object of her fascination. Mount Fuji is not revealed directly or in its deepest mystery (not even photographs can do that) but it is conjured for us nonetheless. Tan has solicited, sifted and sorted all manner of images and set them in motion. It is not the literal motion of the cinematic image but the figural motion of a 'photo-film': a rich weave of associations that are personal, poetic, historical, scientific, anthropological, military, geological, political, literary and artistic. *Ascent* is a bowl for images, a vortex of images, with Mount Fuji at its centre.

Early in the film we hear these words, spoken by 'Mary':

Emptiness or void, you explained patiently, never has negative connotations in the Japanese language. Just like the shining bamboo, a void has the potential to be filled.

We are then shown an image of the crater of Mount Fuji and we hear the male voice of 'Hiroshi', speaking in Japanese:

> *In Japanese the word for void is* utsuro. *But if you change the last syllable to 'wa', the word becomes* utsuwa, *meaning 'bowl'. A bowl can receive and hold some very important things; a bowl for rice; a bowl for tea. If a 'roi' is added to the end the word then becomes* utsuroi *– 'transience', a word representing a concept of time rather than of space.*[1]

By these words *Ascent* prepares us for what is to come: a sliding in and out of history and memory, facts and impressions; an invitation to exchange space for time, or at least to think about the possibility of such an exchange. Mount Fuji is pictured over and over, but somehow it remains elusive. It is as if the real thing was in another place, another time. Or perhaps it is right there but unknowable.

There are many ways to get to Mount Fuji. Fiona Tan has visited Japan several times, but she has constructed her film in her studio, in Amsterdam. If we are dealing with images, and in particular photographic images that can travel on our behalf, we could reasonably begin anywhere. Let us go via Paris. Here is Roland Barthes:

> *Maupassant often lunched in the restaurant in the Eiffel Tower, though he didn't care for the food: 'It's the only place in Paris', he used to say, 'where I don't have to see it.' And it's true that you must take endless precautions, in Paris, not to see the Eiffel Tower; whatever the season, through mist and cloud, on overcast days or in sunshine, in rain – wherever you are, whatever the landscape of roofs, domes, or branches separating you from it, the Tower is there, incorporated into daily life until you can no longer grant it any specific attribute, determined merely to persist, like a rock or the river, it is as literal as a phenomenon of Nature whose meaning can be questioned to infinity but whose existence is incontestable.*[2]

What Barthes describes of the Eiffel Tower holds at least equally true of Mount Fuji, the stratovolcano on Japan's Honshu Island. It is the nation's highest peak and on a clear day it can be seen from Tokyo, sixty miles to its northeast. It is *there*, always *there*, 'until you can no longer grant it any specific attribute'. Like the Eiffel Tower, the only way to make the mountain disappear from view, is to climb it. But unlike the Eiffel Tower, Mount Fuji really is a phenomenon of Nature.

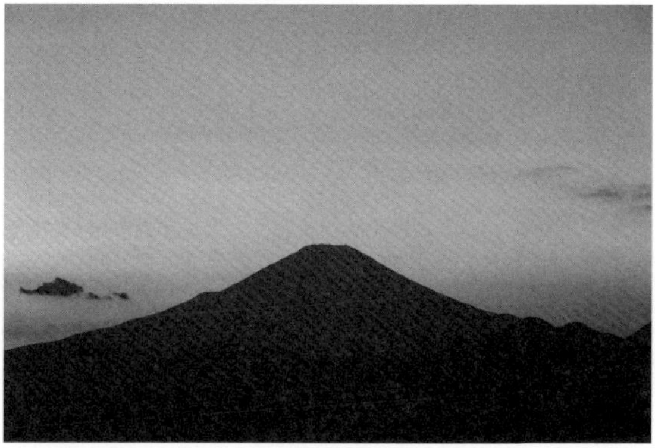

Ascent (still), 2016

As a Parisian, Barthes was pondering the most obvious of Parisian subjects. Mount Fuji could well be the most obvious of Japanese subjects. But when the nimble mind of an artist or writer resolves to contemplate the overly familiar we may feel a kind of disarming excitement. In 2001, the British artist Victor Burgin wrote:

> *I am in Barcelona. I find the genius of the place, which for me is where my internal world and the social and historical reality of the city intersect, in Mies van der Rohe's pavilion for the 1929 International Exhibition. Embarrassing, as if I had gone to Paris and discovered the Eiffel Tower. I must nevertheless accept the fact that the pavilion haunts me. It remains to be seen why.*[3]

We must not fear the obvious, or be embarrassed by it, especially if it haunts us. A cliché may well be a truth worn out by use, but it is better to accept it and find one's own relation to it, find the intersection of one's internal world and the external realities. This is the task Fiona Tan sets herself in the making of her film. In 2015, she writes:

> *I wish to make a new video piece entitled* Ascent *with Mount Fuji as its starting point. I envisage a projection consisting of a carefully edited compilation of photos of Mount Fuji. This work will reflect upon and question the status of this mountain and of all the images there exist of it. For me it is only fitting that I wish to make this*

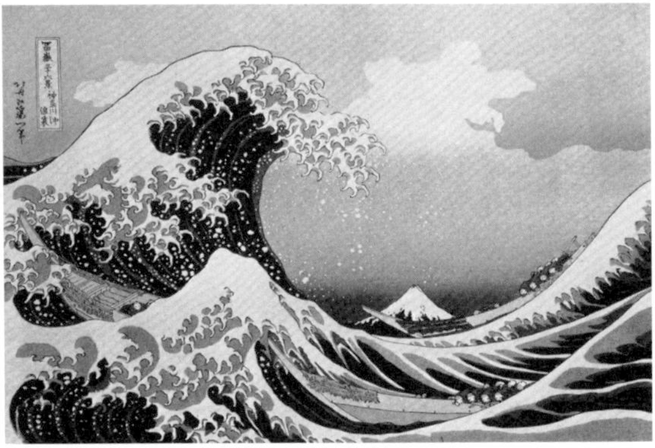

Katsushika Hokusai, *The Great Wave off the Coast of Kanagawa*, c. 1829–31

piece using images which are not mine. Constructing, imagining, mapping the mountain from a distance, through the eyes of others. Strung together all these images will form a composite like frames in a film. This multitude of images represents two paradoxes, both the impossibility of true and complete (photographic) representation and the nature of the mountain itself, always unchanging and yet never the same. These thousands of images encircle the mountain like a cloud; revealing it and hiding it at the same time.[4]

A composite like frames in a film. Remember that phrase. Tan's words appeared on the website of the Izu Photo Museum, as a call for members of the public to send her their images of Mount Fuji.[5] These images would then be complemented by those from the artist's own research, and from all the gathered material the visual component of *Ascent* would be pieced together.

The most celebrated representations of Mount Fuji are of course those comprising the suite of woodcut prints made by the Japanese *Ukiyo-e* artist Katsushika Hokusai (1760–1849). These views remain so loved around the world that it is tempting to see them as the source of Mount Fuji's enduring hold on the popular imagination. But in many ways Hokusai was emphasising the strange way in which Mount Fuji *always was, always has been,* an image. Many of the world's celebrated peaks resemble themselves only from particular angles. Viewed from the wrong spot, the Matterhorn, on the Italian-Swiss border, is barely recognisable.

Mount Everest (known in Nepal as Sagarmāthā and in Tibet as Chomolungma) has a shape so indistinct it refuses to become a fixed icon. The mysterious allure of Mount Fuji is quite the opposite, hiding in plain sight, we might say. With its near-perfect conical shape it invariably looks like itself, and this puts it into an unusually accommodating relation to its image.

Indeed, Mount Fuji is as much an image for those who live around and within sight of it, as it is for those who have seen it only in pictures. (This is what Barthes was getting at in his contemplation of the Eiffel Tower, which also always resembles itself.) This is not to deny the brute physicality of Mount Fuji, nor the enormous geological forces that created it. What is at stake is an unusual conflation of fact and image. To depict something that always resembles itself is to *re-depict*, to make an image of an image, taking the viewer over the lip of representation and into its vortex. Each and every picture of Mount Fuji has something of this quality. We point, with our finger or our eye: *There it is ... see how it looks the way it is supposed to look, the way it always looks.*

We can never know for sure but it is reasonable to assume that it was something of this phenomenon that finally attracted Hokusai, so late in his life, to encircle Mount Fuji with his own series of depictions. He produced at first thirty-six views, and then added a further ten. Each image would be its own masterwork but seen together they would form a composite. This composite would be the appropriate way to show moments from life around an unchanging and instantly recognisable landmark. It would also be a profound contemplation of what images really are, a challenge that all visual artists must face sooner or later.

With Japan isolated from the rest of the world, Hokusai worked on his project right through the period of the invention of photography in Europe. As his project grew, and as his images were being multiplied through woodblock printing, a whole new epoch of the reproducible image was coming into being.[6]

In the West at least (I am writing from London), the two best known of Hokusai's views of Mount Fuji are *The Great Wave off Kanagawa* and *Ejiri in Suruga Province*. Both are notable for their depiction of sudden moments of human danger: a wave at its peak before it crashes down upon small boats; a gust of wind catching people by surprise. In both images Mount Fuji is present as a small but definite shape on the horizon. Hokusai created these works around 1830, when photography's exposure times were still measured in minutes, not fractions of a second. And yet, to a contemporary audience there is something 'proto-photographic' in Hokusai's moments. Moreover, to leaf through a book of his views of Mount Fuji, or to see them projected as a slideshow, or to scroll through them online, is to assemble a mental composite. Mount Fuji becomes the pivot around which life and art revolve.

Consciously or not, Hokusai was anticipating some of the fundamental qualities of experience in the modern world: the proliferation of images, the misfit between permanence and transience, the paradox of the copy without an original, and the tensions between the centre and the whole, the one and the many. A century after Hokusai, in what turned out to be a fragile moment between one world war and another, T.S. Eliot described a similar set of feelings. I cannot quote all of his 1935 poem, 'Burnt Norton', but in the following section you can sense the magnitude of what Eliot was attempting to express:

At the still point of the turning world. Neither flesh nor fleshless;
Neither from nor towards; at the still point, there the dance is,
But neither arrest nor movement. And do not call it fixity,
Where past and future are gathered. Neither movement from nor towards,
Neither ascent nor decline. Except for the point, the still point,
There would be no dance, and there is only the dance.
I can only say, there we have been: but I cannot say where.
And I cannot say, how long, for that is to place it in time.[7]

Eliot is taking ideas of common wisdom and undoing them, twisting apparent opposites until they do not feel like opposites but do not quite reconcile either. In words he suggests what Hokusai was alluding to in images. Whatever its charms, no single image, no single representation, no single way of fixing or viewing the world will suffice. No single conception of time will suffice either. It is into the gaps between representations that modern life falls, and meaning falls. Art, be it printmaking, painting, sculpture, film, photography, literature, music or theatre, will have to address these gaps and make them palpable, make them thinkable. Hokusai's suite of images may be one way of doing this. Eliot's collisions of almost-opposites may be another. Viewing one medium through the prism of another might be a third way, and this is where we find the work of Fiona Tan, which is so often made in the uncharted places where photography and film intersect.

It is tempting think of still photography and the moving image existing in some kind of opposition, and we can easily to draw up a list of binaries to reinforce the differences: photography is always in the past whereas the moving image is experienced in the 'now'; photography fixes but the moving image remains fluid; photography is a ready substitute and prompt for memory but the moving image absorbs us in its own time; and so on. But there are other possibilities that complicate such oppositions.

The first is what we might call the *photographic encounter* in which filmed people appear to be posing for a still image. The second is the filming of a static world in such a way that we cannot be entirely sure whether we perceive the image in a filmic or a photographic way, not knowing if time is coursing through what we see or if it has been stopped for us. The third is the temporal arrangement of photographs within a filmic structure. The fourth is the *spatial* arrangement of multiple photographs either in the gallery space or across the pages of a book. Such practices scramble any strict opposition between the photographic and the filmic. In different ways Fiona Tan has explored all these approaches. [...]

This tension between photography in general and photographs in particular has shaped our visual culture profoundly. It has also shaped critical discussions and artistic practices. Susan Sontag's book *On Photography* (1977) and Vilém Flusser's *Towards a Philosophy of Photography* (1983) both avoid any specific photographs, preferring to approach the medium as a technical/social phenomenon at large. John Szarkowski's *Looking at Photographs* (1973) and Roland Barthes' *Camera Lucida* (1980) attend to specific images in great detail. The artist Jeff Wall makes singular images, each for careful contemplation on its own terms. Hans-Peter Feldmann orchestrates hundreds of images in a critical parody of mass image consumption. Macro or micro, each approach suspects the other of missing something.

Fiona Tan offers an alternative to this false choice. She is deeply attentive to the specifics of each and every image that she makes or selects, and she invites you to be equally attentive. At the same time, her work is mindful of the social parameters of imagery (genre, use, convention) and the technical parameters (cameras, darkrooms, screens), and how together they have shaped our image world. In this sense, the figure Tan most resembles is Antonino, the hero of Italo Calvino's remarkable short story 'The Adventure of a Photographer' (1955). Antonino tries to get to the heart of photography, to solve its deepest mysteries. He watches other people making images. He makes his own images. He stares at individual images. He steps back and contemplates the near infinite number of images. He contemplates how they have determined his understanding of himself and the world.

He re-photographs pages from newspapers and magazines. He looks at domestic snapshots. 'Perhaps true, total photography, he thought, is a pile of fragments of private images, against the creased background of massacres and coronations.'[8] Are the 'true' and the 'total' the same thing? Is the truth of a photograph the same as the truth of photography? Does the truth of photography reside in the one or the many? Both. Are photographs about their subject matter or are they about photography? Both.

In Fiona Tan's *Ascent*, we move over the surface of Mount Fuji and its surroundings. We do so by moving over the surface of hundreds of photographs presented as a film, over which a episodic story is recounted. We move across time, memory and history. Across attitudes, across cultures, and through so many perspectives. For seventy-seven minutes we are with Mount Fuji. Like a lover or close friend we get to know it so well that we take it for granted and it disappears. And then, suddenly, we are surprised by a minor revelation and it becomes the object of our attention once more. Fascination returns afresh. *Ascent* approaches photography and film in the same way. At times, film seems to be merely the vehicle to bring us photographs that in turn bring us Mount Fuji. But there are moments when we feel how film can treat photography, how photography is and is not film, and how Mount Fuji is and is not its image. Nothing is resolved, everything revolves. It is not a circular revolution. It is more like an ongoing spiral.

Elisa Schaar

On *Ascent* and *Elsewhere* at Frith Street Gallery, London

Exhibition review, *Artforum*, February 2019, 185–6.

With her film *Ascent* (2016), Fiona Tan turned her gaze to landscape, creating an eighty-minute montage from thousands of amateur photographs of Japan's Mount Fuji. For her exhibition 'Elsewhere', she dealt with a different terrain: that of Los Angeles, where she recently spent one year. This time, Tan handled the camera herself, filming from a hilltop studio at the Getty Center. As in *Ascent*, this new project saw her grappling with a mythical subject: the notoriously sprawling city has not only featured in countless cinematic representations, but it has also continuously generated new images of itself. As the exhibition's title suggests, the very condition of Los Angeles is one of being constantly on the move to another place, literally as well as metaphorically. [...]

If the freeways signify constant circulation in a place without a centre, they also point to Los Angeles' self-presentation as a city of the future. Tan's film *Elsewhere* (2018), which is just over sixteen minutes long, begins with a new dawn. Shots of the cityscape gradually take on colour as the sun rises through the clouds; meanwhile, the screen's peculiar installation – floating in the middle of the gallery space – and an ambient crackling noise suggest that this is a remote place, an idea rather than an actual location. During long, absorbing takes – sunlight reflects on skyscrapers and bathes the valley in a golden sheen, until the sky slowly grows dark and the stream of white headlights begins flowing again – a narrator explains that this city has no crime, no poverty, no pollution. And, in a trope borrowed from classic utopian literature, it can only be reached after an arduous journey. Only at one point does the speaker express doubt, wondering about the absence of history in a place eternally perfect, but then ultimately praising the bliss of oblivion. Would imperfect reality be better? But then, as Norman Klein once said, isn't the real Los Angeles, with its freeways, actually a city of erasure?

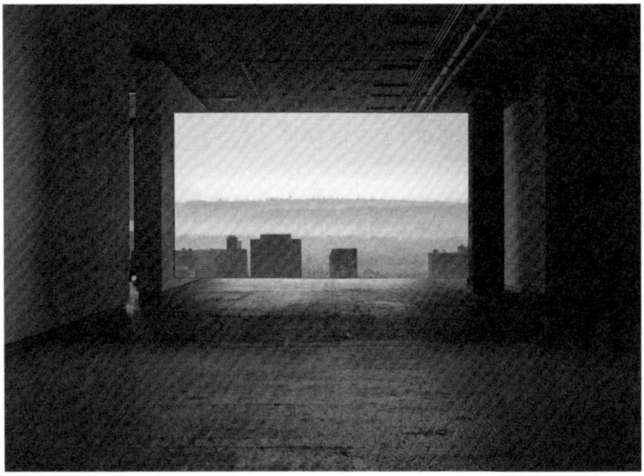

Elsewhere (installation view), 2018

The disjunction between image and audio in *Elsewhere*, reminiscent of Chantal Akerman's *News from Home* (1977), lets the viewer experience the city's contradictions – until image and audio sync up unexpectedly in the end, yielding an unsettling moment of stability. Even when all we see is only beautiful surface, the troubled context still impresses itself on the viewer. As post-truth politics, artificial intelligence and climate change encroach on everyday reality, and while compelling visions of a better future are hardly forthcoming, Tan's work is disturbingly timely. Asking how to get a true representation, it reminds us that utopia and dystopia can be hard to tell apart.

Fiona Tan
'Shadow Archive'

Fiona Tan: L'Archive des ombres / Shadow Archive, Musée des Arts Contemporains, Grand-Hornu, 2019, 27–35.

Umbra sumus
We are but shadows

742.4 (SHADOWS)

For several years now I have been carrying a book around with me. It has an intriguing illustration on its cover and a title that was bound to catch my attention: *The Art of Memory*. Written by Frances A. Yates and published in 1966, it is a history of mnemonic practices. Central to the book are Yates' translations and interpretations of a book by Giordano Bruno. According to Bruno, 'The knowledge or art about to be revealed' by his hermetic text 'is like a rising sun before which the creatures of the night will vanish.' Written originally in Latin and published in Paris in 1582, Bruno's book is known in English as *The Art of Memory*. It is a fitting title; the author claimed that its reader would be able to magically learn and memorise anything and everything. But the original Latin title is, for me, even more beautiful and inspiring: *De Umbris Idearum*, literally, *The Shadows of Ideas*. Are not, I ask myself, all works of art in some way the shadows of ideas?

I arrived at Giordano Bruno through reading Sir Thomas Browne, whom I discovered, in turn, from reading W.G. Sebald's *The Rings of Saturn* (1995). Browne's *Bibliotheca abscondita*, or *Musaeum Clausum* (1684), is a wonderful inventory of an imagined library of 'rare and generally unknown' books, which no longer exist or perhaps never did. In the list of books from his 'sealed museum', Browne attributes *De Umbris Idearum* to no one lesser than King Solomon. I look once more at the cover of my copy of Yates' *Art of Memory*. It shows a detail of her sketch of Bruno's hermetic secret, his memory wheel. Creased along folds and covered with minuscule handwriting as it is, I had originally mistaken it for a drawing by

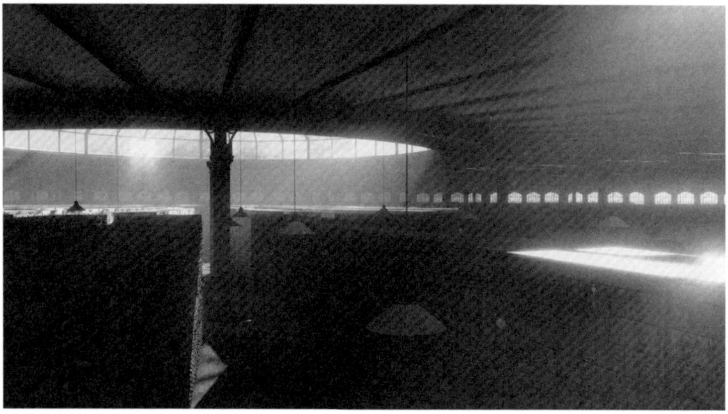

Archive (still), 2019

Bruno himself. Since then I have drawn my own version of this diagram. Neatly organised in a spatial geometry, Bruno's graphic mnemonic scheme was based on a series of concentric circles and considered to have magical, even divine, properties. For the publication of *De Umbris Idearum*, Bruno, a former Dominican friar from Naples, was charged by the Catholic Church with heresy and burned at the stake in Rome on 17 February 1600.

To memorise is to learn to understand. At a time when it was crucial that any scholar be able to memorise entire speeches and long tracts of knowledge, the ancient Greeks and Romans attributed great importance to the practice of mnemonic techniques. And in their footsteps, mediaeval and Renaissance scholars continued to be fascinated by these ideas. But with the invention of the printed book, memory became externalised, and these techniques have largely been lost and forgotten. Currently, there is renewed interest in mnemonic schemes such as the so-called memory palace, or *loci* method of memorisation. Via the sequential linkage of striking images to specific places, usually rooms in an imaginary building or palace, it is possible to memorise long lists of information and recall them perfectly. Thoughts, feelings and memories become connected to physical places – a physical rendering, a geography of thought and memory. As an artist I am particularly interested in this concept. The shadows of memories: a catalogue, or an archive, of a different kind.

So, here is my first circle. Ideas connecting images with knowledge and memory. The elusive idea of a parallel world of shadows, of images that cannot be captured but nonetheless may be experienced and perceived. Images of fleeting and ungraspable beauty. 'Imagination', wrote Giambattista della Porta in 1558, 'draws images as with a pencil in memory.'

930.25 (ARCHIVE, HISTORICAL)

The Mundaneum is a museum and archive currently situated in Mons, Belgium, just ten kilometres away from the Musée des Arts Contemporains in Grand-Hornu. This archive, or what is left of it today, grew out of the International Office of Bibliography founded in Brussels by Paul Otlet and Henri La Fontaine and endorsed by King Leopold II in 1895. Its mission was ambitious: a universal bibliography, 'an inventory of all that has been written at all times, in all languages, and on all subjects.' All knowledge would be freely accessible and readily available. The end result: world peace.

The basis of the Mundaneum is the Universal Decimal Classification, or UDC, a numerical cataloguing system devised and developed by Otlet and La Fontaine. It is similar to the Dewey Decimal System for libraries but more complex and able to show cross-references between subjects. Paul Otlet, now considered by many to be a pioneer in the field of documentation, dedicated his life to the Mundaneum. Books, he felt, were outdated; knowledge needed to be extracted from them and subdivided into single, useful parts. The UDC made it possible to give every piece of information, each bit of knowledge, a unique and logical numerical code. Numbers, digits, held the key to the future.

Otlet described the Mundaneum's bibliographical repertoire as a 'mechanical brain'. Over the years his plans and visions grew. Not only was he involved in numerous international associations, he also ran a museum, worked on an encyclopaedia and a universal atlas, and collaborated with architects on plans for his *Cité mondiale*, or World City (an echo of the Renaissance *città ideale*). The Mundaneum started to collect not only all printed words but all published images – postcards, glass-plate negatives, pamphlets and posters. As is reflected in his many notes and papers, Otlet worked tirelessly on this grand undertaking until his death in 1944. At its peak the Mundaneum housed approximately sixteen million index cards. Requests received were dealt with in writing, the responses supplied within a few weeks.

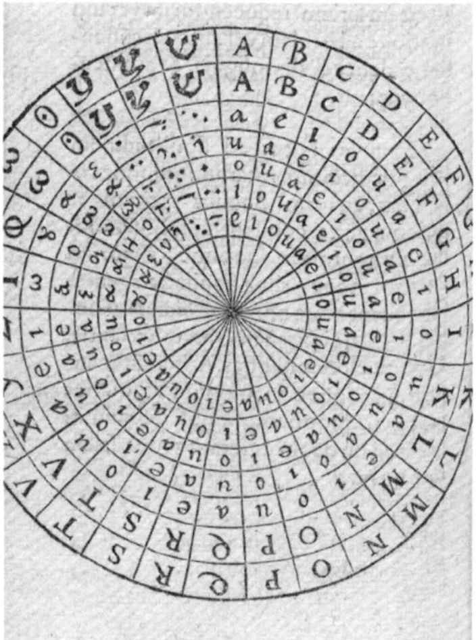

Giordano Bruno, *Ruota della Memoria* (Memory Wheel), 1582

Over the years I have repeatedly delved into archives of both still and moving images. I have collected many images and compiled my own small archives. The titles of some recent works reveal my increasing interest in questions of what makes a collection, what a museum is, what an archive is, and what purpose and potential they can embrace. An archive always holds the idea of promise to me, like a treasure chest. I wonder what secrets it hides and whether I will be lucky enough to find something worth looking at. But I am also aware that no archive is ever complete and that, even though some kind of order or structure is always its defining principle, any archive also houses some form of chaos or is in danger of being engulfed by it.

I can no longer remember how I first heard about the Mundaneum, but I know that many years ago I tried without success to visit it. The car I was travelling in broke down soon after crossing the Belgian border, and I ended up pitching a tent in the backyard of a very kind family somewhere near the ring road around Brussels. Some twenty years later I stand on the cool, polished stone floor of a former department store in front of a long line of dimly lit mahogany filing cabinets. My gaze travels along rows and rows of small drawers, each labelled with a number written neatly by hand in faded ink on a yellowed card. Inside each drawer are hundreds, thousands, of index cards, each with its own unique number and a brief informational text. 'Do not touch' signs are posted at regular intervals. My curiosity is on fire, but I also feel daunted by the sheer weight and magnitude of so many cabinets. Knowledge here seems both displayed in its full physical reality and, at the same time, closed and locked, inaccessible and out of reach. [...]

528.9 – 023.47 (CARTOGRAPHY, MAPPING, CIRCULAR)

Central London, early May. I am on the fourth floor of the Warburg Institute at the University of London, before me boxes containing notes and files from Frances Yates' estate. Behind me are the beautiful catalogue drawers covered with cloth by Aby Warburg himself, each with its own individual pattern and colour, making it easy and intuitive to remember which box to reach for. A large piece of thick paper approximately 120 × 120 cm in size has been unrolled and weighed down at the edges with a few pebbles and antique terracotta fragments. Drawn on it in red ink and pencil are six concentric circles, each divided into thirty segments. Each segment is subdivided into five, creating on the outermost ring one hundred and fifty divisions in all.

Giordano Bruno's memory palace is a graphic scheme that was intended to be committed to memory. Each subdivision of each circle has a name and an image; there are the symbols of the planets, the mansions of the moon, images of the decans, *et cetera, et cetera*. It is, I eventually realise, a schematised map of the universe, the ultimate organisation of the known world. The six circles can function like clockwork rings. In the mind's eye you can rotate the interlocking rings to any number of combinations. Each of these is a *locus*, a place and image in which to store whatever knowledge it is you wish to memorise. The only stumbling block for the reader is that she is first required to memorise in perfect detail this considerably complex memory map. But I am already getting dizzy and lose my orientation, peering closely at the tiny handwritten Latin words.

'The observer', wrote Bruno, 'is always at the centre of things.' All I can see are circles all around me, everywhere I go. In Paul Otlet's multitude of diagrams and papers, in Frances Yates' papers and photographic reproductions, in my own notes and sketches. 'The observer is always at the centre of things.' This implies that the observer has power and perhaps control over her universe, an idea I immediately call into question. Bruno was thinking of Giulio Camillo's famed memory theatre, an architectural mnemonic device in which one stands as if on the stage of a Roman theatre, with tiers for the public rising up and around you. Camillo's wooden model, semicircular in shape, was large enough for two men to stand inside. He described it as a 'mind machine', where knowledge was visible at a glance because it was represented not in words but in peculiar and memorable images. The circularity of his model is even encapsulated in the word 'encyclopaedia', literally, 'training in a circle'. As a student you stand in the middle, surrounded by knowledge, visible on all sides.

001.18 (FUTURE, FUTURE OF KNOWLEDGE)

Paul Otlet wrote in *Traité de documentation: Le livre sur le livre* in 1934:

> *Everything in the universe, and everything of man, would be registered at a distance as it was produced. In this way a moving image of the world will be established, a true mirror of its memory. From afar, anyone would be able to read text, expanded or limited to the desired subject, that could be projected on his individual screen. Thus, from his armchair, anyone would be able to contemplate the whole of creation or particular parts of it.*

Currently receiving financial support from the internet giant Google, the Mundaneum has been called a precursor to the internet and described as the 'paper Google'. It cannot be denied that in his writings, Otlet, who was very interested in technological developments, expressed some appealingly familiar visions for the future, and it is tempting to draw the conclusion that he anticipated computers, television and networks like the internet. In several ways, both he and Henri La Fontaine were ahead of their time: La Fontaine was a feminist and a Nobel Peace Prize winner, and both La Fontaine and Otlet were confirmed pacifists. But Otlet was also a nineteenth-century man from Brussels whose mind was pervaded by Eurocentric thought. His ideas and convictions could arguably be called imperial, simplistic and, at times, even colonial. Indeed, I have come to realise that it is no coincidence that international institutions such as the European Union, NATO and the United Nations have grown out of this kind of thinking, out of this era, out of minds like Otlet's. We currently view the world through such a dystopian frame of mind, but Otlet was a true utopian – he really was trying to come up with a better future, something that feels nigh impossible today. In his quest he must have felt increasingly lonely.

592 (261.6) (493) (JELLYFISH FROM NORTH SEA, BELGIUM)

There is an anecdote Otlet's grandson tells about his grandfather, shortly before his death in 1944. Belgium is occupied, and the Mundaneum has been ransacked by the Nazis. Otlet is a tired, stooped old man with a wispy white beard and spectacles. He and his grandson are walking along the beach at Ostend shortly after a storm. Jellyfish have washed up onto the sand. Otlet takes an index card and a fountain pen from his pocket. Without speaking a word, he writes down a UDC number and places the card gently on top of a dead jellyfish. Then, he turns on his heels and walks away.

I like to think that 5 was Otlet's favourite UDC category. Jellyfish, after all, are not so far removed from 599.89 – the hominids, including, of course, us, *Homo sapiens*. In class 5 the melancholic planet, Saturn, can also be found: 523.46. And this, in turn, is very close to everything – 524, the universe. My field, fine art, is listed in class 7, together with recreation, entertainment and sport. The UDC is still being updated and augmented – for example, 004.738.5 is the code for the internet. Class 4 is currently kept vacant as its subject, linguistics, was moved to class 8 alongside literature. I think this amendment took place after Otlet's death, but I for one appreciate that there is now so much room left in his archive for the unknown, for the not-yet-imagined. To my disappointment I note that the categories 'fool' or 'folly', I cannot find listed.

'We are each at the centre of the universe', wrote Damon Krukowski in 2017. 'A lonely place.'

Hettie Judah
'The Materiality of Information: Fiona Tan's Odes to Bygone Data Systems', on works 2012–9 at MACS, Grand-Hornu

Exhibition review, *frieze*, June 2019.

In the closing years of the nineteenth century, Belgian lawyers Paul Otlet and Henri La Fontaine commenced a project to classify all human knowledge and make it universally accessible. Many decades before big business dubbed data 'the new oil' and the emergence of the information economy, Otlet and La Fontaine imagined their index-card system as a powerful tool for world peace: with understanding, they believed, would come an end to antagonism and destruction.

Otlet and La Fontaine's utopian Mundaneum was never finished – how could such a Borgesian project ever reach conclusion? Until the German occupation of Brussels in 1940, their growing archive was housed in the city's Palais du Cinquantenaire. By then, it extended to some twelve million index cards, arranged according to their Universal Decimal Classification system. What survives is now in the Belgian city of Mons, where the artist Fiona Tan immersed herself in Otlet and La Fontaine's world for two years ahead of her exhibition at nearby Grand-Hornu.

This is not Tan's first deep archival dive. Included here are her earlier works *Depot* (2015) and *Inventory* (2012), in which she explores, respectively, the assembled worlds of marine history collections and Sir John Soane's Museum in London. The Mundaneum offers the artist-filmmaker none of those archives' intriguing visual flair: here are no jars of baby turtles, no cracked classical statuary – only

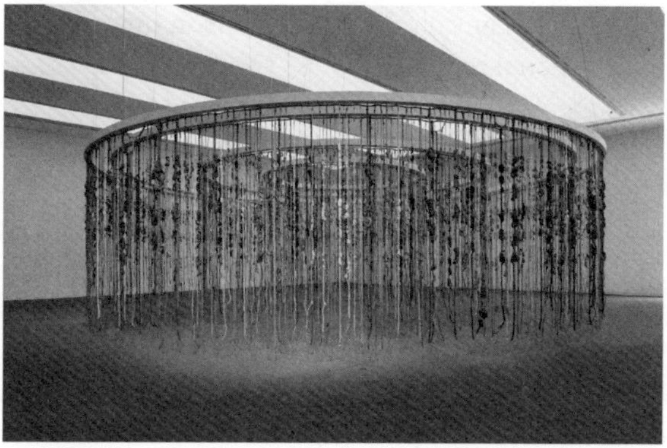

Circular Ruins (installation view), 2019

the inscrutable façades of wooden cabinets. Setting aside her camera, Tan has instead turned to virtual space to realise the architectural structure Otlet dreamed of for his grand bibliography. *Archive* (2019) leads us through a digital labyrinth of filing cabinets, fanning out like a vast, multi-layered panopticon beneath a leaded-glass dome.

Tan's digital rendering of the Mundaneum is gloomy, deserted, sinister: a relic of an era when world knowledge still seemed within human grasp. Arranged in vitrines in the real space of the gallery are Otlet's notes and correspondence. We see him redrafting near-identical plans and schematics over decades, lobbying indefatigably, his obsession bordering on mania. It has become a commonplace to describe the Mundaneum as a precursor to the internet. Tan's selection from Otlet's paper suggests the project as something closer to a proto European Union: a centralised bureaucratic scheme promoting peace between nations from its Brussels headquarters.

Politics is never faraway in Tan's elegantly conceived exhibition. Each work explores subtly different power dynamics of research, collecting, naming, archiving, display and interpretation. Filmed in six different media, and focusing on the cluttered oddness of Soane's collection, *Inventory* raises questions about why certain objects are prized, and what logic should dictate their arrangement. As Tan's camera pans across starfish and cephalopods, the voice-over in *Depot* describes naming as a colonial act: a taking of territory. While ostensibly a peace project, the Mundaneum's panopticon form immediately suggests Jeremy Bentham's late-eighteenth-century designs for prison surveillance and Michel Foucault's discussion of penal regimes.

Systems of classification, however utopian, impose values and viewpoints on the entities and ideas that fall within them. Western Europeans are long used to being the imposers. In the final work, *Circular Ruins* (2019), Tan creates a system according to another key. Concentric circles of suspended ropes relay the titular 1940 short story by Jorge Luis Borges in Quipu, the Inca language of knots. Cast suddenly into illiteracy, we read the sculpture instead through sense memory. The suspended ropes recall changing rooms in old coal mines; their smell of tar smacks of the harbourside; the circular form apes the modern industrial ruins of Grand-Hornu itself. All echo the temple and cycle described in Borges' 'The Circular Ruins': generations without end pouring knowledge into new life, only to discover the futility and illusoriness of their existence.

Fiona Tan
'A Walk Among Ruins'

LOST AND FOUND

In Ariosto's epic poem *Orlando Furioso* (1516–32), the English knight Astolfo undertakes a voyage to the moon, where everything once lost on earth can be found. In his fury, Orlando has lost his wits, and so Astolfo mounts a chariot and rides to the moon in search of them. The lunar satellite serves as an eternal storage depot, halting all decay and disintegration. As it turns out, the moon is more like a cosmic rubbish dump filled with all manner of random items: lost fishing hooks, discarded vessels, abandoned ideas. And also

> *Ruins of cities and of fortresses*
> *Lay scattered all about, with precious stores,*
> *Plots ill-contrived, broken alliances,*
> *Feuds and vendettas and abortive wars, [...]*

Astolfo's journey is not in vain, for he returns to earth with Orlando's wits, and Orlando's sanity is restored. I imagine Ariosto's moon as the ultimate endless archive: a lunar holding facility with room for all manner of bits and pieces and bric-a-brac, forgotten artefacts, and obsolete technologies. I like to think that if I ever took a trip to the moon, I would finally find the mates to a lifetime's supply of my children's odd socks.

DUST AND SCRATCHES

I am in the Dutch town of Hilversum, working in a traditional cutting room. I flick on the power switch of the Steenbeck film-editing table, and also the lamp. I thread the film from left to right across a series of sprockets and rollers and in front of a rotating prism and mirror that projects each frame onto a small screen. The film table emits a humming sound and rattles softly, as if acknowledging my presence. Over and over, I move the handle forward and back, appraising each shot, getting to know the footage, then slicing through the film at the end of each shot. Each of my actions produces its own distinctive sound. There is a clear mechanical analogy between the physical, the visual and the temporal. I can literally see the length of a shot in the strip of film that I cut and then hang from individual pegs on a rack. I can hold the image between my cotton-gloved fingertips, and its colours and the contrast are vivid, beautiful – the blacks have depth and intensity, the film's grain is tactile, warm, organic. And, like riding a bicycle or playing the piano, editing moving images in this way is a motor skill that my hands remember and my senses recall, one that cannot be forgotten.

The first time I held a reel of film in my hands was when I was still a student in Amsterdam. I had a job in a movie theatre for twenty hours a week, and was taught how to operate the projector so I could work in the projection booth. The week's films would arrive in heavy square boxes. Each reel, which weighed at least ten pounds, made up one segment of the film and was about ten minutes long. We would splice together the feature, compile the advertisements, and wind the celluloid onto the huge flat tiers of the non-rewind tables or 'platters' that occupied half of the space in the projection booth. Film struck me as something very physical, material; each frame of a 35 mm film can be easily viewed with the naked eye. Celluloid film is simultaneously durable and delicate: it is impossible to rip or tear by hand, yet is so easily damaged. If a film is loaded incorrectly, it gets eaten up inside the projector and is ruined. A speck of dust caught in the film gate will result in a long vertical 'cable' that will permanently deface the scene. Dust and scratches are inadvertently added to the film, damaging it slightly with every screening.

After a couple of days in the cutting room, concentration comes easily. My efforts are accompanied by satisfying mechanical sounds, and, like a car mechanic, my ear has become attuned to them. Click, slice, purr – the gentle rhythm of the winding rollers and pulleys, the high-pitched ping as the loose end of the celluloid swings round and hits the aluminium baseplate, the feel of the teeth fitting neatly into the perforations, the tug of the reel, taking up any slack. Nothing can be rushed. The resistance offered by the material is a valuable asset in this working process. Step by step, frame by frame, I can speed up or slow down, and I can wind forwards and backwards, but I cannot skip frames or jump across time. I can work only at walking speed, and this feels natural, like second nature. Because the act of physically cutting the film has its own inherent violence, no decision to cut is taken lightly. The blade is sharp and precisely aligned. Like a guillotine, it slices neatly through the celluloid. I have destroyed one long thread of film by cutting it into many pieces. Then, patiently and painstakingly, I attempt to construct and create something new out of the sum of its parts.

RAVENOUS TIME

Ruins are an invention of the Renaissance, or so it is said. Certainly in the West, our interest in and preoccupation with ruins can easily be traced back to that period, a time of rebirth, of renewed interest in the classical past. A ruin is a lesson in vanity, for time – ravenous time – is 'the devourer of all things'. In the fifteenth century, Rome, the 'broken city', lay literally in ruins and was undergoing excavation and reconstruction. Only that which becomes buried and forgotten manages to escape erasure. All artworks exist as potential ruins.

Some years ago, while preparing to film for my installation *Inventory* (2012), I spent several days doing research in the library of Sir John Soane's Museum in London. As a neoclassical architect, Soane was fascinated with ancient Rome. Soane owned a complete set of Piranesi's etchings, including the *Carceri d'Invenzione*, his fantastic depictions of impossible architecture. I was particularly struck by a watercolour sketch that Soane had commissioned and which was based on his own design for the Bank of England (1830). The bank was his magnum opus, and he had worked on the project for forty-five years, 1788–1833. Inspired by Piranesi and the Renaissance convention of the cutaway perspective, its walls have been partially demolished, columns toppled and the roof lifted, rather than displaying this grand building all shiny and new. How surprising that an architect would wish to represent his creation in this way. To my eyes, this looks like a future ruin.

I am drawn to ruins for several reasons. First, there is the view of the sky framed by the coincidental architectural remains. Standing inside a ruin, I am within a structure that has lost its function and is in the process of being stripped bare. What was once interior, private and protected has been undressed and disrobed. Rooms, walls, corners and niches are exposed to the elements. The building has been inverted and turned inside out, as it were. I become keenly aware of negative spaces and of what is missing. Like *terra incognita*, the blank spaces on a map, each gap or hole is a puzzle, and may point to potential creative possibilities. Second, there is the gentle, gradual but inevitable clash with nature. An analogy is often made between architecture and the human body, and buildings too must age and die – ashes and cinder, dust to dust. Man-made structures slowly erode into dust, weeds and trees assert themselves, insects, birds and other fauna take over. For me, a ruin is always a very physical, tactile, material place.

But perhaps most importantly, I feel as though I can glimpse time in motion. I am witness to a drawn-out collapse that is taking place before my very eyes in agonisingly slow motion. As gravity reclaims each stone and brick, I observe time on a much larger scale than usual. If a building such as a cathedral or monastery was wilfully destroyed, time paradoxically appears to have been both halted and accelerated. In fact, I see several moments in time at once. To look at a ruin is to watch it slowly disappear, and at the same time be alerted to its former and presumably complete self. A ruin simultaneously shows me a building's past, present and future. I see time moving forwards and backwards as if on film. Like Bruegel's wonderful painting of the Tower of Babel, I see both its rise and its fall, its fragmentary state and its impossible completion. A ruin is, after all, materially both present and absent, a monument to its own past and thus revealing both its end and its beginning.

Andrew Hui has written insightfully on this:

> *'To ruin' is active and passive, transitive and intransitive; remnants can be pondered, reflected on, meditated upon, or removed, recycled, and further destroyed. A ruin is an ontological paradox: as the degeneration of material and form, its perfection is its very nonexistence. The ruin exists to remind one of what has endured, what has been lost, but most importantly, what is yet to be. Floating at the edge of nonbeing, the fallen monument embodies an intriguing set of binaries: transient and persistent, a source of alienation and recognition, upright and fallen, scarce and abundant, visible and invisible, matter and metaphor. In short, a thing that is and is not.*[1]

PERFECTION IS TERRIBLE

Our ears, eyes and brains are excellent but highly subjective filters. No camera or sound recorder is capable of recording sound and image in quite the same way

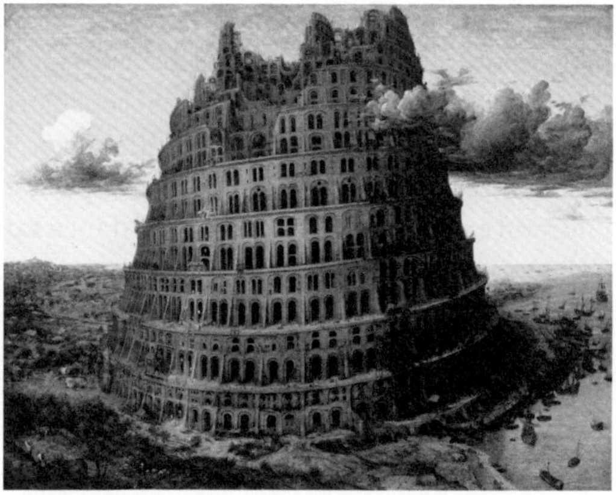

Pieter Bruegel the Elder, *The Tower of Babel*, c. 1563–5

that we, as human beings, perceive the world around us. Just as it is impossible to record only the intended sound (a microphone will pick up anything in its proximity), it is equally impossible to capture a perfect image, a pure picture devoid of any interference or manipulation. Although it sounds blatantly obvious, this is still regularly overlooked. Contrary to the critical description Maxim Gorky wrote after his first visit to a film screening in 1896, we have come to accept the flattened grey ghosts of black-and-white film as an accurate portrayal of our visual world, and not – as he disparagingly described it – as a mere 'kingdom of shadows'.

Film grain – the random optical texture of processed photographic film – is a necessary imperfection inherent to the chemical process of analogue film. In the century since its invention, makers and viewers grew accustomed to the presence of granularity in film, and grew to appreciate and even love it. There is a strong argument to be made for the desirability of imperfection. I can wholeheartedly agree with Sylvia Plath, who wrote, 'Perfection is terrible, it cannot have children.' In an interview recorded in 1966, the French film director Jean Renoir makes a striking comparison between filmmaking and mediaeval tapestries. Renoir argues that technical perfection results in ugliness. He misses the grain of old film, the tonal quality of film stock no longer in production. The Bayeux Tapestry, he argues, is beautiful precisely because of its primitive nature. It is the imperfection of its execution, the manual labour of thousands of hours of weaving and embroidery, which lends the tapestry its unique beauty. However, in the centuries that followed, techniques for making tapestries improved and the tapestry's aesthetic quality declined considerably.

When I first started working with video, it, too, was analogue, just like film. Visual information was recorded onto plastic tape that was thinner than celluloid, and coated with a magnetic substance rather than light-sensitive materials. A chemical process made way for an electromagnetic one. The editing method employed was known as tape-to-tape, and in this way was not so different from reel-to-reel film editing, even if the physical splicing of celluloid was replaced by the pressing of a few buttons and recording from one tape to another. However, the sharpness, contrast and resolution of the image decreased dramatically. So the transition from analogue film to analogue video initially and primarily resulted in loss: loss of quality, loss of colour, loss of contrast, brightness and mobility. But it soon became cheaper and more mobile, and television sets made their victorious entry into our living rooms.

MODERN RUINS

Just like Sir John Soane's architecture, the film location I chose for this work is a ruin that is by no means ancient. Although the locals call the site *la cathédrale*, it is the former machine room of a Belgian coal mine dating from the 1820s. The architectural floor plan of the structure that I was sent dates from 1929, and shows various machines, spare parts and stones from the building marked for sale. *Spolia* up for grabs, just like in Rome in the fifteenth century, when the city's reconstruction simultaneously resulted in its partial deconstruction, and stone walls, columns, and other remnants were readily recycled and incorporated into new structures. Even the Colosseum was mined like a quarry: one fifteenth-century contractor is reported to have removed over 2,500 cartloads of stone over a period of only nine months.

During the shoot my crew and I are blessed with good weather, and we start filming as early as possible, at the crack of dawn. It is surprisingly challenging to film on both analogue 16 mm film and high-definition video at the same time. Shooting both forms simultaneously requires considerable discipline and attention from me and my small crew. Time passes quickly; the sun rises swiftly. The sky turns a steady blue, intense and clear. The length and direction of the sharp, dark shadows mark the time of day like a sundial. The arches remind me of paintings by de Chirico. Thankfully, the ruin's remnants are silent and patient subjects.

A TRUE AND ORIGINAL COPY

Video is now digital. The analogue fluctuating line of light of varying brightness has been replaced by a pixel, a dot of coloured light, a bit of data, an electrical charge, a zero or a one. For eyes accustomed to viewing grainy analogue film, digital imagery often feels too clean and clinical, sometimes too sharp, too detailed. It is this seeming perfection that is at fault, and I am reminded once more of Renoir's thoughts about tapestries. In order to project a film, it is halted twenty-four times a second, but this is technically very challenging. As a result, analogue film jitters and wobbles inside the gate, but ironically, it is this very restlessness that aids the viewing of analogue film. Perhaps this mirrors the tiny high-speed movements of the finely tuned muscles of our own eyeballs. High-definition video of a fixed scene can feel dead or frozen: time appears unnaturally stopped, as if removed from the frame. It is not surprising, then, that all post-production software offers the possibility of adding cosmetic artefacts such as film grain, or indeed, even dust and scratches, later on. This can only be achieved by damaging and partially destroying the recorded image data at pixel level with the use of a series of complicated algorithms.

For some years now, I have been thinking about making a work that consists of and reflects upon both the analogue and the digital image. My primary concern here is with images – not with technology, but with how we perceive images and how they affect us, what they taste like, how they feel. I am not saying that one is better than the other. Both of them are translations – the images these media give us are different than how our human eyes perceive things. But they are translations into two different languages, and I want to pause and reflect upon this while it is still possible.

The terminology we use on a daily basis lags behind the technological developments that engineers have come up with. Our language is lacking. We take, we capture. We shoot and film, we do not video. Within the constraints of dialectical philosophical thought, analogue and digital technologies appear doomed to oppositional positions: analogue as opposed to digital seems to imply old versus new, physical versus immaterial, actual versus virtual, real versus fake. Never was there a phrase more fitting than the strange oxymoron 'a true and original copy'.

Digitally, I can film and edit faster; the process is also less costly, although not by much. I can do most of the editing in my own studio, but I miss the teamwork and the interaction with other professionals in the field – the people in the film lab, the colourist – and I miss the slowness and the resistance of materiality. It is no coincidence that the average length of each cinema shot is now considerably shorter. I miss the physical, geographical or spatial memory that aids me when I am editing an analogue film. In the digital world, I am much more forgetful.

RESISTING TIME

Poets from ancient times as well as those from more recent centuries have been inclined to believe that words had more longevity than buildings. Words were 'the only monuments that do not know how to die.' As du Bellay wrote in 1558, 'Whatever stands firm is destroyed by time. And whatever flees resists time.' A projection feels to me like the most ephemeral of images. Like the light of a candle, projected moving images flicker, burn, fade and die. They cannot escape time, for it is time that carries them. The very word 'projection' implies both a future vision and a non-physicality. I think about all of the verbs associated with moving images: to project, to throw, to cast, to broadcast (and scatter like seeds), to disseminate and then to disappear.

In film, as in video, each projected frame is thrown out onto the screen only to disappear $\frac{1}{24}$th of a second later. Trapped in a time- and lens-based medium, a motion picture film is both stuck in time and forever lost to it. For me, its inevitable transience is also an inherent part of its beauty. 'That which lives by dying', as Rilke once wrote, bringing to mind the ephemeral, fragile beauty of temporal objects like flowers. In displaying itself, analogue film is forever in the process of destroying itself. Every run through the projector results in further damage, in more cables, dust and scratches. It is a ruin in the making.

I find it hard to imagine what digital ruins will look like, and what creative possibilities they might contain. But digital imagery is equally finite, and susceptible to decay and destruction. Digital video is stored as a complex string of electrical charges on a microscopic level inside millions of tiny chips (bits corresponding to the zeros and ones of binary data). Each chip is a switch, a transistor that has been

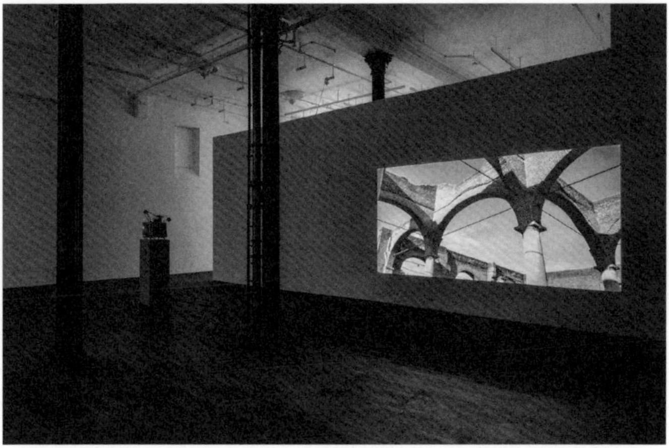

Ruins (installation view), 2020

turned on or off, powered by an electrical charge that is guarded by a capacitor, a simple battery. But transistors always leak energy, electromagnetic memory is constantly dying and must regularly be refreshed. Celluloid film has been shown to last up to 100 years, whereas data on most digital storage has a life expectancy of less than ten years. Digital erasure happens faster than we care to countenance – but hopefully this, too, is a ruin in the making.

Endnotes

Gilda Williams, 'Open Letters'

1 Jorge Luis Borges, 'The Garden of Forking Paths' (1941), cited in Italo Calvino, *Six Memos for the Next Millennium*, Cambridge, MA: Harvard University Press, 1988, translated by Patrick Creagh, 119–20.
2 Tan, '*Saint Sebastian* (2001), Work in Progress', 2005, see in this volume 112.
3 Tan, 'Letter to Chantal Akerman', 1998, see in this volume 32; excerpt from the voice-over to *Ascent*, 2016, see in this volume 254; 'A Walk Among Ruins', 2019, see in this volume 282.
4 Tan, 'On *Provenance*', 2008, see in this volume 196; '*Inventory* (2012) – Some Notes', 2013, see in this volume 225; '*Diagonal Composition*, Jeff Wall, 1993', 2019, see in this volume 54.
5 Tan, 'Letter to Chantal Akerman', 1998, *op. cit.*; Tan and Bos, 'Other Facets of the Same Globe: A Conversation', 2009, see in this volume 176.
6 Tan, *'Smoke Screen'*, 1997–8, see in this volume 96.

Fiona Tan, 'Women in Storage, or GAAF' (references)

Joan Didion, *The White Album*, New York: Simon & Schuster, 1979.

Rüdiger Overmans, *Deutsche militärische Verluste im Zweiten Weltkrieg* [German Military Losses in World War II], Munich: Oldenbourg, 2004.

Betty Friedan, *The Feminine Mystique*, New York: W. W. Norton & Co. Inc., 1963.

Matthew Weiner (creator), *Mad Men*. Aired 2007–15 on cable network AMC; currently available on Netflix.

Malcolm Gladwell, 'True Colors. Hair dye and the hidden history of post-war America', *The New Yorker*, 22 March 1999, 70–82.

Russell W. Belk and Richard W. Pollay, 'Materialism and Magazine Advertising During the Twentieth Century', *NA – Advances in Consumer Research*, vol. 12, eds. Elizabeth C. Hirschman and Morris B. Holbrook, Provo, UT: Association for Consumer Research, 1985, 394–8.

Doris von Drathen, 'Aerial Roots'

1 I first became aware of the notion of 'plants with aerial roots' when reading W. G. Sebald, *Die Ausgewanderten*, Frankfurt/Main: Fischer, 1994, 145. (In English, *The Emigrants*, 1996.) It is a common term in biology and listed in all standard works on plant growth.
2 I refer here to the theory of exile formulated by the sociologist and philosopher Shmuel Trigano in *Le temps de l'exil*, Paris: Manuels-Payot, 2001.
3 *Ibid.*, 21.
4 Hermann Broch, *Tod des Vergil*, Frankfurt: Suhrkamp, 1976, S. 315. In English, *The Death of Virgil*, translated from German by Jean Starr Untermeyer, London: Routledge, 1945/95, 336.
5 Trigano, *op. cit.*, 13.
6 Fiona Tan in an unpublished interview with the author, Paris, December 2008.
7 Martin Buber, *Weg des Menschen*, Frankfurt: Rütten und Loening, 1984, 16.
8 Trigano, *op. cit.*, 42–3.
9 *Ibid.*, 80.
10 Robert Ornstein, *Multimind*, Paderborn: Junfermann, 1989, 37. (Original English edition, Boston: Houghton Mifflin, 1986.)
11 Fiona Tan, cited from the voice-over for the film *Island* (2008), as are all the other quotes relating to this work.

12 Henri Bergson, *Sur les données immédiates de la conscience*, Paris: Les. Presses universitaires de France, 1970, 57–8. In English, *Time and Free Will: An Essay on the Immediate Data of Consciousness*, translated from French by Frank Lubecki Pogson (1910), 1996, 100–1.

Thomas Elsaesser, 'Place After Place'

1 The reference is to Michel Foucault's discussion of Jeremy Bentham's plans for an optimised regime of incarceration and surveillance in *Discipline & Punish: The Birth of the Prison* (1975), New York: Vintage Books, 1995, 195–228.

2 There is no critical edition of Béla Balázs' *Visible Man* available in English. Extracts have been translated in *Screen* 48–1 (Spring 2007), 91–108 and in *October* 115 (Winter 2006), 46–60.

3 Béla Balázs, *Der Sichtbare Mensch* (1924), translated by Erica Carter and Rodney Livingstone, *Screen* 48–1 (Spring 2007), 96.

4 Originally published in Jean Epstein, *Bonjour Cinéma*, Paris: Editions de La Sirène, 1921. Here quoted from, Epstein, 'Bonjour cinéma and Other Writings', translated from French by Tom Milne, *Afterimage* 10 (1981), 20.

5 Roland Barthes, 'Le Visage de Garbo', *Lettres nouvelles*, 26 (1955), 632–3.

6 Jacques Lacan, 'Le stade du miroir comme formateur de la fonction du Je', in *Écrits*, Paris: Seuil, 1966, 93–100. In English, 'The mirror stage as formative of the function of the I', translated from French by Alan Sheridan. *Écrits: A Selection*, London: Tavistock, 1977, 1–7.

7 Michel Foucault, 'Las Meninas', in *The Order of Things* (1966), New York: Random House, 1973, 3–16.

8 Bettina Bergo, *Emmanuel Levinas*, 2006 (revised 2007), https://stanford.library.sydney.edu.au/archives/spr2009/entries/levinas/ (accessed 6 July 2020).

9 Tan, Interview with Ana Finel Honigman, *Kultureflash* 06-04-2005 http://www.kultureflash.net/archive/118/priview.html (last accessed: Feb 16, 2009)

10 Tan, quoted in Philip Gefter, 'Is That Portrait Staring at Me?', *New York Times*, 10 April 2005. See in this volume 147.

11 Gilles Deleuze, *Cinema 1: The Movement Image*, translated from French by Hugh Tomlinson and Barbara Habberjam, and *Cinema 2: The Time Image*, translated from French by Hugh Tomlinson and Robert Caleta, Minneapolis: University of Minnesota Press, 1986/1989. Original in French, *L'image-mouvement. Cinéma 1*, 1983; *L'Image-temps. Cinéma* 2, 1985.

12 Roland Barthes, *Camera Lucida* (1980), translated from French by Richard Howard, New York: Hill and Wang, 1981.

Brian Dillon, 'Different Voices'

1 Thomas De Quincey, *Confessions of an English Opium-Eater* (1821), London: Macdonald, 1956, 426–7.

2 'Other Facets of the Same Globe: A Conversation between Fiona Tan and Saskia Bos', in *Fiona Tan: Disorient*, Mondriaan Foundation, Amsterdam, 2009, 22. See in this volume 176.

3 Samuel Beckett, *Krapp's Last Tape* (1958), in *The Complete Dramatic Works*, London: Faber, 1986, 223.

4 Tan, voice-over to *Rise and Fall*, unpublished text quoted in *Fiona Tan: Rise and Fall*, Vancouver Art Gallery, 2009, 36.

Fiona Tan, *'Smoke Screen'*

1 Original Dutch commentary: 'een oude Balinees met 'n markanten kop; een jonge hofvrouw; zuigelingen profiteren van de geleegenheid van moeder inkoopen doet; vrouwen!, thuis hebben wij kinderen in een schommel slendang 't eigenlijk veel beter, zodra we wakker worden, worden wij doodeenvoudig omgekeerd en dan zijn we weer een uur zoet.'

Lynne Cooke, 'Fiona Tan: Re-take'

1 'First contact' refers to the first time a so-called 'primitive' culture/tribe came in contact with people from the West, usually as a result of a scientific expedition.
2 Italo Calvino, *Invisible Cities* (1972), Orlando, FL: Harcourt, 1974.
3 For Marcel Mauss, Marcel Griaule and other early twentieth-century anthropologists, the camera is a supplementary tool in the ethnographer's store of equipment, one which affords great accuracy and flexibility in recording rites and customs. Hence it is considered capable of avoiding or correcting undue subjectivity in the field worker. Through her work with Gregory Bateson in Bali, Margaret Mead, too, became an advocate of the use of film as a 'note-taking tool' in the practice of ethnographic research.
4 See James Clifford, *Routes: Travel and Translation in the Late Twentieth Century*, Cambridge, MA: Harvard University Press, 1997, 319.
5 *Ibid.*, 320.
6 *Ibid.*, chap. 10, 'Diasporas', 244–77. Also Edward Said, 'Reflections on Exile', in *Altogether Elsewhere*, ed. Marc Robinson, Boston: Faber and Faber, 1994, 137–49.
7 Cited in Mick Eaton, ed., *Anthropology-Reality-Cinema: The Films of Jean Rouch*, London: British Film Institute, 1979, 8.
8 Ewa Kuryluk, *Veronica and Her Cloth: History, Symbolism, and Structure of a 'True' Image*, Oxford: Basil Blackwell, 1991, 144–5.
9 Marina Warner, 'Stolen Shadows, Lost Souls: Body and Soul in Photography', in *Raritan*, Fall 1995, 35.

Fiona Tan, '*Saint Sebastian*, Work in Progress'

1 Eugen Herrigel, *Zen in the Art of Archery*, 1948. Translated from German by R. F. C. Hull, New York: Pantheon Books, 1953.

Mark Godfrey, 'Fiona Tan's *Countenance*'

1 The DAAD is an international exchange programme in which artists working in the fields of visual arts, music, literature and the performing arts spend a year in Berlin.
2 In 'The Metropolis and Mental Life' (1903), George Simmel noted the ways in which urban life produced changes in subjectivity. 'One nowhere feels as lonely and lost as in the metropolitan crowd.' Simmel, in eds. Charles Harrison and Paul Wood, *Art in Theory 1900–1990*, Oxford: Blackwell, 1992, 130–5.
3 August Sander, 'Remarks on My Exhibition at the Cologne Art Union', in *The Weimar Republic Sourcebook*, eds. Anton Kaes, Martin Jay and Edward Dimendberg, Berkeley and Los Angeles: University of California Press, 1994, 645–6.
4 See Blake Stimson, 'The Photographic Comportment of Bernd and Hilla Becher', http://www.tate.org.uk/research/tateresearch/tatepapers/04spring/stimson_paper.htm
5 Allan Sekula, 'Reading an Archive', in *Blasted Allegories*, ed. Brian Wallis, New York: New Museum of Contemporary Art and Cambridge, MA: MIT Press, 1987, 118.
6 Benjamin Buchloh, 'Portraits/Genre: Thomas Struth' in *Thomas Struth – Portraits*, Munich: Schirmer Art Books, 1997, 150.
7 'In portraiture, a seemingly natural and guaranteed nexus between object and representation had appeared particularly evident: in fact, mimetic resemblance had been one of the category's founding conditions. The desire for the lasting depiction of subjects took the possibilities of physiognomic truth as a natural given, limited, if at all, by the painter's hand, or, conversely, superbly enacted by the painter's mimetic skills.' Benjamin Buchloh, 'Residual Resemblance: Three Notes on the Ends of Portraiture', in *Face-Off*, ICA Philadelphia, 1994, 54.

8 'We can tell from appearance the work someone does or does not do; we can read in his face whether he is happy or troubled, for life leaves its trail there unavoidably.' August Sander, 'Lecture 5: Photography as a Universal Language', in *Massachusetts Review*, Winter 1978, 677.

9 'It is possible to record the historical physiognomic image of a whole generation and – with enough knowledge of physiognomy – to make that image speak in photographs. The historical image will become even clearer if we join together pictures typical of the many different groups that make up human society.' *Ibid.*, 678.

10 Ulrich Keller, 'The Portfolio Arrangement' in *Citizens of the Twentieth Century*, Cambridge, MA: MIT Press, 1989, 37.

11 Hal Foster, *The Return of the Real*, Cambridge, MA: October books, MIT Press, 1996, 196.

12 Roland Barthes, *Camera Lucida* (1980), London: Vintage, 1993, 14.

13 Graham Clarke, 'Public Faces, Private Lives: August Sander and the Social Typology of the Portrait Photograph', in ed. Clarke, *The Portrait in Photography*, London: Reaktion, 1992, 82. Clarke's essay ends with an account of Sander's *Secretary (Cologne)* (1914) where 'the casual title ("Secretary") belies the individual context ... [A] private, not public, identity inhabits the Sander frame.' 93.

14 Of course this phenomenon predates photography. See Harry Berger, *Fictions of the Pose: Rembrandt Against the Italian Renaissance*, Stanford University Press, 2000.

15 Though Mario Merz does not stay in one place during Tacita Dean's film, it is precisely his minor movements like these that dramatise the work.

16 See the essays gathered in *Fiona Tan: Correction*, MCA Chicago, 2004.

17 Think, for instance, of Matthew Buckingham's deployment of nostalgic found film in *Situation Leading to a Story* (1999) or Marine Hugonnier's treatment of the surveying pan in *Ariana* (2003).

Christophe Gallois, 'On Fiona Tan's "Visual Letters"'

1 Tan, 'Brief aan Chantal Akerman', *Skrien* 228, November 1998, 56. Translated from Dutch into English by Frans van Woerden. See in this volume 32.

2 Tan and Saskia Bos, 'Other Facets of the Same Globe', in *Fiona Tan: Disorient*, catalogue for the Dutch Pavilion, 53rd Venice Biennale, Heidelberg: Kehrer Verlag, 2009, 1.23–4. See in this volume 176.

3 Tan, 'Brief aan Chantal Akerman', *op. cit.*

4 Tan, 'The Changeling, Voice-over for an Installation', in *Fiona Tan: Mirror Maker*, Heidelberg: Kehrer, 2006. See in this volume 150.

5 *The Changeling* has been made in English, Dutch, German, Danish, Swedish, Canadian, Norwegian, Finnish and Japanese language versions.

6 Tan, '*The Changeling*, Voice-over for an Installation', *op. cit.*

7 *Ibid.*

8 Tan, *'A Lapse of Memory'*, in *Fiona Tan: Time and Again*, Lunds Konsthall, 2007, 39. See in this volume 174.

9 *Ibid.*

10 *Ibid.*

11 Magdalena Malm, 'Interview with Fiona Tan', in *Island* exhibition leaflet, Stockholm: Mobile Art Production, 2008, n. p.

12 Marguerite Duras and Xavière Gauthier, *Les Parleuses*, Paris: Éditions de Minuit, 1974, 88. English translation quoted from *Jump Cut* 5 (1975), 13–5.

13 Malm, *op. cit.*

14 Tan, 'Brief aan Chantal Akerman', *op. cit.*

15 'Sicilian storytellers use the formula *lu cuntu nun metti tempu* (time takes no time in a story) ...' Italo Calvino, *Six Memos for the Next Millennium*, Cambridge, MA: Harvard University Press, 1988, 35.

16 *Ibid.*

17 Tan and Bos, 'Other Facets of the Same Globe', *op. cit.*, 123–4.

18 Tan, '*The Changeling*, Voice-over for an Installation', *op. cit.*

19 *Ibid.*

20 *Ibid.*

21 Malm, *op. cit.*
22 Tan, 'Brief aan Chantal Akerman', *op. cit.*
23 Chantal Akerman, 'Le frigidaire est vide. On peut le remplir', in Claudine Paquot, ed., *Chantal Akerman. Autoportrait en cinéaste*, Paris: Centre Pompidou and Cahiers du Cinéma, 2004, 32.
24 Tan, '*Island*, Voice-over', https://fiona tan.nl/project/island/.
25 *Ibid.*
26 Tan, 'Brief aan Chantal Akerman', *op. cit.*
27 Jean-Christophe Bailly, *L'Instant et son ombre*, Paris: Éditions du Seuil, 2008, 99.
28 Tan, *'A Lapse of Memory'*, *op. cit.*
29 Irit Rogoff, 'Island: Neither Police, nor Pirates', in *Fiona Tan: Rise and Fall*, Aargauer Kunsthaus, 2010, 55–61.
30 Tan, 'Brief aan Chantal Akerman', *op. cit.*

Stéphane Carrayrou, 'Images Murmuring'

1 'No es música solamente / la de la voz que callada / se escucha, música es / cuanto hace consonancia'
2 In her review of the exhibition, Cecilia Bezzan describes this as an 'endlessly repeated mantra', see 'Fiona Tan', *Art-press* 348, September 2008, 81–2.
3 '... una red creciente y vertiginosa de tiempos divergentos, convergentes y paralelos.' Italo Calvino studies this aspect of the short story in his *Six Memos for the Next Millennium* (1988).
4 André Green, *Le temps éclaté* (Exploded Time), chap.1, 'Réveil: les temps du rêve', Paris: Editions de Minuit, 2000, 11.
5 Jean-Christophe Bailly, *Le propre du langage. Voyages au pays des noms propres*, Paris: Le Seuil, 1997, 187.
6 Jean-Christophe Bailly, *Regarder la peinture*, Paris: Hazan, 1992, 5. Bailly revised this text in *L'atelier infini: 30 000 ans de peinture*, Paris: Hazan, 2007.
7 Roland Barthes, *Le Bruissement de la langue (The Rustle of Language)*, 'Collection Points – Essais', Paris: Le Seuil, 1984, 101.

Okwui Enwezor, 'Allegory in Fiona Tan's *A Lapse of Memory*'

1 This is how Tan describes herself in her autobiographical documentary film *May You Live In Interesting Times* which was first presented on Dutch television in 1997.
2 Craig Owens, 'The Allegorical Impulse: Toward a Theory of Postmodernism', in *Beyond Recognition: Representation, Power, and Culture*, Berkeley: University of California Press, 1994, 52.
3 *Ibid.*, 53.
4 *Ibid.*

Fiona Tan, *'On Provenance'*

1 John Berger, *Ways of Seeing* (1972), London: Penguin, 2008, 88–9.

Fiona Tan, ` Introduction to *Disorient*, with excerpt from Marco Polo, *The Travels*'

1 A kind of steel. See Jean Le Coze, 'About Wootz – The Question of Hinduwani/ Ondanique', *Indian Journal of History of Science*, 45.3 (2010), 403–10.

Juliana Engberg, 'Infinite Crossroads'

1 Gilles Deleuze and Félix Guattari (1987), *A Thousand Plateaus: Capitalism and Schizophrenia*, translated from French by Brian Massumi, London: Athlone, 1988, 479.

Sabine Maria Schmidt, 'Below the Water Line'

1 Stuart Hall, *Questions of Cultural Identity*, London: Sage, 1996, 276–7.

Adelina Vlas, 'Fiona Tan's *Inventory*'

1 *The American Heritage Dictionary of the English Language*, ed. William Morris, Boston: Houghton Mifflin Company, 1979, 688–9.
2 See Peter Thornton and Helen Dorey, *Sir John Soane: The Architect as Collector, 1753–1837*, New York: Harry N. Abrams, 1992, ix.
3 Helene Furján, 'Sir John Soane's Spectacular Theater', in *AA Files*, no. 47, Summer 2002, 12.
4 Furján is quick to note that Soane's architectural extravaganza is partially lost to us today, as some of the spaces are gone and others have shifted or were poorly reinstalled. The museum's current administration is actively engaged in restoring part of the building to its original state, as much as that can be determined.
5 Carol Duncan, *Civilizing Rituals: Inside Public Art Museums*, London and New York: Routledge, 1995, 85–7.
6 Thomas Elsaesser, 'Fiona Tan: Place after Place', in *Fiona Tan: Disorient*, Heidelberg: Kehrer, 2009, 2.24. See in this volume 74.

Denis Gielen, 'Memory, Too, Holds Its Breath'

1 Charles Baudelaire, 'Man and Sea', in *The Flowers of Evil*, translated from French by Richard Howard, Boston: David R. Godine, 1988, 22.
2 Jean-Claude Ameisen, *Sur les épaules de Darwin*, Paris: Les Liens qui libèrent / France Inter, 2012, 38–9.
3 Jules Michelet, *The Sea* (1861), translated from French by W. H. D. Adams, London: T. Nelson and Sons, 223 and 21, respectively.
4 *Ibid.*, 224.
5 Jean-Baptiste Lamarck, *Terminologie pour les coquilles et Méthode de conchyliologie*, Paris: Muséum national d'histoire naturelle/ Centre de recherche en histoire des sciences et des techniques (CRHST), n. d. (c. 1817), vol. 7, 413.
6 The attraction was also sometimes called 'The Ostend Whale' or 'The Royal Whale', the former after it was offered as a gift to the king of the Netherlands. Tan included an image of the pavilion, bearing the caption 'Pavilion of the Whale at Charing Cross, 1831', in her film *Depot*; see *Fiona Tan: Depot*, Gateshead, UK, BALTIC Centre for Contemporary Art, 2015, 17.
7 Michelet, *op. cit.*, 225. Translator's note: The passage is Michelet's free rendering of *Paradise Lost* (1.201–209).
8 *Ibid.*, 233.
9 Tan, voice-over to *Depot*, 2015, see in this volume 236.

David Campany, 'Still Point of the Turning World'

1 Tan, voice-over to *Ascent*, 2016. See in this volume 254.
2 Roland Barthes, 'The Eiffel Tower', *The Eiffel Tower and Other Mythologies*, translated from French by Richard Howard, Berkeley: University of California Press, 1979.
3 Victor Burgin, *Components of a Practice*, Milan: Skira Editore, 2008.
4 http://www.izuphoto-museum.jp/fiona tan/en.html
5 Tan, http://www.izuphotoproject-fionatan.jp; and http://www.izuphotoproject-fionatan.jp/?page_id=1013 (English version). Accessed 1 April 2016.
6 This was before the appearance of the Eiffel Tower, which opened in 1889.
7 T. S. Eliot, 'Burnt Norton' (1935), *Four Quartets*, New York: Harcourt, 1943.
8 Italo Calvino, 'The Adventure of a Photographer' (1955), in *Difficult Loves*, translated from Italian by William Weaver, Boston: Mariner Books, 1985.

Fiona Tan, 'A Walk Among Ruins'

1 Andrew Hui, *The Poetics of Ruins in Renaissance Literature*, New York: Fordham University Press, 2016.

Monographs / Artist's books

2020 *A Walk Among Ruins*, 'A Walk Among Ruins' by Fiona Tan. Peter Freeman Inc., New York

2019 *Fiona Tan: Goraiko*, 'Ascent, voice-over transcript' by Fiona Tan and text by Stefan Gronert. Sprengel Museum Hannover and Van Zoetendaal Publishers, Amsterdam (in German and English)

Fiona Tan: L'Archive des ombres / Shadow Archive, 'Introduction' and 'L'Archive des ombres / Shadow Archive' by Fiona Tan and texts by Sophie Berrebi, Patricia Faguières, Denis Gielen, Ellen Mara De Wachter. Musée des Arts Contemporains, Grand-Hornu BE (in French and English)

Fiona Tan: GAAF, Museum Ludwig, Cologne; Verlag der Buchhandlung Walther König, Cologne (in German and English)

2018 *10 Madnesses*, '10 Madnesses' by Fiona Tan. Roma Publications, Amsterdam

2016 *Fiona Tan: Ascent*, 'Ascent' (draft script) by Fiona Tan and texts by David Campany, Toshiharu Ito, Shin-ichi Takemura. Izu Photo Museum, Shizuoka JP, De Pont Museum, Tilburg NL and NOHARA, Tokyo (in English and Japanese)

2015 *Fiona Tan: Depot*, artist's book. 'Depot' by Fiona Tan and text by Angela Jerardi. BALTIC Centre for Contemporary Art, Gateshead UK,

Fiona Tan: Geography of Time, texts by Ruth Direktor, Christophe Gallois, Eva Klerck Gange, Peter Gorschlüter, Jenny Hval, Angela Jerardi. Nasjonalmuseet – Museet for samtidskunst, Oslo; Mudam Luxembourg; MMK Museum für Moderne Kunst, Frankfurt am Main; and Tel Aviv Museum of Art (in English, Norwegian, German and Hebrew)

2014 *Fiona Tan: Terminology*, texts by Matsui Midori, Yoko Hayashi, Asako Fujioka, Miyuki Endo, Keiko Okamura, Yasuyuki Nakai. Tokyo Metropolitan Museum of Photography; The National Museum of Art, Osaka; and Bijutsu Shuppan-sha, Co., Ltd., Tokyo (in Japanese and English)

Fiona Tan: Options & Futures, texts by Hendrik Driessen, Sacha Bronwasser. Rabo Kunstzone, Utrecht (in Dutch and English)

2013 *Fiona Tan: Ellipsis*, voice-over scripts to *Linnaeus' Flower Clock, A Lapse of Memory, Brendan' s Isle* by Fiona Tan and texts by Hiromi Kurosawa, Okwui Enwezor. 21st-Century Museum of Contemporary Art, Kanazawa, and Nitta Shoin Honsha Co. Ltd., Tokyo (in Japanese and English)

Fiona Tan: Inventory, '*Inventory* – Some Notes' by Fiona Tan and texts by Monia Trombetta, Andrea Lissoni, Adelina Vlas, Anita Seppä. MAXXI Rome and Philadelphia Museum of Art (in English and Italian)

2012 *Fiona Tan: Point of Departure*, texts by Peio Agirre, Juan Antonio Álzares Reyes, Sabine Maria Schmidt. Centro Andaluz de Arte Contemporáneo, Sevilla and Koldo Mitxelena, San Sebastián ES (in Spanish, German and English)

Fiona Tan: Vox Populi London, artist's book. Text by Brian Dillon. Book Works, London

2011 *Fiona Tan: Essays*, 'Of Clouds and Islands' and 'The Changeling' by Fiona Tan, with an interview by Saskia Bos and texts by Lynne Cooke, Bruce Grenville. Wako Works of Art, Tokyo (in Japanese)

2010 *Fiona Tan: Rise and Fall*, texts by Bruce Grenville, Madeline Schuppli, Irit Rogoff, Michael Newman, Okwui Enwezor. Vancouver Art Gallery and Aargauer Kunsthaus, Aarau CH (in English and German)

Fiona Tan: Coming Home, texts by Anita Taylor, Gene Sherman, Juliana Engberg. Sherman Contemporary Art Foundation, Sydney

Fiona Tan: Vox Populi Switzerland, artist's book. Text by Madeline Schuppli. Book Works, London

2009 *Fiona Tan: Disorient*, 'Introduction' by Fiona Tan, with extracts from Marco Polo (1298) and texts by Saskia Bos, Bruce Grenville, Dominic van den Boogerd, Doris von Drathen, Thomas Elsaesser. Catalogue for the Dutch Pavilion, 53rd Venice Biennale, Heidelberg: Kehrer Verlag

2008 *Provenance*, artist's book. 'On *Provenance*' by Fiona Tan. Rijksmuseum, Amsterdam (in English and Dutch)

2007 *Fiona Tan: Vox Populi Tokyo*, artist's book. Text by Chris Keuleman. Book Works, London

Fiona Tan: Time and Again, text by Anders Kruge. Lunds Konsthall SE (in English and Swedish)

Fiona Tan: Images Murmuring, text by Stéphane Carrayrou. Le Carré, Château Gontier (in French and English)

2006 *Fiona Tan: Vox Populi Sydney*, artist's book. Text by Rachel Kent. Book Works, London

Fiona Tan: Vox Populi Norway, artist's book. Text by Suzanne Cotter. Book Works, London

Fiona Tan: Mirror Maker, voice-over script to *The Changeling* by Fiona Tan and texts by Thorsten Sadowsky, Martin Hochleitner, Dag Erik Elgin. Kehrer Verlag, Heidelberg (in English, German, Danish and Finnish)

Disassembling the Archive: Fiona Tan, text by Philip Monk. Art Gallery of York University, Toronto and Distributed Art Publishers Inc., New York

2005 *Fiona Tan: Countenance*, texts by Suzanne Cotter, Andrew Nairne, Mark Godfrey. Modern Art Oxford

Fiona Tan, with an interview by Annie Fletcher and texts by Johan Pousette. Baltic Art Center, Visby SE (in English and Swedish)

Fiona Tan: Saint Sebastian, '*Saint Sebastian*, Work in Progress' by Fiona Tan and text by Pierre Landry. Musée d'Art Contemporain, Montréal (in English and French)

2004 *Fiona Tan: Correction*, 'Carceri d'Invenzione' by Fiona Tan and texts by Francesco Bonami, Tessa Jackson, Julie Rodrigues Widholm, Joel Snyder. Museum of Contemporary Art, Chicago; New Museum of Contemporary Art, New York; Armand Hammer Museum of Art and Cultural Center at UCLA, Los Angeles

2002 *Fiona Tan, Akte 1*, 'Saint Sebastian, Work in Progress' by Fiona Tan with texts by Beatrice von Bismarck, Els Hoek. De Pont Foundation for Contemporary Art, Tilburg (in Dutch, English, French and German)

Marebito, artist's book. 'Excerpts from a Personal Diary' by Fiona Tan, with extracts from Heinrich Schliemann (1865) and texts by Nosongdang, Cornelis Jansz-Coen. Wako Works of Art, Tokyo (in English and Japanese)

2000 *Fiona Tan: Scenario*, 'Exchange of Letters' by John Berger and Fiona Tan with texts by Lynne Cooke, Dominic van den Boogerd, Heddy Honigmann, Stephan Schmidt-Wulffen, ed. Mariska van den Berg. Vandenberg & Wallroth, Amsterdam and NAI Publishers, Rotterdam

Selected list of works

Archive, 2019
Video installation
High-definition video (3-D animation, b & w, stereo sound)
5 min. 45 sec. (loop)
High-definition projector, media player
Dimensions variable

Ascent, 2016
2-part installation
Room 1 – 16:10 projection (colour, 7:1 surround sound), 77 min.
High-definition projector, media player, amplifier, 5 hifi speakers and subwoofer, seating, projection screen
Room 2 – 150 mounted colour photographs (4 × 5⅞, 5⅛ × 7⅛, 7⅛ × 9½ in. [10 × 15, 13 × 18, 18 × 24 cm]), shelf

Brendan's Isle, 2010
Sound work
6 min. 52 sec.
mp3 or Compact Disc player, headphones
English version spoken by Fiona Tan
German version spoken by Inge Krichau Sadowsky

The Changeling, 2006
Two-channel digital installation
Digital files (b & w / tinted, mono sound)
12 min. (loop)
2 LCD monitors, 2 media players, built-in hifi speaker
English version spoken by Fiona Shaw / Dutch version spoken by Johanna ter Steege / Danish version spoken by Birgitte Raaberg / Swedish version spoken by Anita Björk / Canadian English version spoken by Martha Burns / German version spoken by Hanna Schygulla / Norwegian version spoken by Andrine Sæther / Finnish version spoken by Outi Maenpaa / Japanese version spoken by Junko Uchida

Circular Ruins, 2019
Sculptural installation
Ropes, wooden structure, steel cables, stereo amplifier, 4 hifi speakers
11 ft. 5¾ in. × 39 ft. 4 7/16 in. (3.5 × 12 m)
Commissioned by Musée des Arts Contemporains au Grand-Hornu, BE

Cloud Island I, Project for the Venice Architecture Biennale 2010, 2010
Two-channel video installation
High-definition video (colour, 5:1 surround sound)
2 high-definition projectors, 2 media players, 2 stereo amplifiers, 4 stereo speakers
Double-sided white projection screen, dimensions: 44¼ × 78¾ in. (112.5 × 200 cm)
Filmed on location on Inujima and Teshima, JP
Commissioned by the Naoshima Fukutake Art Museum Foundation, JP
Supported by Naoshima Fukutake Art Museum Foundation and Wako Works of Art, Tokyo, JP

Cloud Island, 2010
Video installation
High-definition video (colour, surround sound)
46 min. (loop)
High-definition projector, media player, surround amplifier, 4 hifi speakers and subwoofer
White projection screen, dimensions: min. 6 ft. 5¼ in. × 11 ft. 5¾ in. (1.97 × 3.5 m)
Filmed on location on Inujima, JP

Correction, 2004
Six-channel video installation
Video (colour, mono sound)
Approx. 3 hours total running time, between 25 min. 2 sec. and 35 min. 7 sec. (varying loop lengths)
6 video projectors 4:3, 6 media players, 6 amplifiers, 6 hifi speakers
6 rear projection screens, dimensions: 4 ft. 9⅛ in. × 3 ft. 7¼ in. (1.45 × 1.1 m) each
Commissioned by the Museum of Contemporary Art, Chicago, IL, as part of a collaborative programme with the New Museum of Contemporary Art, New York, NY, and the Hammer Museum, Los Angeles, CA, US
Filmed on location in various US prisons

Countenance, 2002
Four-channel, 2-room video installation
Film, 16 mm (b&w / tinted, mono sound), transferred to video
Approx. 90 min. total running time
4 video projectors (4:3), 4 media players, 4 hifi speakers
Room 1: rear projection screen, dimensions: 23⅝ × 17⅜ in. (60 × 44 cm)
Room 2: 3 rear projection screens, dimensions: 6 ft. 2¾ in. × 4 ft. 7⅞ in. (1.9 × 1.42 m) each
Commissioned by Documenta 9, Kassel, DE, and supported by DAAD, Berlin, DE, and Frith Street Gallery, London, GB

Cradle, 1998
Film installation
Film, 16 mm (b&w / tinted, silent)
Tripod table, white handkerchief, 16 mm film projector, no-rewind, electronic sensor / timer

De Umbris Idearum
As described by Giordano Bruno, after Francis Yates, 2018
Ink on paper
46½ × 40⅛ in. (118 × 102 cm)

Depot, 2015
Video installation
High-definition video (colour, stereo sound)
22 min. 40 sec. (loop)
High-definition projector, media player, amplifier, stereo speakers
Dimensions variable
Voice-over spoken by Andrew Bennett
Commissioned by the BALTIC, Gateshead, GB

Disorient, 2009
Two-channel video installation
High-definition video (colour, 5:1 surround sound)
17 min. and 19 min. 30 sec. (loop)
2 high-definition projectors, 2 media players, 2 surround amplifiers, 8 hifi speakers and subwoofer
2 white projection screens, dimensions: min. 5 ft. 10 9/10 in. × 10 ft. 6 in. (1.8 × 3.2 m) and 8 ft. 10 3/10 in. × 15 ft. 9 in. (2.7 × 4.8 m)
Voice-over spoken by Michael Maloney
Screen 1 filmed on location in the Dutch Pavilion, Venice, IT
Commissioned by the Mondriaan Foundation for the Dutch Pavilion, 53rd Venice Biennale
Supported by Frith Street Gallery, London, GB, and Peter Freeman, Inc., New York, NY, US

Elsewhere, 2018
Video installation
High-definition video (colour, stereo sound)
16 min. 10 sec. (loop)
High-definition projector, media player, amplifier, stereo speakers
Projection screen, dimensions variable
Voice-over spoken by Laurel Lefkow
Filmed on location in Los Angeles, CA, US

Facing Forward, 1999
Video installation
Film, 35 mm (b&w / tinted, stereo sound), transferred to video
11 min.
Video projector, amplifier, stereo speakers
Projection dimensions: approx. 8 ft. 10¼ in. × 12 ft. 9½ in. (2.7 × 3.9 m)
Voice-over spoken by Owen Oppenheimer

A Fool's Paradise, 2010
Sound work (site-specific)
22 min.
mp3 player, headphones
Commissioned by de Hoge Rielen, Kasterlee, BE
Voice-over spoken in Dutch by Johan Leysen

History's Future, 2015
Film (colour, surround sound, DCP, English, French or Dutch subtitles)
95 min.
Produced by Family Affair Films, Antithesis Film, Rohfilm & Vico Films

Inventory, 2012
Six-channel high-definition and standard-definition video installation
Film, 35 mm, 16 mm and Super-8 (colour, stereo sound), transferred to high-definition and standard-definition video
Video, Video-8, DV (colour, stereo sound), transfered to standard-definition and high-definition video
16 min. 30 sec. (loop)
3 video projectors (4:3), 3 high-definition projectors (16:9), 6 sync media players, network hub, amplifier, stereo speakers
Dimensions: 13 ft. 9⅜ in. × 32 ft. 9¾ in. (4.2 × 10 m)
Filmed on location at the Sir John Soane Museum, London, GB
Commissioned by MAXXI, Rome, IT, and Philadelphia Museum of Art, Philadelphia, PA, US

Island, 2008
Video installation
High-definition video (b&w, 5:1 surround sound)
15 min. (loop)
High-definition projector, media player, surround amplifier, 5 hifi speakers and subwoofer
Dimensions variable
Voice-over spoken by Heathcote Williams
Filmed on location on Gotland, SE

A Lapse of Memory, 2007
Video installation
Film, 16 mm (colour, 5:1 surround sound), transferred to high-definition video
24 min. (loop)
High-definition projector, media player, surround amplifier, 5 hifi speakers and subwoofer
Front projection screen, min. dimensions: 5 ft. 6½ in. × 9 ft. 10⅛ in. (1.69 × 3 m)
Filmed on location at the Brighton Pavilion, GB
Commissioned by Brighton Photography Biennial

Levensloop, 2011
Seven-channel video installation
High-definition video (b&w, silent)
7 LCD monitors 42", 7 media players, network hub and sync connection, 7 monitor mounts
Dimensions: 26 ft. 3 in. × 10 ft. 6 in. (8 × 3.2 m)
Commissioned by Jeroen Bosch Hospital, 's-Hertogenbosch, NL

Leviathan, 2015
Video installation
Video (colour, stereo sound)
4 min. 30 sec.
Video projector, media player, amplifier, stereo speakers
Dimensions variable

Lift, 2000
Two-channel film and video installation
Film, 16 mm, and video (colour, silent)
Table, monitor 14", media player, 16 mm film projector, no-rewind, electronic sensor
Front projection screen, dimensions: 6 ft. 9⅞ in. × 9 ft. 1⅞ in. (2.08 × 2.79 m)

Linnaeus' Flower Clock, 1998
Video (colour/tinted, stereo sound)
17 min.
Monitor 27", media player, amplifier, stereo speakers

May You Live In Interesting Times, 1997
Video (colour, stereo)
60 min.
English, Dutch, French, Spanish versions

Nellie, 2013
Video installation
Video (colour, stereo sound)
3 min. 9 sec. (loop)
Video projector, media player, amplifier, stereo speaker
Dimensions variable
Commissioned by Museum van Loon, Amsterdam, NL

News from the Near Future, 2003
Video projection
Video (b & w / tinted, stereo sound)
9 min. 30 sec. (loop)
Video projector, media player, amplifier, stereo speakers
Projection, dimensions: min. 9 ft. 10 ⅛ in. × 13 ft. 1½ in. (3 × 4 m)
Commissioned by Netherlands Film Museum, Amsterdam, NL

n. t. (Leidsestr.), 1997
Video (colour, silent)
Endless loop
Plinth, monitor 21", media player

Projection, 2009
Video installation
High-definition video (colour, silent)
1 min. (loop)
High-definition projector, media player
Rear projection screen, dimensions: 15 ¾ × 8 ⅞ in. (40 × 22.5 cm)

Provenance, 2008
Six-channel digital installation
Digital files (b & w, silent)
Between 3 min. 36 sec. and 5 min. 10 sec. (varying loop lengths)
LCD monitor 17", LCD monitor 19", 4 LCD monitors 21", 6 media players, mounts
Commissioned by the Rijksmuseum, Amsterdam, NL

Rise and Fall, 2009
Two-channel video installation
High-definition video (colour, 5:1 surround sound)
26 min. (loop)
2 high-definition projectors, 2 sync media players, surround amplifier, stereo speakers
2 back projection screens, dimensions: min. 8 ft. 2½ in. × 4 ft. 7⅛ in. (2.5 × 1.4 m)
Commissioned by the Vancouver Art Gallery, Vancouver, CA

Roll I & II, 1997
Two-channel video installation
Video (colour, stereo sound)
Endless loop
Video projector, monitor 9", 2 media players, 2 speakers
Projection, dimensions: ca. 13 ft. 1½ in. × 19 ft. 8¼ in. (4 × 6 m)

Ruins, 2020
Two-channel film and video installation
Film, Super 16 mm (colour, silent)
High-definition video (colour, silent)
Between 3 min. 50 sec. and 4 min. 10 sec. (varying loop lengths)
Super 16 mm film projector, no-rewind loop device, high-definition projector, media player
2 front projection screens, 2 plinths, dimensions variable

Saint Sebastian, 2001
Two-channel video installation
Film, Super 16 mm (colour, stereo sound), transferred to high-definition video
Between 4 min. 52 sec. and 9 min. 50 sec. (varying loop lengths)
2 video projectors 16:9, 2 media players, 2 amplifiers, 8 hifi speakers
White double-sided projection screen, dimensions: 8 ft. 3⅝ in. × 14 ft. 9⅛ in. (2.53 × 4.5 m)
Filmed on location at Sanjûsangen-dô temple, Kyoto, JP
Commissioned by the Yokohama Triennale

Shadow Archive I–IV, 2019
Photogravures
Set of 4 small prints
Each 11¼ × 14¾ in. (28.5 × 37.5 cm)

Shadow Archive V–VI, 2019
Photogravures
Set of 2 large prints
Each 30¾ × 39⅜ in. (78 × 100 cm)

Smoke Screen, 1997
Film installation
Film, 16 mm (b & w and colour, silent)
3 min. 12 sec. (loop)
16 mm film projector, no-rewind
Dimensions variable

Tuareg, 1999
2-room video installation
Video (b & w, stereo sound)
Endless loop
Video projector, media player, 2 amplifiers, 4 speakers, glass
Rear projection screen, dimensions: 5 ft. 10⅞ in. × 7 ft. 10½ in. (1.8 × 2.4 m)

Vox Populi London, 2012
Photographic installation
267 individually framed colour photographs
Each 5⅛ × 7⅛ in. (13 × 18 cm), installation dimensions: 6 ft. 10¾ in. × 22 ft. 11⅝ in. (2.1 × 7 m)

Vox Populi Norway, 2004
Photographic installation
267 individually framed colour photographs
Each 5⅛ × 7⅛ in. (13 × 18 cm), installation dimensions: 7 ft. 6¼ in. × 23 ft. 7½ in. (2.3 × 7.2 m)
Commissioned by the Norwegian Parliament

Vox Populi Switzerland, 2010
Photographic installation
254 individually framed colour photographs
Each 5⅛ × 7⅛ in. (13 × 18 cm), installation dimensions: 9 ft. 10⅛ in. × 26 ft. 3 in. (3 × 8 m)
Commissioned by Aargauer Kunsthaus, Aarau, CH

Vox Populi Sydney, 2006
Photographic installation
301 individually framed colour photographs
Each 5⅛ × 7⅛ in. (13 × 18 cm), installation dimensions: 7 ft. 6¼ in. × 27 ft. 10⅝ in. (2.3 × 8.5 m)
Commissioned by Sydney Biennial

Vox Populi Tokyo, 2007
Photographic installation
305 individually framed colour photographs
Each 5⅛ × 7⅛ in. (13 × 18 cm), installation dimensions: 7 ft. 6¼ in. × 27 ft. 10⅝ in. (2.3 × 8.5 m)

Authors' biographies

John Berger (1926–2017) was a noted British-born novelist, poet, screenwriter and art critic, based (from 1974) in the remote community of Quincy, Haute-Savoie, France. His published works of fiction and nonfiction include *Ways of Seeing* (1972) and *G.* (1972), for which he was awarded the Booker Prize.

Saskia Bos is an art historian and curator based in Amsterdam, a former Dean at the School of Art at Cooper Union, New York (2005–16) and Director of De Appel, Amsterdam (1985–2006). Bos was curator of Fiona Tan's solo presentation at the Dutch Pavilion, 53rd Venice Biennale, 2009.

David Campany is a writer, curator, and Managing Director of Programs at the International Center of Photography, New York. A noted specialist on art and photography, his many publications include *On Photographs* (2020) and *A Handful of Dust* (also curated, 2015).

Stéphane Carrayrou is a Paris-based art historian, curator and art critic. Carrayrou curated the group exhibition *Between Fictions*, whose fifteen artists included Fiona Tan (Centre d'art contemporain, Rueil-Malmaison, 1998). On Fiona Tan he also published texts in *Art Press* (no. 280, 2002) and in the catalogue *Appel à témoins*, Le Quartier, FR (2004).

Dawn Chan's criticism and journalism has been published, among others, in *The New York Times*, *thenewyorker.com*, *Paris Review* and *Artforum*, where she was an editor (2007–18). Winner of a 2018 Warhol Arts Writers Grant, Chan is a member of the Visiting Faculty at CCS Bard, Annandale-on-Hudson, NY.

Lynne Cooke is Senior Curator, Special Projects in Modern Art, National Gallery of Art, Washington DC. A renowned curator and scholar, Cooke was formerly curator at Dia Art Foundation, New York (1991–2008); artistic director of the 10th Biennale of Sydney (1994–6); and Chief Curator / Deputy Director, Museo Nacional de Arte Reina Sofia, Madrid (2008–12).

Laura Cumming has been the chief art critic of *The Observer* (London) since 1999. Her many books include *A Face to the World: On Self-Portraits* (2014) and the bestselling memoir *On Chapel Sands: My Mother and Other Missing Persons* (2019).

Brian Dillon is an art critic, editor and essayist whose books include *Essayism* (2017), *In the Dark Room: A Journey in Memory* (2005) and *Objects in This Mirror* (2014). He is UK editor of *Cabinet* magazine and Visiting Professor at the Royal College of Art, London.

Doris von Drathen is an art historian and professor at the École Spéciale d'Architecture in Paris. Publications include *Vortex of Silence: Proposition for an art criticism beyond aesthetic categories* (2004) and monographs *Marina Abramović* (1998) and *Rebecca Horn: Cosmic Maps* (2008).

Thomas Elsaesser (1943–2019) was a prominent film theorist, professor at the University of East Anglia and the University of Amsterdam and visiting professor at Yale University and Columbia University, among others. His many publications include the prizewinning *New German Cinema: A History* (1989; reprinted 1994) and *European Cinema: Face to Face with Hollywood* (2005). Elsaesser was co-founder and first chairman of the Martin-Elsaesser-Foundation.

Juliana Engberg is a curator and writer. She has been Programme Director, European Capital of Culture Aarhus (2017); curator of the Australian Pavilion, Venice Biennale (2019); and Artistic Director of the Sydney Biennial (2014) and the Australian Centre for Contemporary Art (2002–15).

Okwui Enwezor (1963–2019) was among the most influential curators of his generation, whose groundbreaking exhibitions often foregrounded non-Western Modernist and late 20th-century artistic practices. Enwezor was at the helm of many major international institutions, among them documenta 11 (2002); the Venice Biennale (2015); and Munich's Haus der Kunst (2011–18).

David Frankel is an art critic and former Editorial Director of Publications at The Museum of Modern Art, New York. He was previously Senior Editor at *Artforum* magazine, where he remains a Contributing Editor.

Christophe Gallois is, since 2007, Curator / Head of Exhibitions at Mudam Luxembourg. His curated projects include the group show *L'image papillon* (2013), on the relationship of image to memory through W. G. Sebald's writings, and solo exhibitions of Fiona Tan (2016), Su-Mei Tse (2017) and Katinka Bock (2018).

Philip Gefter is an American photography critic and author of *What Becomes a Legend Most: The Biography of Richard Avedon* (2020); *Wagstaff: Before and After Mapplethorpe* (2014; awarded the Marfield Prize); and the collection of essays *Photography After Frank* (2009). For over fifteen years Gefter was an editor at the *New York Times*, where he wrote regularly on photography.

Denis Gielen is a curator and writer and has been Director of the Museum of Contemporary Arts, Grand-Hornu, BE since 2016. Curated exhibitions at the Museum include *S. F. [Art, Sciences and Fiction]* (2012) and *Fiona Tan: Shadow Archive* (2019). Publications include the *Atlas of Contemporary Art for Use by Everyone* (2007).

Massimiliano Gioni is Artistic Director, New Museum of Contemporary Art, New York, and Director, Nicola Trussardi Foundation, Milan. His many curated exhibitions include Manifesta 5 (2004), Berlin Biennale (2006), Gwangju Biennale (2010), Venice Biennale (2013) and, at the New Museum, *The Generational Triennial: Younger Than Jesus* (2009).

Mark Godfrey is Senior Curator of International Art, Tate Modern, London. He is author of *Abstraction and the Holocaust* (2007) and *Alighiero E Boetti* (2011) and his curated exhibitions include, at Tate, *Soul of a Nation: Art in the Age of Black Power* (2017) and *Franz West* (2019).

Hettie Judah is senior art critic on the British newspaper *The I* and contributor to *Frieze*, *The Guardian*, *Vogue*, *The New York Times*, *Art Quarterly* and more. Among her books are *Art London: A Guide to Places, Events and Artists* (2019) and *Lives of the Artists: Frida Kahlo* (2020).

Midori Matsui is a Tokyo-based art critic whose books include *Art in a New World* (2002) and *Winter Garden: The Exploration of the Micropop Imagination in Contemporary Japanese Art* (2009). She has contributed to such publications as *Ice Cream: Contemporary Art in Culture* (2007) and *Little Boy: The Art of Japan's Exploding Subculture* (2005).

Philip Monk has been Director of the Art Gallery of York University (2003–17), curator at The Power Plant (1994–2003) and the Art Gallery of Ontario (1985–94), Toronto. His books include *Glamour is Theft: A User's Guide to General Idea* (2012) and *Is Toronto Burning?: Three Years in the Making (and Unmaking) of the Toronto Art Scene* (2016).

Elisa Schaar is an art historian, writer, curator and Visiting Tutor at the Ruskin School of Art, Oxford University. She is a London contributor to *Artforum* and her writing has appeared in *Art History* and *American Art*. Curated exhibitions include Günther Förg (Venice Biennale, 2019).

Sabine Maria Schmidt is an art historian, museum curator and art critic working in Düsseldorf and Chemnitz. Her monographs include *Aernout Mik. Communitas* (2010), *Korpys/Löffler. PIOS* (2017) and *Christoph Faulhaber: A Golden Age* (2018).

Adrian Searle has been chief art critic for *The Guardian* (London) since 1996, and he has also written for *Artforum*, *Parkett*, and *frieze*, among others. Books include *Peter Doig* (2007) and *ON & BY: Luc Tuymans* (2013). Searle was a juror for the Turner Prize (2004).

Joel Snyder is Professor Emeritus in History of Photography and Film in the Department of Art History at the University of Chicago. Among his many publications is *One/Many: Western American Survey Photographs by Bell and O'Sullivan* (2006). Snyder was a co-editor of *Critical Inquiry* for thirty-five years.

Adelina Vlas is an Associate Curator at the Art Gallery of Ontario, Toronto. Often focusing on conceptual and time-based media practices, her curated exhibitions include *Haegue Yang: Emergence* (2020) and *Hito Steyerl: This is the future* (2019).

Gilda Williams is Senior Lecturer at Goldsmiths College, London and critic for *Artforum*. Her books include *How to Write about Contemporary Art* (2014, in seven languages) and *ON & BY Andy Warhol* (2016). In 2020 Williams is an evaluator for the Arts Writers Grant Program, The Andy Warhol Foundation / Creative Capital, New York.

List of images

All images of Fiona Tan courtesy the artist; Frith Street Gallery, London; Peter Freeman, Inc., New York; and Wako Works of Art, Tokyo.

p. 130, Fiona Tan, *Countenance*, 2002. Four-channel, 2-room video installation, film, 16 mm (b&w/tinted, mono sound), transferred to video, approx. 90 min. Commissioned by Documenta XI, Kassel, and supported by DAAD, Berlin, and Frith Street Gallery, London

p. 133, Andy Warhol, *Screen Test: Edie Sedgwick* [ST308], 1965. Film, 16 mm (b&w and colour, silent), 4 min. 30 sec. © 2020 The Andy Warhol Museum, Pittsburgh, PA, a museum of Carnegie Institute. All rights reserved. Film still courtesy The Andy Warhol Museum / Bildrecht, Wien, 2020

p. 134, August Sander, *Young Farmers*, 1914. Gelatin silver print, 10 ¼ × 7 ⅛ in. (26 × 18 cm). © Die Photographische Sammlung / SK Stiftung Kultur – August Sander Archiv, Köln / Bildrecht, Wien, 2020

p. 140, Giovanni Battista Piranesi, *Le Carceri d'Invenzione*, 1761. Etching, from *The Gothic Arch*, 2nd edition, plate XIV, 16 ⅜ × 21 ⅝ in. (41.5 × 54.8 cm). Princeton University Art Museum. WikiCommons

pp. 145/148, Fiona Tan, *Correction*, 2004. Six-channel video installation, video (colour, mono sound), approx. 3 hrs total running time, between 25 min. 2 sec. and 35 min. 7 sec. (varying loop lengths). Commissioned by the Museum of Contemporary Art, Chicago, as part of a collaborative programme with the New Museum of Contemporary Art, New York, and the Hammer Museum, Los Angeles

p. 153, Fiona Tan, *The Changeling*, 2006. Two-channel digital installation, digital files (b&w/tinted, mono sound), 12 min. (loop)

p. 167, Fiona Tan, *Vox Populi Norway*, 2004. Photographic installation, 267 individually framed colour photographs, each 5 ⅛ × 7 ⅛ in. (13 × 18 cm). Commissioned by the Norwegian Parliament

pp. 170/171, Fiona Tan, *Vox Populi London*, 2012. Photographic installation, 267 individually framed colour photographs, each 5 ⅛ × 7 ⅛ in. (13 × 18 cm). Commissioned by The Photographers' Gallery, London

p. 179, Fiona Tan, *A Lapse of Memory*, 2007. Video installation, film, 16 mm (colour, 5:1 surround sound) transferred to high-definition video, 24 min. (loop). Commissioned by Brighton Photography Biennial, GB

p. 201, Jacob Gerritsz. Cuyp, *Portrait of Margaretha de Geer (1585–1672)*, 1651. Oil on panel, 29 ⅛ × 23 ⅝ in. (73.9 × 59.9 cm). Rijksmuseum, Amsterdam. © Rijksmuseum Amsterdam

p. 201, Rembrandt van Rijn, *Portrait of Margaretha de Geer, Wife of Jacob Trip*, c. 1661. Oil on canvas, 51 ⅜ × 38 ⅜ in. (130.5 × 97.5 cm), part of *Portraits of Jacob Trip and his Wife Margaretha de Geer*. The National Gallery, London, Acc. No. NG1675. Bought, 1899. © 2020. Copyright The National Gallery, London / Scala, Florence

p. 209, Fiona Tan, *Disorient*, 2009. Two-channel video installation, high-definition video (colour, 5:1 surround sound), 17 min. and 19 min. 30 sec. (loops). Commissioned by the Mondriaan Fund for the Dutch Pavilion, 53rd Venice Biennale

p. 220, World map from one of the Leipzig Codices showing various cities, rivers and seas, 11th century. Mary Evans Picture Library, London. © Mary Evans Picture Library

p. 227, Fiona Tan, *Inventory*, 2012. Six-channel high-definition and standard-definition video installation, film, 35 mm, 16 mm and Super-8 (colour, stereo sound), transferred to high-definition and standard-definition video, video (colour, stereo sound), 16 min. 30 sec. (loop). Commissioned by MAXXI, Rome, and Philadelphia Museum of Art

p. 241, Page from the journal kept by Captain Samuel B. Devoll onboard the bark *George and Mary*'s 1855–7 whaling voyage out of Westport (Massachusetts, US), 19th century. Courtesy of the New Bedford Whaling Museum, New Bedford, MA, US

p. 243, Jack Leeson, *Jonah the Whale Show*, Rugby Fair, GB, front view, March 1954. Photograph, 2⅛ × 1⅜ in. (5.5 × 3.5 cm). Copyright University of Sheffield Library, National Fairground and Circus Archive

p. 249, Fiona Tan, *Depot*, 2015. Video installation, high-definition video (colour, stereo sound), 22 min. 40 sec. (loop). Commissioned by the BALTIC, Gateshead, GB

p. 253, Fiona Tan, *Depot*, 2015. Exhibition view. Commissioned by the BALTIC Centre for Contempoary Art, Gateshead, GB

p. 265, Fiona Tan, *Ascent*, 2016. 2-part installation, 16:10 projection (colour, 7:1 surround sound), 77 min., and 150 mounted colour photographs

p. 266, Katsushika Hokusai, *The Great Wave off the Coast of Kanagawa*, c. 1829–31. Colour woodblock print, from the series: *36 Views of Mount Fuji*, 10⅛ × 14⅞ in. (25.7 × 37.9 cm). State A. Pushkin Museum of Fine Arts, Moscow. © 2020. Photo Fine Art Images / Heritage Images / Scala, Florence

p. 272, Fiona Tan, *Elsewhere*, 2018. Video installation high-definition video (colour, stereo), 16 min. (loop).

p. 274, Fiona Tan, *Archive*, 2019. Video installation, high-definition video (3-D animation, b & w, silent), 5 min. 45 sec. (loop)

p. 276, Giordano Bruno, *Ruota della Memoria* (Memory Wheel), 1582. From the publication *De umbris idearum. Implicantibus artem, Quaerendi ... & Applicandi: Ad internam scripturam explicatis ...*, Paris: Apud Aegidium Gorbinum, 5¾ × 3½ in. (14.7 × 9 cm). Österreichische Nationalbibliothek, Vienna, Sammlung von Handschriften und Alten Drucken, Inv. Nr. 71.X.15 © Österreichische Nationalbibliothek, Wien, Sammlung von Handschriften und Alten Drucken

p. 281, Fiona Tan, *Circular Ruins*, 2019. Sculptural installation (mixed media, audio), 39 × 6 ft. (12 × 3.5 m).

p. 285, Pieter Bruegel the Elder, *The Tower of Babel*, c. 1563–5. Oil on oak panel, 23⅝ × 29⅜ in. (60 × 74.5 cm). Museum Boijmans Van Beuningen, Rotterdam

p. 291, Fiona Tan, *Ruins*, 2020. Two-channel film and video installation, film, Super 16 mm (colour, silent), high-definition video (colour, silent), between 3 min. 50 sec. and 4 min. 10 sec. (varying loop lengths)

Index

Colophon

Published in conjunction with the exhibition

Fiona Tan
With the other hand

31 October 2020 – 21 February 2021
Museum der Moderne Salzburg

21 November 2020 – 14 February 2021
Kunsthalle Krems

Museum der Moderne
Salzburg

Director: Thorsten Sadowsky
Curators: Thorsten Sadowsky, Marijana Schneider
Registrar: Susanne Greimel
Assistant Registrar: Lena McFadden
Conservation: Marcella Steinbichler
Exhibition Installation: hs art service Austria
Media technicians: Michael Krupica, Ivo van Stiphout
Technicians: Oliver Wacht (Head), Christian Hauer, Alija Salihovic, Max Wittmann
Marketing and Public Relations: Martin Riegler (Head), Saskia Sikabonyi, Susanne Susanka
Art Education: Mirabelle Spreckelsen (Head), Victoria Fahrengruber, Elisabeth Ihrenberger

KUNST HALLE KREMS

Managing directors: Eva Engelberger, Julia Flunger-Schulz (on maternity leave), Stefan Mitterer
Artistic director: Florian Steininger
Curator: Nina Schedlmayer
Exhibition management: Elke Pehamberger-Müllner (Head), Helene Fehringer
Media technicians: Hermann Amon, Ivo van Stiphout
Marketing and communication: Sigrid Wilhelm (Head), Matej Gajdos, Laura Kudrnovsky, Sabine Soban, Franziska Treml, Elisabeth Zettl
Art Education: Stefanie Fröhlich (Head), Isabell Fiedler (Head, on maternity leave), Claudia Pitnik and team

Publications

Edited by Thorsten Sadowsky for the
Museum der Moderne Salzburg
Mönchsberg 32
5020 Salzburg
Austria
T +43 662 84 22 20 -0
F +43 662 84 22 20 -700
info@mdmsalzburg.at
www.mdmsalzburg.at

Edited by Florian Steininger for the
Kunsthalle Krems
Kunstmeile Krems Betriebs GmbH
Museumsplatz 5
3500 Krems an der Donau
Austria
T +43 2732 9080 10
F +43 2732 90 80 11
E office@kunstmeile.at
www.kunsthalle.at
www.kunstmeile.at

Volume 1: Exhibition Catalogue
Texts by: Ruth Horak, Nina Schedlmayer, Thorsten Sadowsky, Marijana Schneider
Interview by: Eva Sangiorgi with Fiona Tan
Editing and Production Management: Tina Teufel
Translations: Bram Opstelten
English copy-editing: Susie Hondl

Volume 2: Reader
Editor: Gilda Williams
Texts by: John Berger, Saskia Bos, David Campany, Stéphane Carrayrou, Dawn Chan, Lynne Cooke, Laura Cumming, Brian Dillon, Doris von Drathen, Thomas Elsaesser, Juliana Engberg, Okwui Enwezor, David Frankel, Christophe Gallois, Philip Gefter, Denis Gielen, Massimiliano Gioni, Mark Godfrey, Hettie Judah, Midori Matsui, Philip Monk, Elisa Schaar, Sabine Maria Schmidt, Adrian Searle, Joel Snyder, Fiona Tan, Adelina Vlas, and Gilda Williams
Project editors: Ali MacGilp and Tina Teufel
Production Management: Tina Teufel
Translations: Bram Opstelten (pp. 9–10)
English copy-editing: Gilda Williams, Ali MacGilp

Graphic design and typesetting: Studio Victor Balko, Frankfurt
Production: Snoeck Verlagsgesellschaft mbH, Köln

Published by
Snoeck Verlagsgesellschaft mbH
Nievenheimer Str. 18
50739 Cologne
Germany
www.snoeck.de

ISBN 978-3-86442-324-6 (exhibition catalogue)
ISBN 978-3-86442-325-3 (reader, English)
ISBN 978-3-86442-326-0 (reader, German)

Printed in Germany

Cover: Fiona Tan, *Ascent*, 2016, still. Two part video and photographic installation. Photo: Nakano Yuko

Acknowledgments

With the kind support of
Mondriaan Fund
Netherlands Embassy

Special thanks to: Marianne Breuer and Gabriele Conrath-Scholl, Die Photographische Sammlung / SK Stiftung Kultur der Sparkasse KölnBonn – August Sander Archiv, Cologne, DE; Ciarán Finlayson and *Artforum*, New York, NY, US; Katja Lehmann, Scala Archives, Scala Group Spa, Florence, IT; Matthew Neill, National Fairground & Circus Archive, University of Sheffield, Scheffield, GB; Gertrud Oswald, Österreichische Nationalbibliothek – Sammlung von Handschriften und alten Drucken, Vienna, AT; Mark Procknik, New Bedford Whaling Museum, New Bedford, MA, US; Patrick Seymour, The Andy Warhol Museum, Pittsburgh, PA, US; Miriam Szwast, Museum Ludwig, Cologne, DE; Amanda Wilkinson and Gavriella Abekassis, London, GB

The Museum der Moderne Salzburg is sponsored with funds provided by the Province of Salzburg.

The Kunsthalle Krems is supported by